ADELAIDE

Independent Monthly Literary Magazine
Revista Literária Independente Mensal
Year IV, Number 21, February 2019
Ano IV, Número 21, fevereiro de 2019

ISBN-13: 978-1-950437-11-5
ISBN-10: 1-950437-11-6

Adelaide Literary Magazine is an independent international monthly publication, based in New York and Lisbon. Founded by Stevan V. Nikolic and Adelaide Franco Nikolic in 2015, the magazine's aim is to publish quality poetry, fiction, nonfiction, artwork, and photography, as well as interviews, articles, and book reviews, written in English and Portuguese. We seek to publish outstanding literary fiction, nonfiction, and poetry, and to promote the writers we publish, helping both new, emerging, and established authors reach a wider literary audience.

A Revista Literária Adelaide é uma publicação mensal internacional e independente, localizada em Nova Iorque e Lisboa. Fundada por Stevan V. Nikolic e Adelaide Franco Nikolic em 2015, o objectivo da revista é publicar poesia, ficção, não-ficção, arte e fotografia de qualidade assim como entrevistas, artigos e críticas literárias, escritas em inglês e português. Pretendemos publicar ficção, não-ficção e poesia excepcionais assim como promover os escritores que publicamos, ajudando os autores novos e emergentes a atingir uma audiência literária mais vasta.

(http://adelaidemagazine.org)

Published by: Adelaide Books LLC, New York
244 Fifth Avenue, Suite D27
New York NY, 10001
e-mail: info@adelaidemagazine.org
phone: (917) 477 8984
http://adelaidebooks.org

FOUNDERS / FUNDADORES
Stevan V. Nikolic & Adelaide Franco Nikolic

EDITOR IN CHIEF / EDITOR-CHEFE
Stevan V. Nikolic
editor@adelaidemagazine.org

MANAGING DIRECTOR / DIRECTORA EXECUTIVA
Adelaide Franco Nikolic

GRAPHIC & WEB DESIGN
Adelaide Books LLC, New York

CONTRIBUTING AUTHORS IN THIS ISSUE

Nick Farriella, Michael Trobich, Anna Brassky, Zak Block, Rees Nielsen, Don Dussault, Rina Sclove, Torrie Jay White, Paul Perilli, John C. Weil, Pauline Duchesneau, Joel Worford, Sana Mojdeh, Ruth Deming, Anita Haas, P. J. Gannon, Samuel Buckley, David Massey, Eric Massey, Claudia Piepenburg, Eric Lutz, Maggie Gleason, Jordan King, Allen Long, Rachel Cavell, Robert Steward, Patrick Hahn, Kirby Michael Wright, Dr. Raymon Fenech, Noel Williams, Margo Poirier, Korkut Onaran, Luke Francis Beirne, Jonathan Dowdle, John Casey, Dave Nielsen, Sophie Chen, Barry Silesky, Katharine Studer, Howard Winn, Luke Skoza, John Horváth, Gary Beck, Mark J. Mitchell, Scott Thomas Outlar, Ryan Havely, William Welch, John Grey, Frederick Pollack, Dmitry Blizniuk, David Dephy, Madison Smith, Jane Varley

CONTENTS / CONTEÚDOS

Editor's Notes

STEVAN V. NIKOLIC

"TRUTH ACCORDING TO MICHAEL" QUOTES

"God wants you to be truthful and humble to yourself and others. He made you good and industrious, but you can't benefit from it if you always stumble on pride."

"... for miracles to happen, God needs our co-operation. As Pastor Charles once told me, God can throw us a rope to save us, but we have to hold to it."

"...leaving a book behind keeps your thoughts alive in this world forever. So, in some ways, your spirit never dies. It is the best way to achieve immortality."

"Sometimes, he thought of himself as an elephant walking through the china store, breaking everything in his path and still expecting people not to be angry with the damage he made, but rather to admire his strength and his endurance."

"I think that both our lives and the potential directions our lives may go are predestined. By using our free will in making our life choices, we do nothing else but picking up one of many already predestined options. To us, it seems like we were making the decision, while in reality, we just selected one of many possibilities that were already a part of our destiny."

"Don't you think God is so powerful that he can make us believe that we made some choices, when in actuality, he had made a choice for us?"

"How far we can go with our liberty of conscience, without offending God, and disturbing the natural order of things..."

"Strangely enough, he didn't feel any guilt for separating himself from his past. Five years ago, he clearly heard in his dream a message brought to him by Archangel Michael from the God Almighty, telling him he should get up and leave everything behind; that his place was not there; that it was time to go in search for his true self and for his true destiny. Now, five years after, he was sitting in the Bowery chapel, a broken and homeless man, still trying to find that which he was looking for. But he didn't regret anything he had done in those five years. In his mind, it wasn't his doing. He sincerely believed that he surrendered his own will to the will of God and that everything that happened to him, good or bad, had to happen for some reason. It was God's doing. It was his destiny. He just had to figure out why."

"I was going after a woman believing that the key is in being with her. But the key is in writing about her. The key is in words and words are in me. Longing for her is just an impulse for words to come out. And the whole purpose is for words to come out. Words are important. Words about love. About life."

"I don't know why I am doing this. Everybody is saying bad things about you. Wherever you go, whatever you do, there is a noise after you... In spite of everything, I respect your courage to go after your ideals, no matter what. Men like you make this world move. I know that the road you go is covered with thorns. But I also know that it must be a road to the stars."

KNOCK
by Nick Farriella

Esme was a charity care worker or "charity care officer" as she'd like to call it when discussing her job with relatives at family functions. She'd been doing it for twenty-two years, approving or denying thousands, if not millions of people Medicaid or health care assistance. At first, she felt like her job was a public service that she, an immigrant herself, was helping her people get the medical attention they needed. But now, a seasoned American citizen, Esme felt more like a gatekeeper, a guard of America's wealth. How things change.

Esme has been suffering from panic attacks lately. Call it menopause, or hot flashes, or low level anxiety since her twenties, but whatever you call it, Esme has had to rise from her desk chair, stagger across her office gasping for her breath, and turn over the deadbolt on her door. The simple click was a quick relief. Next came crouching behind her desk and hyperventilating into a brown paper bag until her breathing settled, her heart rate lowered, and the world aligned with itself again. She remembered thinking, briefly during her first panic attack, it was as if the uncertain state of her home country of Colombia had found its way into her mind and took a small bite. Slowly, this anxiety ate at her, until she felt it had consumed her thoughts entirely. Even her office— a small, broom closet-like office in the basement level of St. Katharine Drexel's hospital— had felt as if it were shrinking, closing in on her to the point where it felt her ear was steadily against the door and with each knock of a new patient, came a dreadful thud of panic.

Her husband, Paul, a gringo always comfortable with the ground he stands on, had told her to relax, to chill out. But honestly, Esme thought, *Callate la fucking boca*, because she hasn't been able to chill out since she left Colombia in 1978.

When Esme decided to tell her son Jorge about the panic attacks, on the phone while attempting to eat her lunch at her desk in between patient visits, spooning the refried bean casserole into her mouth while tears hardened in streams on her cheeks, she expected that he would offer her some type of console. Instead, his voice cracked and quivered. *Panic attacks, Mija?* His worry had made Esme worry; anxiety over anxiety, the loop continued.

It was usually after lunch when Esme would find herself feeling sluggish. It was easy to blame the greasy cafeteria food or the three to four hours of attempted sleep where she was half conscious, hearing her heartbeat in the canals of her ears as she tried to drift off, but the thing that depleted her energy entirely was the fact that she was *tired*. She was tired of seeing patient after patient, always wanting something from her. Whether it was a pregnant Muslim woman, dressed in a burka, who traveled from Saudi Arabia to New Jersey to have her child be born an American citizen; with only eyes looking back at Esme that said, "You better make this happen, white woman, or it will be your life," or the slender man from Nigeria with gorgeous facial features, dazzling jewelry, and a royal complexion, that refused to look at her because she was a woman. She imagined him lifting her off the ground by her throat and sliding an elephant's tusk through her chest if she denied him Medicaid. People assumed, because she was on one side of the desk wearing a suit with an ID badge around her neck, that she wasn't one of them, that she was simply some white bitch.

"It's mentally exhausting," she had admitted to Jorge over the phone one night, pouring herself a glass of wine.

The job wasn't like this at first. In the late nineties, when Esme had just graduated from college at thirty-eight, she would proudly say, even before a drink, with all seriousness, "I love my new job." That, she did. She loved all the different kinds of people who would come to her with their illnesses, their flaws, and she was the one to fix them. Well, not *actually* do the procedure, but she at least got them through to the next round, as if she was an interviewer or a talent scout. The patients would knock on her door, enter with sunken eyes of helplessness, and she would be sitting behind her desk, back straight and sincere smile, and think something like, "No need to frown, dear human, there is hope. This is America and you are in good hands. Now let's see what you've got."

What a wonderful time that was. A time when patients would offer her gifts, bracelets, fruit baskets, even cash; which she always denied. The smiles she accepted, the gracious stamp that another good deed was done, another person saved. Gratitude was always enough.

What had changed?

It wasn't her drinking. She always kept that in moderation with the help from a doctor's opinion that one to two glasses of red wine per day helps keep the blood pressure down and the overall health up. So, what was one more extra glass going to do? She still went to work every day, she kept her son and her husband fed, the house clean, the laundry done. It was definitely not the wine.

She wondered if it was *her* that had changed. At times she would stare at herself in the mirror and think, "Has my skin always been this white?" Her hair, chemically straightened and blonde, opposed to the voluminous dark curls of her youth. She sometimes would cry and think of her home country. It tore her up to realize that she had been in the United States for almost thirty years longer than she was in Colombia. "That seems like another life," she once admitted to Jorge, before any wine was had at all.

It *was* another life. Life on a farm for the youngest girl of 4 sisters and 6 brothers was not easy, a life where she had to give up a childhood for work and routine. Every day felt like a life in itself; born into a task to retire by dusk. This was all she knew. She was the dirty farm girl in school with a big nose and crusty ponytails. Her friends were the animals on her father's farm, not the kids that picked on her because of her smell or her rotten shoes. After a long day of farm chores, school, then house cleaning, she would welcome the death of sleep each night. It was there where she would dream of a foreign place; one where she felt like she belonged, one that didn't feel like a struggle to exist in, one that looked like America in Time Magazine.

Often, usually on nights when Paul was away on business trips, she wondered if it was the distance from who she was to who she is that broke her apart, like two continents splitting and drifting away. Over time did she erase who she was to be who her new country wanted her to be? These were questions that a fourth glass of wine would bring up, which Esme never poured.

What *had* changed her job was the change in the country. Prior to 2008, her patients were mostly immigrants from Mexico, undocumented workers who got hurt on the job or pregnant women who had been in the country illegally for years. This was no problem, they needed help. She would file the proper paperwork along with her stamp of approval, to ensure these people got the best health care that was available to them. They were survivors just as she was; hardworking, *kind* people, who one day will seize the opportunity to become legal citizens, just as she had. But for them, there was always a nasty tooth, a broken femur, or an unexpected baby in the way of that goal. It was Esme's job to keep them on that path, a path to freedom. This is what she loved about America, its dutiful responsibility to immigrants; that you can come here and belong, that after bubbling in George Washington as the first president on a Scantron test, you will be accepted.

After 9/11, this ideology would change in a devastating way. It seemed foreigners were not to be trusted, but vetted with a nationalistic scope of judgment. This seemed to be a global sized problem, an issue to be worked out over time by future presidents and world leaders. How was it possible for Esme, in the charity care department of a Catholic hospital, to end up with a small scope of judgment herself? It started with a change in her patients, then a change in Paul to cause her scope to grow in size.

It was in early 2009 when Esme started to get an increase in volatile patients. The outbursts were nothing new; this part of the job was expected when someone's health was on the line. It was the knife that was new, pulled on her behind a closed door. Luckily she had a panic button beneath her desk. After the knife, it was spitting. She had been spat on by all races. People denied healthcare because of expired visas, criminal records, or because they already received a certain amount of money for their last child, their last surgery, their last visit to the ER. After spitting came death threats, not just to her personally but to the country of America. "No wonder why they bombed the towers. They *ought* to do it again," a woman had said. Esme froze and felt offended. She had lost a friend in 9/11. It was hard to hide her smile as she stamped DECLINED on the woman's application, as security dragged her out.

At times she didn't know who to blame, so she blamed Paul. After all this time he still didn't understand her. It didn't help that he naturally rejected anything Hispanic. "Turn that crap off," he'd groan, when Esme would play Salsa music while mopping the kitchen. "This is disgusting, I'm ordering pizza," he said, pushing away the plate of Bandeja Paisa, a famous Colombian dish of red beans cooked with pork, white rice, ground meat, chicharron, fried egg, plantain, chorizo, arepa, hogao sauce, black pudding, avocado, and lemon. One may ask, who would tolerate this? Well, Esme saw in Paul what she saw in America. She saw his dark history, one of liberation, misguidedness, racism, triumph and glory, but what she saw most was great potential.

At first, her marriage with Paul marriage was good. Paul was a good man, a man full of life. He was always laughing. They met when they were both nineteen. Paul would play his records, they would smoke some pot. Esme would sit in silence, admiring his grandiosity. He was big, he was strong, and he was American. He was a hard worker like she was and had great taste in music. Esme would attest to learning English from Paul's Led Zeppelin collection. They were married by twenty-two. That was thirty years ago, now. And much like the state of race in America, Paul hadn't made the changes necessary to accept Esme as an equal. Paul could never really grasp the idea that Esme was from a different world. To him, it was as if she was from a small suburban town similar to his, just one that was too far to drive to. When Esme brought him to Colombia, the first thing he said of Bogota was, "Oh, it's like a shitty New Brunswick."

Over time it was these micro-assaults on Esme's ethnicity that built a wall between them. Esme felt like a foreigner in her own house. As the news became more intense, more polarizing, Paul grew angry and cold. He no longer laughed with her. He no longer reached across the table for her hand at dinner to look at Esme with his wide green eyes to say things like, "We'll make it happen together."

She no longer saw potential in him nor sought comfort in his words. She only heard his outbursts, as if every single person who comes into the country to use America's services for their benefit was a personal attack on his character. She became an attack on his character. It showed in his flushed face, in his salivating mouth.

"Es, are you kidding with that shit? Do you really believe that America could be just this open door mat? Get a grip."

Esme would sink into herself like a turtle and mutter to herself that he just didn't understand.

Maybe it was her too that didn't understand. Maybe this is how it was. She understood that getting older brought opportunities to become someone new, but she could never adopt new things like going to baseball games, using credit cards, and celebrating the Fourth of July with tequila shots and a stars and stripes bathing suit. She struggled to learn that a good patriot is loyal to her country. Even though no matter where she was from, America was her country now, her home and she was incredibly lucky to have that. She'd relinquished her past and wanted to believe that made her strong. She just could never see, not even in the cards of her fate, that she would eventually tolerate knitting besides an American husband, as he drank beer and watched Fox News. It was impossible. And as Esme struggled to accept this, the further away she felt from it all. It was as if America was some bus that she had missed, and Paul was the driver.

Slowly over time, Esme began to hide her ethnicity from her husband, as if it was a secret lover or a private smoking habit. She would play the Salsa or the Cumbia while in the car or in her headphones at the gym. She would enjoy the foods of her country only on Sundays with her son. But eventually, she would go to the gym less and less, her headphones would lay dormant in her nightstand drawer, and Jorge would go off to college.

***

"This is the new world," Paul was saying. They were on the couch, watching TV together. Esme had just finished making hamburgers. Fox News was running a segment on immigration about how illegal immigrants "drain" the healthcare system. "It's time to close the borders," Paul declared.

Was this true? Esme thought, sipping her wine in distress. The more she sipped, eventually finishing her glass, and then the bottle, it started to make sense to her. It gave reason to the influx of volatile patients, patients who seemed ungrateful.

"It wasn't like this for *me*," she blurted out, sort of snobbishly, the way older generations speak of younger ones.

"That's right," Paul agreed.

"I struggled," she said.

"Yes."

"I *never* took advantage of the system like this."

The next day at work, Esme had her first panic attack.

***

That was six months ago. She tried therapy, but was put off when having to talk about her childhood. Some scars just run too deep. The death of her father at age six. Being raped at age thirteen in Medellín. The loss of her mother at sixteen. She couldn't understand how things that happened fifty years ago could ever impact her now, especially in her new country. Paul said that she had a point. Her primary care physician agreed and went the scientific route, the biology behind it all.

"It's clear that your hormones are at play here; menopause, along with your history of anxiety. Is your job very stressful?"

Esme contained her laughter.

"Doctors are quacks," Paul said later that night, flicking on the TV, "Have another glass of wine."

By this point, her and Paul were like two passing ships. The idea of sitting with him as he consumed his media repulsed her, so she retreated to her bedroom to text her sister in Colombia using an app that doesn't charge long distance through Wi-Fi.

-Hola, it's been awhile, what's up?

It was strange to her that even now, after all these years, she and Rodika spoke to each other through text in English when Spanish came out naturally over the phone and in person. It was as if Spanish was strictly reserved for intimacy.

-Hi!!! Que Paso…

-Not much. It's just me and Paul. Jorge is back at school. How's everything?

-Wonderful! We have new chickens :^)

For some reason, Rodika always correlated the wellness of her life with the stock of her farm. This made Esme miss home and jealous of the simplicity.

-Question… have you ever had a panic attack before?

Esme felt foolish for having asked this through text and wished she never did. She wanted to delete it, but Rodika started typing.

(…)

(…)

Rodika would start typing then stop, building the suspense. Esme hoped that a break in connection caused her last text to fail before sending.

-How are the kids? Esme sent quickly.

-Of course I've had panic attacks Mija. We all have. Have you tried meditation?

Meditation to Esme was for hippies and Buddhists. She didn't understand how sitting in silence, legs crossed like a pretzel, could relax the mind. What does that even mean? Relax the mind. Anytime Esme closed her eyes, it was as if she could feel her thoughts whooshing by

in her head. She could never sit still listening to all of that chatter.

However, with help from a few Facebooks posts, shared by Rodika, Esme found herself using an iPhone app to assist her with guided meditation. The first session was for ten minutes. Esme put on stretchy pants to signify that some type of exercise was about to be done. She shouted out to Paul, "I'll be in the basement for ten minutes doing some yoga."

"Whatever," he said.

She wondered why she felt like she had to lie and thought that that wasn't a very good start.

Esme sat on the faded beige carpet next to the broken treadmill that had old winter coats thrown across it. She sat as legs crossed as she could, feeling completely ridiculous, feeling like a child in time out. She followed the instructions from the soothing voice in her earphones; focused on her breath, let thoughts come and go. She was surprised that for about fifteen seconds out of the entire session, her mind seemed to be thoughtless. She decided to meditate again the following day.

The next morning at work, Esme was twisting her hair behind her desk, trying to focus on her breath. She was waiting for the next knock on her door. The previous patient was a pregnant woman from Dubai. She had brought along her husband; they were expecting twins. They were approved for Medicaid and when they received the amount due, $14,676, the husband said, "I cannot pay this. This is absurd."

"I do apologize, Mr. Antar," she said.

He seemed stunned.

She apologized once more.

"I'm sorry, Mr. Antar. It shows here that this is your fourth Medicaid request and that you have been approved twice before. It seems that you were able to pay your last amount due with no problem, in cash. There's nothing else I can do."

"Fucking bitch," he said, then spat across her desk.

As soon as the door slammed, Esme felt her breath escaping her. She could feel her heart hammering inside of her chest, feeling it pulse in her neck and her arms. She began to sweat and lose focus visually. Her office felt like it was melting away.

Despite her racing thoughts, Esme tried to follow the meditation guide: focus on your weight in the chair, feel your feet against the floor, concentrate on your breath. How does one focus on what they cannot catch? *Inhale on one, exhale on two.* It's like trying to chase the wind. Her eyes gaped with fear, her ears felt nearly closed, until a knock on the door brought her back.

Knock knock.

A couple entered, slouching over to the chairs at Esme's desk. They had a skittish demeanor, the way one can scrunch in the presence of someone of a higher class. They were Hispanic. The woman was small, slightly wounded looking with a youthful face. The man was rugged looking, dirty with sunken eyes. He was missing his left hand. Esme, coming down from her panic attack, was unimpressed. She had seen it all and by now she was numb to it.

"How may I help you?" she said.

"We would like to apply for charity care," the woman said.

"The two of you?"

"For our daughter. She is sick."

Usually she doesn't like to hear patient's stories. It puts an unnecessary context to the entire process and the last thing Esme needed was to feel guilty for denying someone their coverage. An application was enough. Medical history, immigration status, financial status; these were concrete things attached to no emotion, but the woman went on.

"We are from Nicaragua," she said, in clear English.

"I see," Esme said, "undocumented?"

The couple's eyes found the floor.

"Yes," the woman said.

"Have you filed for a green card?" A Diversity Visa?"

"No."

"Unfortunately, I cannot assist you until the proper paperwork has been filed."

This is when Esme expected the spit, the knife, or the cursing. Instead, the woman leaned in close and spoke in a direct manner.

"It took us twelve days to travel here by train. You see, our daughter was awoken in the middle of the night with a fever and a deep cough. We figured she had caught a cold from school. It is winter in Nicaragua, the temperature sometimes drops suddenly. It affects our farm, we farm sugarcane."

Esme began to focus on her breath, listening with half an ear, more so concerned with how much longer until the end of her shift.

"The fever no passed even after a full day. I spent all night at her side, patting a soaked towel on her forehead and rubbing menthol cream on her chest. This went on for two more days. We went to the village doctor. After a day of tests, he was sure she had cancer. He referred us to the shaman for prayer and a dose of pills."

By this point, Esme was studying the woman's face. She was looking into her eyes thinking, "Okay, what else? My first three patients this morning were children, all under the age of two, all with terminal cancer."

"We did not want our daughter to suffer anymore. We knew that she needed the best health care. Cruz, my husband," she said, "had heard that America was advanced. There were surgeries, better tests, more certainty."

"That was when I made a deal with the Devil," Cruz said in Spanish, lifting his left arm in the air, showing a curve of skin and stitches where his hand used to be.

This had struck a nerve with Esme; it had broken the rhythm of her breath and allowed a flood of thoughts to enter her mind. She was always quick to assume that missing limbs, like scars, had stories behind them. When her uncle had lost his foot from gout, he said it was because he danced with the devil for too long. *Did the Devil always take limbs?,* she wondered, then started to listen to Cruz with intent.

"My cousin knew a route to America, a freight train that went from Nicaragua to Mexico City, then Mexico City straight through to Texas. It was called The Beast."

Esme has heard of such trains, they were almost mythicized, where hundreds of immigrants would board the train, sometimes tucking themselves underneath the beams below the freight cars, but usually laying on the roofs like excess baggage thrown above for convenience. She had heard that a lot of people had died before getting into America, some struck with illness or starvation, some were sucked under the train in motion, and some were even murdered. She compared this to her migration to the states, a coach flight from Bogota to Miami.

"We met a man in the Mexican desert who went by the name of El Diablo. He said for one-hundred thousand pesos he could get us a spot on the train to get us to the U.S. border. From there, it was up to us. At the border, the train running at full speed, a man with a bandana tied around his face like half of a mask, blew an air horn. That meant it was time to jump. I held tight around my wife with our daughter between us and leapt into the darkness, directly into the hands of God. Aminta and Lana landed in some shrubs; they were scratched up, but no serious injuries. I smacked the desert ground so hard, my teeth rattled, my hand was badly broken."

By this point, Esme was one with her breath. She was a vessel being filled with her surroundings. When Cruz explained the eighteen mile hike out of the desert, the infection, the amputation, the train ride from Texas to Chicago then to New Jersey, Esme was full, bursting with emotion. She heard this story and saw herself alongside Cruz, Aminta, and Lana on their journey. *It's the sacrifices we make that mark us for eternity,* Rodika posted to Facebook after their text conversation. Esme understood it, and even hit "like." It was the result of these sacrifices that was left unknown. Had Cruz sold his soul, exchanging his hand for his daughter's health? Unfortunately, she still had to deny them coverage. They had none of the right paperwork, and their only U.S. residency was Cruz's cousin, who had a criminal background of theft and arson. So, what was it all for? All of that sacrifice just for an opportunity?

When Esme saw what she had given up for her life of freedom, it doesn't seem like much in comparison to Cruz and Aminta, who smiled and thanked her for her time as they left her office. *Such gratitude.* Perhaps what she found here in the land of the free wasn't freedom at all, but different ways by which she was imprisoned. Perhaps she will never understand what else she has left to give, just as her husband may never understand her, and maybe her panic attacks will never go away. This is uncertainty that she would have to learn to live with, like a scar or an amputated hand. "Dios que da la llaga, de la medicina," Aminta had said. God, who gives the wound, gives the salve.

She left work that day feeling what she had felt in the airport leaving Colombia all of those years ago. Her body trembling. Her mind racing. It was these physical symptoms that always reminded Esme it was time for action, like an alarm clock waking her up. But this time it wasn't begging her to leave her country, but to leave herself; whatever idea of herself as an American. She had called Jorge on her way home and let out everything that has been troubling her. It felt as if she had split open an artery. His voice sounded encouraging through the speakers of her car, filling up the space around her almost god-like, embodying the words she needed to hear. "It's okay if you divorce," he said. "I can't say I didn't see this coming. I'm old enough now to take it. I just want you to be happy."

At home she had went straight to her room, ignoring Paul's request for dinner and his demanding poison tipped arrows trying to infiltrate her, trying to pierce her skin with his negativity. She locked the door then found a place in the center of the room to assume the lotus position. She closed her eyes and focused on her breath. She felt her weight on the floor, observed the tension of her shoulders, her neck; she felt the weight of her entire being. It seemed like so much, too much to bear. But she stayed focused on her breath. Soon, breath after breath, the floor beneath her feet fell away, along with Paul's high-pitched yelling and thunderous knocks against the door. She felt weightless.

About the Author:

Nick Farriella's fiction has appeared in Barrelhouse, X-R-A-Y, Maudlin House, and elsewhere. He lives in New Jersey and works as a copywriter and a flash fiction reader for Split Lip Magazine.

CANDID

by Michael Trobich

Kate Gibbons likes to take pictures. She doesn't know how it started, closing shutters and toggling flash, but she loves the way that each photo has every pixel in place and captures moments in amber. She sees the way her friends quietly fear age, the gym memberships and expensive cars and spa weekends, and she takes her comfort in the small army of family photos around her home. They're her way of remembering who she is, her mind fighting back against the body's inevitable betrayal.

Her family, for the most part, either appreciates or indulges this habit. Her husband Scott is a salesman, and so always has a winning smile on demand. Molly is just getting to be seven, and likes dressing up and having fashion shows for Mommy. Ty is one year old, and still getting used to the peculiar experience that is having toes, so he's registered no serious objections. Even her mom lets her take the pictures when they visit. Kate has always had a talent to pose people just so, and with a bright "Smile!" She takes photos in which people look, if not the best they ever have, certainly the best they can today.

Her dad is the one exception. When Arthur was young, he had been a bit of a hell-raiser, shooting out the stoplight in his one stoplight town, and though he's mellowed with age, rules remain his favorite thing to break. Whenever Kate's taking pictures, he's sure to be close, and he'll jump in at the last second, laughing. There's never a quiet moment when Arthur is around the rest of his family. He has never quite known how to relate to his daughter, his only child. Nowadays, he often acts like a schoolboy with her, doing small things just to get a rise or a smile.

Today, though, he has a new idea. It is Ty's first birthday party tonight, and Arthur and his wife Rose are lucky enough to be in town. So, while Molly goes shopping with her grandma and Scott and Kate decorate furiously, he pops into town for an hour or so. The nice young man at the electronics store helps him pick out a camera that's nice and practical, quick enough to catch a hummingbird at the feeder, sturdy enough to take a few falls when his hands swell in the mornings.

During the party, he takes it out of the intricate packaging and walks over to his daughter.

"Katie," he asks, "can you show me how to use this thing?"

She sees the camera and laughs.

"Dad, why'd you buy a camera? I'm taking plenty of pictures already."

"I know, but you seem to enjoy it so much I thought I'd give it a shot."

So she shows him the settings she thinks he'll want to use and asks him to take some pictures of the kids, thinking he wants to feel useful. Arthur, though, knows what he wants to do.

For the rest of the night, he is furtive, lurking around corners or across the room. Somehow, his daughter's talent has been passed up to him, but instead of delicately posed photos, he takes candid shots. He captures the moments that people look the most like themselves. Ty laughs as his hand extends leftward, sending his plate of cake flipping away. Molly hugs the family dog close, burying her face in his shoulder fur. Scott watches his wife snap a picture of their son as he leans on the doorframe, simple contentment in his eyes and on his lips.

These are what greet Kate when she wakes up in the morning. Her work means she gets up before anyone else in the house, and they are there in the soft light of the early morning. There is one on the inside of her door, one in the hallway, one on the kitchen table. He must've gone out last night to get them printed, after everyone had gone to bed. Kate has never known how to think of her dad as a person and not her father or a grandfather, and so every photo to her is like a little miracle, preserving moments she didn't even know she missed.

When Arthur comes down that morning, he sees that all the photos have been collected. He smiles. His daughter is not someone who lets things get lost, and he is sure the photos have been put away somewhere, stowed for a rainy day.

Time passes, as it does, and more pictures are taken. Kate and her father grow closer, the way you do to people with whom you share a passion, and they talk about the way the light is best in the early morning, how one of the best parts of pictures are the things you see in them that you never saw the first time.

At some point or another, she asks Arthur why he started taking photos.

"Well, why did you start?" he replies.

"I don't know. I've never really thought about it," she says.

There is a moment of comfortable silence between them.

"I don't know why I started, but I think I take pictures now to remember things," she says.

"That's funny," he says. "I was going to say the same thing."

Kate had a different reason when she began to take photos. She has always been this way, the way where the world feels always a little out of place around her. Scott calls it "nervous". To Kate, it feels the way she feels whenever she breaks open a Pop-Tart.

When Kate was younger, she had the same nightmare on the second Saturday of every month. She would be holding a Pop-Tart in her mother's kitchen, brown sugar cinnamon, her favorite. She would sna it in half, the way that children who eat Pop-Tarts do to make them feel like they last longer. She would break it, and out would come a colony of ants, a steady stream of tiny black marching insects, rows and columns and regiments and battalions and she couldn't drop the Pop-Tarts, all she could do was let the ants crawl over her body, cover her skin, and scream silently.

Kate does not call the way she is "nervous". Kate does not call it anything. She takes photos of the best that people can be because people, she has decided, are like Pop-Tarts. Sometimes, they are horrible and terrifying. But most of the time, they're pretty okay, and they deserve to see that.

More time passes and even more pictures are taken and Rose, her mother, dies. Arthur speaks at the funeral, but begins crying halfway through the eulogy, and struggles through the rest of it. Years weigh down his shoulders like sandbags. The picture beside the coffin, the one beside the priest who performs the service, is one Kate took a few years ago, of her mother in her Sunday best. At the reception afterwards, there are pictures Arthur took: Rose gardening, or tasting soup, or reading in her armchair with her glasses on, the dusty lamp beside her spilling a soft light over the page. Neither one of them have any photos of her in her hospital bed, when the cancer took hold. It seemed cruel then, to capture a moment they had all hoped so long would never come.

Soon, Arthur finds himself in a similar situation. He has always had arthritis and now gout begins to creep into him through his toes. They give him a wheelchair, but osteoporosis soon makes it difficult for him to push himself around. Kate and Scott do an admirable job of ignoring the ways in which his body is failing, but he can feel it, and he asks them to help him look into assisted living. At first, they protest, thinking that he wants them to tell him why he doesn't need it. He doesn't. They come around, Kate more slowly than Scott.

The assisted living home is very nice and the nurses are very nice and everything there is very nice and smells like cleaning supplies. Arthur tires quickly of the preplanned activities, and begins to stay in bed more and more often. Soon, he spends entire days there, writing in a journal or doing crossword puzzles. He doesn't bother anyone, and his condition doesn't seem to worsen. He convinces the nurses one by one to let him take just two walks a day. Whenever Kate visits, they take a walk in the hour after sunrise and the hour before sunset, when the light from the sun filters best through a camera. They find squirrels gathering supplies for the winter, hummingbirds flitting through flowers, and once, the shadow of an old wolf stretching like a tree trunk through the twilight. They take a lot of pictures.

She visits often, sometimes with Scott, sometimes with the kids. Molly is in college now, and Ty is starting high school. They are too preoccupied discovering young adulthood to think too much about their grandfather.

On one visit, he asks her to bring him some of his old photographs.

"I'm getting old," he says. "Can you bring me some pictures? I'd love to see if I can rustle up a few fond memories."

So she brings him the pictures, all put to-gether in a nice album. He flips through every page, growing gradually frustrated as he begins to encounter photographs he doesn't remember taking. Eventually, he gives the album back to Kate and turns away. The sun is setting outside.

"I remember this one," she says. "Ty's first birthday party. It was when you first went out and bought that camera."

He turns back to her. "Which camera?"

And so she tells him about the camera that was both nice and sturdy and the way that she thought he had just wanted to be useful. She shows him the picture of Molly and the picture of her and Scott and she tells him about coming down in the morning to the photos scattered throughout the house. And he remembers the nice young man in the electronics store, the one who had helped him print out those photos that night, and the way that Ty's cake had spattered the nice white tablecloth with specks of blue icing that never quite came out.

He makes his way through his memories like this, some slower than others. If he doesn't have pictures for something he wants to know about, she shows him hers, and he relives his life one event at a time. Kate learns some of the things about a person you don't learn when they're your father if they can help it, like how infuriating he's always found Scott's habit of drumming his fingers on the table, or how he had drunkenly lost several thousand dollars to a man in poker a few days after Rose's funeral. He finds the times in his life when everything seemed like it was going wrong, and he makes his way to now, to spending sunsets and sunrises with his daughter.

Scott and the kids begin to visit less frequently. Arthur's place in assisted living has become a regularity now, and this decline in activity is understood and quietly accepted by everyone involved.

Before a particular visit, the doctor who is

in charge of Arthur's case takes Kate aside in the lobby.

"Kate, I hate to tell you this, but your father's getting worse," he says. Kate wonders how many times a day he has to say that.

"What do you mean?"

"His physical condition is fine, nothing new there. But his mental state is slowly deteriorating. He's getting plenty of mental exercise, but he's reached the age where some decline is inevitable."

"What exactly does that mean, Doctor?"

"He may begin to forget things. Things he shouldn't forget, I mean."

"Like?"

"Significant events in his life. People. The other day, he asked how his daughter's baby boy was doing."

"Is there anything you can do?"

"We can give him medication," he says. "But eventually, this is just what his mind is going to do. We see it every day here. People are like everything else. They break slowly over time."

Kate comes away from the conversation thoroughly unimpressed with the doctor's bedside manner. When she goes in to see her dad, she can see in his face that it takes a second for him to recognize her. They talk about the way that the bird feeders are set up so that he can't take good pictures. They take a walk in the hour before sunset. Kate is still getting used to pushing her father around in the wheelchair. He is still getting used to not being able to jump into pictures.

When they get back, she takes out the album she brings to every visit, but before she can get it out of her bag, she hears him start talking.

"Scott, what are you doing here? I thought you had a business trip?"

Kate looks up with a start. Scott isn't here.

He's away on a business trip, and Arthur is looking at a picture of Scott on his bedside table, a picture that Kate had given him. There is a smile on his face and for a moment, Kate can't tell if he's joking or not, but then he starts to speak again.

"Well, I'm happy you made it, and I'm sure Katie appreciates the time you're taking away from your job."

And he turns to her and the smile on his face is so full and she knows in that moment that he is not joking. In this moment, Kate doesn't know what to do, and Arthur does, so she goes along with it.

"It's definitely not easy getting time away," she says, doing her best Scott impression. "But it's worth it."

Arthur laughs. "Coming from someone who took plenty of off days in my time, you never end up regretting them."

They have a three-person conversation. After a while, it is easier for Kate to look at the picture of Scott when she is speaking in his voice, for her to act as if Scott was really speaking. It doesn't get easier for her to understand what is going on, and when she's left, making sure to say goodbye to the picture of Scott as well ("I think I'll stay a little later this time, Kate, why don't you go ahead and get back home?"), she is too rattled by the experience and her previous conversation with him to ask the doctor what precisely just happened. When she gets back home, though, she tells Scott, and spends the rest of the night sitting with him at the kitchen table, alternately crying and exhausted.

"What do I do?" she asks him. "There has to be something I can do."

"Just keep visiting him," Scott says. "He'll know it's you. He'll remember you."

Kate keeps visiting her dad, and he keeps remembering her. She asks Scott and the kids not to come, hoping not to destabilize her father's perception of reality even further. She hopes that the kids are old enough to mostly remember their grandfather when he was not dying in a nursing home. There are times when Arthur thinks that Kate has left the room, and he will have conversations with other people, all of whose voices come out of her mouth. Still, these things all begin and end with her and her father saying hello and goodbye. She asks the nurses, and they tell her that he doesn't do this when she's not visiting. He's happier when you're here, they say. He knows somewhere inside him that you're here, they say.

They no longer go on walks after sunrise and before sunset. If her dad isn't asleep, it's too hard to get him out of bed.

Time passes. Kate begins, to a certain extent, to think this is normal.

Kate walks into her father's room for the last time before he dies, although, of course, she doesn't know that. Arthur is writing in his journal, and doesn't look up.

"Hey Dad," she says. Arthur still doesn't look up. She thinks of the room as it must look to him: empty, with only the growing shadows of dusk for company. She goes over to the side of his bed, and takes out a picture from her bag which she had never hoped to talk about.

She holds it up, and a posed picture of herself on a family vacation, in a sundress at the beach, her favorite photo of herself, says with her voice, "Hi Dad."

He looks at it and smiles. "Katie! How are you?"

Her voice breaks several times when she is talking to him, but she passes it off as recovering from a sickness. Her arm begins to get tired holding the picture up in front of her face, but she does not want to look at his eyes, so when she lowers it she looks out of the window. He asks her to tell him stories about her life, says he's begun to forget things that he wants to know about her. So she says words and the picture tells him stories, tells him about her

wedding, about the days her children were born, about how happy she was when he started taking pictures because that was something she loved and now he loved it too. How both of their reasons for taking pictures were to remember things, and the picture sniffled a little bit on that one. When he hears that, he laughs.

"Oh Katie," he says. "I really started taking pictures to have something worth remembering. Of course, Rose meant the world to me, but at that point, I barely knew my daughter. Sure, I knew who you were, and I knew what you did, but I didn't have any memories of you that weren't posed, you know? I wanted to know who you were when you were doing something you really loved. So I started taking pictures because I wanted to take them of you. I wanted to see you the way you see someone when you see a photo of them they weren't expecting. I've always thought that's how you know someone best, when they're not expecting it."

Katie is focusing very hard on the fact that she is not crying. Focusing so hard on this, in fact, that she misses the first time her dad says, "Excuse me, miss?" He says it again and she starts. She looks around the room, but there are no other pictures, no other people. She lowers the picture slowly from her face and there is her father looking at her, blank and earnest.

"Miss, would you mind taking a picture of me and my daughter? I want something to remember this by." He is handing her a camera, an old one, and she realizes it is the first one he bought, still nice and sturdy. He is taking the photo from her, the one of her, and holding it close to him.

"Of course," she says mechanically. She has been taking pictures her whole life.

She stands and pulls the shutter up in front of her eye. She frames the old man in the hospital bed, cradling the photo of his daughter that she took a few years ago, on the last family vacation he was in good enough shape to go on. Kate Gibbons arranges the picture for herself in the golden light that streams in from the window.

"Smile," she says, and takes the picture.

About the Author:

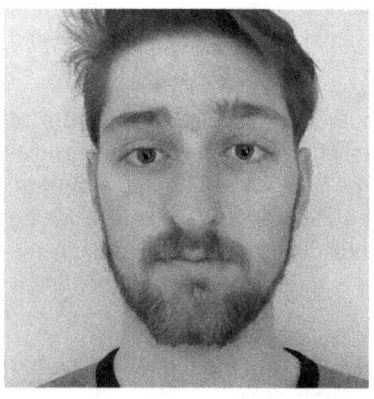

Michael J. Trobich is a North Carolinian by birth, an Ohioan by residence, and a current student at Kenyon College. His fiction has previously appeared in in Polyphony.

PLEASE CONFIRM YOU ARE NOT IN BEAST MODE

by Anna Brassky

A month ago, Chris began to see dwarfs, though not exactly see but rather sense their presence. Just as he was about to spot them, they hid. He could only get a glimpse of their small dark outlines and tiny dirty feet as they ran away.

It'd have been okay if they appeared only outside and during daytime. But they got into his bed at night, rattled his sheets and pinched him. He cried and called his family for help. He was sure that if someone else saw them too, the dwarfs wouldn't trouble him anymore. His brothers and sisters rushed over, turned his bed upside down, but the wicked dwarfs holed up in their crevices - all that his family found was the light fluttering of blankets from their rapid flight.

At least his siblings believed him. Each time he shrieked in his bed they were there by his side, and that comforted him. It meant that they wouldn't let the dwarfs win, because Chris knew what these creatures wanted. When he was asleep, their little bodies snuck to his neck, sat on it and closed his mouth and nose with their filthy palms so he couldn't breathe. The only way to stop their abuse was by waking up, then they disappeared under his gaze, and his breathing returned.

To be helpful, his family signed him into a therapy group. Those people could suggest how to get rid of the dwarfs, they said. They had gone through similar things, and each of them had their own solution. Chris was glad to meet like minds, but as soon as he set foot in the room, he immediately realized he was surrounded by psychos. Was that what his family thought of him?

Not willing to stay in this gray, faceless place soaked in dust and boredom anymore, he walked straight to the corner of the room where a young woman with glasses and a thin mousy ponytail sat at a shabby desk. A few other people joined him; they now stood silently behind making him the undisputed leader of their rebellion. *They've probably figured out this place too*, thought Chris.

'I...We want to leave,' Chris announced loudly, staring at the faded flag on the wall.

The girl looked up at him wearily, her gaze reading, *I'm so sick and tired of you all*, and said:

'Please confirm you are not in beast mode.'

'What?' asked Chris, confused.

'If you want to leave,' the girl repeated with a sigh, 'you need to sign a certificate that you aren't in beast mode. Here it is.' She pushed the paper across the desk; a pen was there too, next to it.

That's crazy, thought Chris, but still reached for the pen and signed the paper.

'This copy is for you,' Specky said when Chris tried to return it to her. 'It's enough for us to know that you've agreed to sign.'

At home, Chris hid the certificate under his mattress. He had a gut feeling it belonged there. *Please confirm you are not in beast mode*. What had she meant? Before he knew it he had fallen asleep. The dwarfs showed up, once they saw he was defenceless. Vile wretches!

Chris realized that the air was coming out of his lungs but was not returning. It was getting harder to breathe. He tried to wake but something hampered him. Calling for help was the only thing that could save him before it was too late.

'AAAH,' a scary animal bellow exploded from his throat while in his head he heard, *Please confirm you are not in beast mode*.

'Will you go?' half-awake Mother asked Father in the neighboring room. Chris's muffled screams had woken her, now she lay on the bed squinting into the blinding moonlight.

'Nah,' Father answered and turned onto his other side. 'Let him wake by himself.'

'AAAH,' Chris continued to shriek but the sound didn't come as clear any more. It rather resembled a growl, a beast's growl. *Please confirm you are not in beast mode*. So that's what it meant. Maybe, he'd gone into beast mode and didn't notice that?

But the dwarfs were gaining the upper hand. His lungs were almost empty, his throat burned and his head became heavy, like a bowling ball. Chris still tried to fight, swung his arms and legs, spun like a top, anything just to shake those little sneaks off. But the bedsheets bound his fierce movements. He ripped them with his teeth but they enveloped him even tighter.

PLEASE CONFIRM YOU ARE NOT IN BEAST MODE! a female voice screamed in his head.

'I can't,' Chris hissed, like a rattlesnake now - these were the last drops of the air leaving his body. He froze.

Chris's body was found in his own apartment where he had lived alone for the last ten years. In his sleep, he had tossed and turned, winding mounting layers of cloth around him. One of the wraps covered his head. Any other man would have thrown a blanket aside even in the deepest slumber - it was a basic survival instinct - but Chris was unable to do that; he was wrapped like an ancient Egyptian mummy. His death throes only tightened the coil strangling him.

'Just like an animal in the coils of a constrictor,' noted Harry, one of the policemen who had arrived on the scene.

'Yeah, poor guy,' Nick agreed. 'Do you know what he watched before going to sleep?'

'What?'

'Snow White and the Seven Dwarfs. Weird, isn't it?'

'Yeaahh,' Harry drawled. 'Let's go, they need our help.'

Harry and Nick picked up Chris's cold, skinny body and put him on the stretcher. Behind them, the dwarfs giggled acidly.

'Turn off this cartoon already!' Harry snapped without turning back. Unpleasant chills ran down his spine.

'It's not on,' replied Nick as he eyed the dark screen curiously.

About the Author:

Anna Brassky is originally from Moscow, Russia but she currently lives and works in Southeast Asia. She studied Linguistics and Psychology and she has always been a fan of science fiction and Russian classic literature. This unusual combination and her adventurous spirit have become her inspiration for creating stories in the genre of psychological science fiction. Anna has recently finished her debut science fiction novel, Nadarri, which hasn't been published yet. She is currently working on her collection of short stories and non-fiction book tentatively entitled, How to Master Your Body. For more information about the author, visit https://twitter.com/ABrassky

THE GERMAN
by Rees Nielsen

It was the summer of 1971 and Murrow and I were stuck in Tehran waiting for the weekly bus to Istanbul. Down the hallway this barrel chested German was leaned up against the north wall smoking a cigarette.

"I'm going to tell you my life story." The German informed me as I passed. He was approaching middle age and had that weathered look that suggested trouble. "I'm not going to lie to you. I need a loan. Not baksheesh, mind you, but a short-term loan. They're about to kick my wife and I out on the street if I don't come up with the rent. I've got a check coming week's end and then I can pay you back." He flicked a cigarette out of his pack and held it out in my direction. "Let me tell you my story then it's your call."

His room was at the far corner of the hall. A chubby Persian boy clutching an accordion was waiting timorously next to the German's door. "This is Hissan," the German explained, "He has come for his weekly lesson." The boy looked at the floor in awe of the maestro.

The German patted Hissan on the top of the head. "Come Hissan, show me what you have learned." The German opened the door and pointed at a chair where I sat down. A woman wearing a turquoise silk sari embroidered with silver thread came out of the bathroom. She stood to the side checking the mirror while braiding the last strands of her long thick black hair. She waved me over to the sink at the other end of the room.

"It is permissible for a man to grow his hair long. That is fine," she said. "You have beautiful hair but you must wash it three times every day. Come to me and bend over the sink." She took a bottle down from the cabinet and, of all things, began to shampoo my hair.

Hissan, who couldn't have been more than eight, strapped on his accordion. He played with enthusiasm but he played like an eight-year old. Hissan wasn't the next Mozart but you had to admire his reverence for his mentor. He hung on every word. Half an hour later he pulled some waded Rials out of his pocket and anxiously asked about his next lesson.

"So you're a musician?" I asked after the boy departed.

The German smiled as I dried my head. He acknowledged the lady in the room sitting stiffly at the edge of the bed. "This is my wife Akter." Akter put her palms together closed her eyes and dipped her head. The German had crossed the room in three quick strides and was holding a large scrap book which he opened at the end of the bed. He waved me over and I sat across from him on the other side of the book.

"What do I call you," the German asked

"Call me Red," I answered, "everybody else does."

"Red, I am no ordinary musician. I am an entertainer. You understand the difference. A musician plays in an orchestra, an entertainer plays for the audience. I can play the accordion or the guitar or the horns, but better than that, I can play the crowd. This is my path. I am a student of songs and also a student of people. Songs can tell you more about people than any newspaper. I can sing songs from anywhere in the world. Anywhere! Name a country and I will sing you a song."

"Look," He flipped rapidly through the scrap book which was pasted with handbills of numerous countries from every hemisphere. He lighted on what he was looking for. "Red, believe me, I know American songs. Look here, I lived in Texas for four years." He pointed at a black and white photograph. It was a photo of the young German on a quarter horse wearing a black Stetson. "That's me," he assured me.

"I know all the melodies. All the everyday songs. I know ditch diggers songs. I know the lullabyes. The love songs. The drinking songs. I know the songs you grew up with in grade school. I know Red River Valley, Streets of Laredo, Strawberry Roan. I know all the cowboy songs and the coal miner songs and the union songs. I can sing about the Civil War. I sing the songs of Ulysses and Robert E."

I took a long look at the photo. It was definitely the German and from what little I could see it looked like Texas. "You're a folk singer then?" I asked.

"Yes, yes I am the volk singer! And my wife Akter, she is a classical Bengali dancer. I play and she dances. We play all over the world. You know the Hilton Hotels. Yes I have played the Hiltons many times, many countries. We have a home but we can't get back until my check comes through. My wife is East Bengali, there's a war going on and we can't cross the Pakistani border. We need to fly direct to Mumbai."

"Let me show you something. I have my own instrument. I invented it," the German explained enthusiastically, "It's what you Americans call, one of a kind." He jumped from his chair without waiting for my reply and pulled this huge contraption from under the bed.

The workings of the instrument were bolted to a large sheet of plywood almost as big as the bed itself. It was crafted with all sorts of piano wire and sitar strings. There were levers at intervals and myriad mechanical devices. Some wires ran diagonally above other sets of strings. These sympathetic strings picked up on the vibrations of the bottom strings and created a harmonic hum echoing off the workings of the instrument. Near the top there were a set of keys that struck the tightly strung wires much like a piano. The German had cut a half circle into the plywood giving him room to reach all the gizmos on the board.

The German began to pick at his contraption slowly but with rising intensity. At one point he threw a bow onto the bed, stopping at times to draw a low deep groan out of the thing. Meanwhile he strummed and picked, as he delicately tuned his creation. The myriad levers seemed to provide him with a range of chords while there were other sets of strings where he plucked, with remarkable dexterity, at individual notes.

It sounded similar to a sitar or a zither, then later, especially when he ran through the scales, it produced a ringing liquid clarity, like a runaway bluegrass mandolin. The thing was filling the room with a sound that was dense and pungent. The German was trapped in the sway of this composition. Then the melody slowed from its frantic pace and became simpler, almost familiar. Without warning he lent his voice to the mix:

I ride an old paint, I lead an old Dan

I'm goin' to Montana for to throw the hoolihan

They feed in the coulees, they water in the draw

Their tails are all matted, their backs are all raw

My uncle used to sing that very song after a long day and a tumbler or two of Canadian

Club. I have to admit hearing Ol Paint in this shabby hotel in Tehran left me missing home for the first time in a long while. There were some borders I couldn't cross either but that's a story for another time.

The German played on for another twenty minutes in a million languages and styles. His shirt was sweated thru and he flung his head from side to side as he played with utter abandon as if we weren't even there. Without warning as the music reached a fevered pitch he abruptly stopped, like pulling the emergency brake on a passenger train. I nearly fell from my seat thunder struck by the abrupt end of the concert as his Stradivarius lay on the bed humming along down a long road that stretched off into what approached forever.

The German looked exhausted. He dragged his instrument back under the bed and sat there contrite. The thing was still vibrating. His shoulders sagged and his voice took a plaintive tone. He turned to the front of his scrapbook and spoke breathless.

"When I came east I was a young man. The same cock sure stupid young man you run into every day. A man not so different from yourself. I owned a Mercedes and a matching trailer and I had 20000 marks in the bank. He pointed to a photo which showed himself standing before just such a rig. Look at me now. I am a child's abandoned doll. I am a mutt with a torn ear that will never mend."

"How to begin?" He thought about this for some time. "In the beginning I was determined to establish some concrete direction. My peculiar ambition being to practice and learn the music of every country along the old Silk road. I did this to foment some historical context to my interests. In the process during a foray into east Bengal, I met Akter and not long after we became man and wife. We began to perform together. It was as if the world with all its troubles had given Akter and I a pass. We had run off to join the circus."

"After two years a child was born. We named our daughter Pavi and we bought a small house in Eastern Mumbai. By the time Pavi was four we gave up the road. We had cultured a network of clubs and hotels in the surrounding area that provided a livelihood. Akter taught school and I gave lessons. We set about raising our daughter properly. We lived in a middle class neighborhood and we had middle class concerns.

Our particular neighborhood was under the control of the Vardha Bhai. They were a local mafia of Tamil criminals. Theirs was an organization of bootleggers, smugglers, opium traffickers and murderers. They operated with impunity. They even had their own courts and they settled their scores as if they were a country unto themselves.

One evening I caught a boy trying to lift my Mercedes. I knew him to be the son of one of the thugs of the neighborhood, so I dismissed him with a swift kick to the pants rather than the beating he deserved.

That's how I ended up in the court of The Vardha Bhai. They captured me with the quick strike of a black jack and a coil of rope. I was hijacked off the street and when I came to, I sat in a dock before the local gangster magistrate. I was told to surrender my Mercedes before the end of the following day in recompense for my offense. I tore open my shirt and pointed to my heart. "Take it now." I screamed, "save yourself the trouble." I considered them duly warned.

That night I sat in my car with a club and a small sword. I kept a pistol in the glove compartment. Just before dawn they set upon me. I sent two of them to hospital before someone landed the deciding blow. I lay there stunned on the street. One of the goons rifled my pockets till he found my keys. He started my Mercedes and sat there patiently waiting.

There was blood running down into my eyes. I managed to get to my knees but I was too wobbly to stand. A third man came crashing through the front door. He had something in his arms. I could hear my wife calling my name frantically from the front door. This last gangster had tied a kerchief over his face, he paused and opened his arms. "Tell Daddy goodnight," the monster said and then he kicked me and the lights went out.

When I came to Akter was shaking me. She looked worse than I did. She held me in her arms for the longest time rocking back and forth with me in her lap trying desperately to clear the cobwebs from my head. Pavi had disappeared and I knew the clock was ticking.

The German took the scrapbook and opened it in his lap. Methodically he turned the pages until he found the place. There was the newspaper photo of a beautiful young girl and the banner headline: KIDNAPPED!!!

"Over the next 5 years I spent all the money I had trying to find our Pavi. I bribed. I begged. I threatened. I made crucial contacts within both the criminal organizations of Mumbai and the police. Through these contacts we discovered she had been sold by the Vardha Bhai to slave traders who dispensed children across Asia as house servants and prostitutes.

I sold the Mercedes and mortgaged our home. I sunk every pisa I owned into her discovery. Gradually we came to know the names and evil histories of the handful of men responsible for this despicable act. Slowly I began to give up hope of her return. I resorted instead to the least transcendent of emotions, personal revenge."

"I murdered five of the perpetrators of my daughters abduction in cold blood. I poisoned the man that did the actual deed. I stole his car, drove it some two hundred miles and handed the keys to a beggar. Over three months time I bankrupted his family.

The others I killed face to face and with my own hands. I snapped their necks like a farmer snaps the neck of a chicken. I came upon them in the dead of night and waited for their eyes to cloud over so that the very last thing they saw was my face and my vengeance." The

German was silent and in this ghastly silence I read the articles in the scrapbook of a beautiful 11 year old girl stolen from her family.

"Red," the German said at long last. "A piece of advice. If you choose to marry, marry a Bengali. The women of Bengal are both beautiful and loyal. They are known for their honesty and they will smoke charas with you. They are not timid in bed either and most important, they protect you from snakes.

As god is my witness I will tell you a true story. We traveled to East Pakistan, the country they call Bangladesh now. Akter's people live there. You would have thought we were royalty the way they received us. We were given a hut at the edge of the village next to the jungle."

"I was tired after the long journey and I ducked my head to enter the hut but Akter refused to let me pass."

"'Babu she said, 'you must not enter here. There are seven Cobra's inside and they will strike you. Wait here while I fetch them.' "And so she did, returning seven times and each time holding a cobra at arms length."

"Akter how did you know there were seven, I asked my wife."

"'I could smell them Babu,' she answered. 'They smelled like seven."

The German looked at me. He looked exhausted. "True story." He said, "Every word."

The German was suddenly played out. He was no longer the hardy barrel chested German I had encountered in the hall an hour or so earlier. He looked older and feebler than I had realized. I stood up to take my leave. Without a word I pulled my wallet and handed over most of my cash.

"It's all I got," I added. "I'll talk to Murrow see how much cash he's got on him."

"Like I said," the German assured me, "I can pay you back come the Thursday."

"That's ok. We have tickets for the Wednesday bus to Istanbul."

"O," the German said and looked down at his hands. He had massive hands and I did not doubt he could snap a man's neck if he took a notion to do so.

"I studied literature in school. I have always loved books. I eat books like Texas eat bar-b-que. I will tell you this secret Red. It is a secret I have discovered after years of study. In this world there are only two books worth reading more than once. There is this," the German held up a well worn Bible. "All great literature springs from here." The German slapped the Bible as if it were a drinking companion and he was slapping it across the shoulders. And there is this," The German opened a drawer in his nightstand. He handed me a dog eared copy of The Lustful Turk. I gathered in a glance that this was a 17th century erotic novel set in the harem of the Dey of Algiers.

The German tore a page out of a notebook and scribbled on it. "Here," he said, "this is our address in Mumbai. Should you ever find yourself in the vicinity call me or just come by. I will personally put myself at your disposal. We can ride the elephant. We can go on a tiger safari. We can go anywhere you want to go. Take our number with the confidence we will never forget you."

I tried to return his copy of The Lustful Turk but he was having none of that. "My gift to you. Thank you for your generosity."

I turned to leave. " Remember," Akter said, "you must shampoo the hair three times every day." She somberly held up three fingers. I held up three fingers in return and nodded solemnly.

I grabbed the doorknob and I heard the German say, "Red, read the book and if you need to don't be shy, use the hand."

About the Author:

For 35 years **Rees Nielsen** farmed stone fruit with his cousins on the family farm 3 miles southwest of Selma, at the heart California's San Joaquin Valley. Three years after the passing of his wife Riina, he moved to Indianola, Iowa where he chauffeurs his grandchildren, Marshall and Adelaide Taylor, to and from elementary school. He has published poetry, fiction and visual art in the USA and the UK.

GUILT MONOLOGUE

by Don Dussault

For me everything is in the present tense. Whatever whoever slips away into the past I yank it back. Here something of me thrives. And him. Too much of him. Straight hair a paler brown than my rich dark walnut. Bright blue eyes. At any moment I revive that most dramatic afternoon with an unexpected visitor, a guest from America.

We dally. I love that word, a sweetener for the sweaty groping gasping noises and smells it connotes and the rumpling of the young man's bed, dally, ah, the scrubbed-clean sound of it, this primary color word, cadmium yellow letters, or red-orange, on a cobalt field, signifying the most pure of pleasures filling us with golden glowing warmth as we look brighteyed at each other afterward, strong young male with smears of dark hair on his chest, mature female thickened, not yet sagging. We relax knowing we won't be alone for long in our overheated universe. I get up first. He watches me getting dressed to resume my role as consort to the aristocratic landowner, really a modern businessman with an antique title anachronistic in an era of capitalist socialist quasi-republics. The Count and the quite young female companion of my bedfellow are riding back to the castle.

A genuine castle in eastern Europe mostly spared by war towering in hills above a city rebuilt in the image of a theme mall. The Count we call him. Acts no, lives the part. My count possesses the circumspection not to flirt nor dally too long with the young quite female half of our guest couple. The verb plays in my mind. Ah, that smile of his! I know little about them. Jerry and Alicia, she a photo-journalist hoping to make her name by recording the rebuilt cities since the world war. I savor the glow of of this young man's body.

As I idle in Jerry's room, reluctant to leave, subconsciously seeking clues to this young traveler's personality, I notice atop his dresser loose paper money, coins, a rumpled handkerchief, his passport. Ever piqued by photographs I open the passport. In the this-is-me square signed across the side he looks younger than his eighteen years, with an innocent infectious grin he now wears in real life, watching me. "I look pretty goofy in that picture, don't I?"

Jerry turns out to be Jeremiah Slade. I'm about to tell him I have a son named Jeremiah when his last name echoing through my mind shivers my pleasant woolly mood, sets me trembling, for my own Jeremiah and his mother—myself!— have not seen each other since he was two, and I ask his father's name, dreading his response to this innocuous question. "Senator Slade."

I can hardly control my voice. "A United States Senator?"

"He's a State Senator now but he's running for the United States Senate."

Impatient I blurt, "Senator Marlon Slade?"

I can write this with some clarity now, recalling my incoherence as old scenes and images swirl and blend into each other and as I assemble them I see satisfaction in his calm features as he reclines with his arms folded behind his head, mildly surprised I've heard of the Senator. I mutter I keep up with American politics. I read his birthdate— the same as my son's! My full weight rests against the dresser. Both hands braced on the dresser. It slides away. I gaze at the white ceiling. His anxious face intrudes. He is kneeling beside me, holding my hand, eyes filled with concern. "Are you OK?"

I shake my head not in reply but to clear it. Steadying myself on my arms I let him help me up, leaning against him, shaky, avoiding his touch while I straighten my clothes. "I'm fine. Truly, I'm fine. I'm going downstairs.

Get dressed. Tell no one what happened. We don't want controversy at dinner, do we? The Count hates controversy."

My son has the intelligence to volunteer no information that could trace our paths to his room. I force a smile and after watching him leave, thinking it would be my last sight of him, I try to stroll with blithe steps, managing not to totter, out into the hallway.

To avoid meeting anyone I take the stairs up to a walkway along a parapet under the roof. A single thought burrows into my mind: I seduced my own son! Leaning outward between crenels, mind whirling, I peer down into the courtyard and the square stones fitting together, imbedded in concrete. Jocasta, wife and mother of Oedipus, a suicide. Could I? Too dear a cost to preserve my awful secret? My duty, proper retribution for having enjoyed my son's youthful maleness in ways no mother should! I curse the horrid impossible coincidence that brought him to me, challenge my courage to fly down to those square stones. See my stiff, crumpled, broken body on the flagstones as Vasile and his servants venture out to stand around in bemused silence. Am I artfully posed, lovely, saintlike, asleep in perfect peace? My sister Eleanor cries out, "You must dramatize yourself as usual! Selfish, inconsiderate this latest stunt of yours, turning yourself into a gruesome mess on those stones

for others to clean up."

Remembrances of my sister halt my plunge into despair. Afternoons of dancing with her, laughing under the backyard arbor of sweet green grapes. Wiser than I ever was, she raised my son well. Vasile and Alicia ride into the courtyard, laughing. From my height I observe their progress toward the stables behind the castle. Handyman, chauffeur Dracul marches across the courtyard and closes the gate. Make a decision— walk downstairs or leap. I can't take a first step. I shiver as mountain shadows creep over the parapet. Fear frazzles the soles of my feet and my ankles tremble and weakness riddles my knees. Too cowardly for the coward's way. Has some time passed? Lighted rooms cast pale-yellow trapezoids across the dim courtyard stones so far far down.

Hours of my madness shiver any semblance of rationality in me. Don't believe the rationality. I'm back to my first days with Count Vasile Grigore when, in Paris, I veer away from the upperclass woman I'm supposed to become, who holds charity events, perhaps joins Suffragist rallies, ages in ease and contentment. Tell Vasile I have a son or await a reply to my letter home, a reply that never arrives, no, I can't. A man of the world, Vasile won't judge me harshly. Can a woman feel certain she understands a man? Or a man a woman? A pleasure-loving wealthy businessman respected in his homeland who adheres to traditional principles of honor, who'd sympathize, probably comfort a woman amid her tangled feelings, might Vasile go so far as to forgive my tryst with Jerry? Irrelevant. I can never tell Vasile what transpired between my son and myself. Words of forgiveness mean nothing when our eyes meet, every day, every year.

During the years between my carefree travels with Vasile and my night of despair in his castle, I surrender at moments to thoughts of returning to Marlon, father of a son forever a small child in my mind. Moving on, willynilly, I can't fathom them moving on from me. Year after year a soft hectoring guilt buttresses my doubts. Returning home to them is another indulgence in fantasy. My sister is a better mother to my son than someone so deficient in maternal instincts as I. How dare I disrupt their lives again! A year is a day. Is a minute. Every delay diminishes any likelihood I'll return. The past enters the present with a vengeance. Today with stunning finality a bizarre improbability has forced the long-avoided confrontation with myself. No choice remains. Protect the innocents, now including my own son.

In the darkness a wavering light appears in the entrance to the walkway. I don't budge, awaiting the inevitable inquiring voice, Vasily's, worried. "Why are you up here alone?" I shrink from the brilliance of his flashlight as if it would burn me to ashes, clinging to my silence, afraid my tone may reveal my distress. He repeats his question, adding, "Are you angry toward me?"

I latch onto any guilt he might or might not feel, hoping he dallied with Alicia in the forest. I chill my entire self, becoming that Biblical pillar of salt not to sound fragile. "Would you have any reason for me to get angry?"

"None that I can think of." I hear sufficient puzzlement in his voice to believe his denial, at any rate caring little. He sounds anxious. "Does something trouble you?"

I steady my voice. "Nothing that should concern you."

"You are missed downstairs. You should not be late for dinner."

"I have no appetite. I wish to forgo dinner tonight."

Over the years, when stressed, I have fallen into his rather formal manner of speaking. He sounds curious, concerned. "Are you well?"

"Tired. I may be coming down with something. I need to go to bed early."

"You do look peaked."

I make my voice weak. "Our guests should leave tomorrow morning."

Unease drifts into his eyes. "Has anything happened in my absence?"

"You have nothing to worry about. I don't feel up to entertaining strangers any longer." I manage a weak smile. I can speak his lingo. "Their limitless youthful energy strains my own."

I walk past him trying not to touch the stone walls, not to seem I rely on them to avoid tottering. In my own private bedroom with the door locked my sleep is fitful. Tormented by images I can't banish, suspicions about myself— did I intuit my special prior connection with this manchild? A profound chill penetrates my being. I stand in my nightgown watching the dawn from a parapet with no recollection of how I got there. Returning to my room I   lay sleepless on my bed. A new notion rushes round and round in my mind, sparked by fear that, without thinking, I may blab to Vasile our American visitor was my son. Around midmorning Vasile knocks, pauses. I know his knock. Through the closed door he tells me our guests have gone. "Good," I call back.

Waking again late in the morning I stay in bed. At noon someone knocks on my door. After several minutes I rouse myself and discover the door locked from the inside. I cannot recall locking it. Walking away, our housekeeper   Sorina turns to frown in impatience. On the carpeting outside my door she   has left a tray containing a dish of mamaliga topped with a fried egg, a small bowl of yogurt and a tall glass of coffee. I eat mechanically and then sleep again until after dark. A light night breeze energizes me. I wander upstairs   and along the ramparts and gaze at the half-moon teasing its way among pale clouds. My torments overflow in spasms of numbness. Emily, admit your genuine attraction to Jerry, beyond maternal. A young male of eighteen can be aroused by almost any bearer of a vagina, especially one who returns his interest, even merely piques it with brightening eyes. He'd have been aware of his physical appeal to a woman living in rural castle isolation. This young Jerry could have been any handsome man of any age, I any promiscuous female. In the courtroom of my heart I argue I shouldn't be faulted, for how in a distant continent could I possibly meet and recognize my own child how old, two? learning to walk, talk, run, whom as a baby I'd pushed in a pram on Westchester sidewalks. A liaison unlikely beyond the wildest chance. I find myself believing, hoping, it never happened, I dream it, while, dreamlike, he and I join as lovers finding each other. My own dear boy Jeremiah, my son, what must you have envisioned in a woman your mother's age tumbling with you in your bed, stirring subliminal remembrances of a mother you lost early? Sincere, romantic, you remark, "We should be strangers but we don't feel like strangers." In believable naive sincerity you reveal the loving man in you capable of winning a woman. Don't lose that gift, dear one, when you recall, as you may, with amusement   and male pride the eccentric middleaged stranger of your fling. If Jeremiah should learn this stranger was his mother, what harm would that knowledge bring! My son must never know. Alone I bear the burden of that afternoon. I may envelop myself in innocent ignorance or wallow in despair at my violation of nature, of human nature, yet never rid my spirit of that night and the images locked into my brain— the easy grin in a handsome face which somewhere certainly contains traces of the baby I gave birth to, the supple young body, the lean yet muscular arms, the surprising stamina of this incipient man...

Hard as I try to avoid moping, I catch surreptitious glances. I avoid the kitchen, the common social area, unless I have instructions to impart. I go horseback riding in the morning while Vasile works in his office, giving myself an excuse not to ride with him in late afternoon, his favorite time. At dinner I labor at contriving

conversation and avoiding extended silences. When we sleep in the same bed, he notices my lack of enthusiasm and my poor attempts to simulate it. Dare he ask what's troubling me, I may blurt oh, I met my son whom I abandoned. His next words? Likely wonderful, we must celebrate the reunion. I clutch at a straw. "I've been away from my family far too many years."

"Then we shall visit America. I would be pleased to meet your family."

"Maybe."

Feigning immunity to my diffidence he makes another offer. "They can come here."

"They never travel."

"After so many years, you cannot know their feelings. Does that frighten   you?"

"Perhaps."

I fear I may explode in rage, and worse, I worry. I've sunken too deep into my sorrow for any anger to surmount it. Tell him, Emily. Truth is reputed to be liberating. Tell Vasile the story of that afternoon. Leave it to him to forgive me or banish me. Emily, overcome your paralyzing fear. I should fear my weakness more than his response and the risk of altering my life   with him. Crossing a Rubicon is no longer a mythic tale about someone else. It's become my story. I must reveal my past to a man of great importance in my life. I owe him that.

How might it go? Tentative, I approach him in midafternoon. "About my life in America, there's something you must know," and he waits, perhaps inquires, "You have a husband?" and I stay calm, "I've never had a husband," hoping I need go no further, aware I must, while he holds his silence, "My parents live in Newport," for whatever that might mean to him, "My sister is married to an attorney," which jogs his memory, "I believe you mentioned a sister once," and now I wait until he continues, "Do they have children? Do you have nieces and nephews?" and in a soft voice I reply, "No," and now I've gone too far to turn back, here goes, "I have a son." I must say it, "By my sister's husband." I can say it. No, not today...

As the quiet and isolation of the castle exacerbates my moods, I fancy bright lights and crowds bringing lifesaving distractions. My passing fear Vasile and I are losing each other is buried among the debris of my disfocused thinking. "Vasile, I need a change."

"I do as well. Tomorrow we may be on the train to Vienna."

Good to be out of the castle and in a bustling city. My melancholy overcomes the best of Vienna. The stolid Viennese architecture displaying the overwrought fervor for an empire that no longer exists fails to conceal the changes brought on by two great wars and an era of social evolution. Telephones of old friends are disconnected. After a magnificent Don Giovanni at the State Opera an acquaintance informs us one of our friends is an actor in Hollywood and another has moved to Prague. In caffes the young chat in excited voices sparked by bursts of laughter. Vasile isn't one to conceal his disappointment. "The lights of Vienna are not as brilliant as I recall."

I understand he means the intellectual illumination of our age. "The splendor has faded, the horrors of war can do that."

"No doubt the world has changed. America may become the center of dialogue."

"We Americans aren't much for daylong conversations in caffes."

I recognize the expression on his features, marked by a brief distant look. "The future is in the beginning."

"One of those ancient ideas you love."

"It originates in nature, as do most good ideas. The seed determines the fruit. The manner of America's entrance on the world stage may tell us much about the role your people will play. The English Bard reveals his hero in his first lines, Keep up your bright swords, for the dew will rust them."

"Is that from Othello?"

"The commanding entrance of a general. So different from Hamlet, who is detached, aloof. Hamlet's first words are an aside. America arrives like Othello, a formidable warrior."

"That seems kind of unfair. Americans love peace."

"In due course we shall see."

With me, briefly he indulges in his moment of intellectual badinage. We cut our trip short and return to the castle. My moods return. Unable to conceal them forever I force myself into activity. I help in the kitchen that I may learn from Sorina how to prepare local dishes. I take an easel outdoors to paint the trees on green slopes, sunsets on undulant ridges. With my mind clouded by guilt I don't quite realize a growing impulse is driving me, until I finally express it to Vasile. "What would you think if I went to Paris by myself for a, oh, a visit to old haunts?"

His eyes darken to flat black and thoughtful. "Paris holds special meaning for you. It is the city where you awoke to yourself."

"Where we met."

Irrelevant now, he gets it. "I understand your longing to revisit Paris."

I can hear his regret. He knows I'm not inviting him. Ever ready to accomodate my wishes, withholding his reservations he lets me go. I deserve no such easy reprieve. Suddenly I want him to sit me down and command me to tell the truth about my past or face his wrath. I want to hear him tell me he loves me too much to let me drift away. Neither are in his nature. Does his reliance on traditional nobless oblige signify he is weak of spirit? My spiritual kin would be one who wouldn't as easily have allowed me to leave. My spiritual kin, yes, with whom I couldn't live any better than I live with myself, now overwhelmed with fear and proddings of guilt.

I project my weakness onto Vasile. More than once I've overheard him berating some business associate on the telephone. Never has he spoken with harshness toward the castle help nor to me, transmitting any displeasure toward us, a rare event, with a look and a curt phrase. He can ask me a hundred questions: did I run to Europe to escape an unloved husband, do I have children in America, what is my family like, why am I not closer to them? So many questions he refrains from asking— whether from courtesy or weakness, no matter— and now, as I gain his approval for my solo trip to Paris I notice in his dark eyes a whirligig of hope I'll return and a sense I won't. In his eyes the blent shades of premonition and loss mirror my dark grief at a past that's a long knife aimed at his heart. No, my dear Vasile, nostalgia is not a primary reason why I must return to Paris. My voice is thankful. "With your blessing, I'll pack tonight and leave tomorrow morning."

As his thoughts cycle through the potential consequences of my departure, he listens to my announcement with weighty calm. "You will not return?"

It's both question and statement. I owe him more than an abrupt departure— the full truth about myself. Dare I repay my happy years with him by telling him the tawdry tale of a mother who abandoned her son, leaving him, my best friend and lover, satisfied to be rid of such a person but defiled by years of my deceit, first by my misrepresentation of myself and now by an incestuous infidelity. He is owed the full truth about me. Now arrives my final chance to confess, to set him free of me forever, to allow him to abandon hope I might return, to wish never again to see me. I manage a pittance of honesty. "Probably not."

I see sorrow in his dark eyes, hear tradition and nobility in his softened voice. We're all captives of something. "Your quest, wherever it may take you, may it bring you happiness."

I love him more than ever for those words, an intimation I may never have loved him as much as we believed. That night an automaton inside me packs two suitcases and restores me to sleep every time restless thoughts jar me until I rise well after the sun. I hear Vasile typing in his office with its door closed as usual. Without a word Sorina fixes me eggs and ham and pours my coffee and then departs for the garden, where Ilie is already at work. Dracul sips coffee in silence until I finish my breakfast and then in response to my inquiring uncertain look accompanies me upstairs to my room, where he lifts my suitcases and we start out to the courtyard. Pausing as I pass Vasile's office I knock at the closed hardwood door and announce I'm leaving and he calls back, "I'm on the telephone. Have a pleasant journey."

In the backseat of the Mercedes I recline, surprisingly tired so soon after a night's sleep and I doze at moments as the car winds down the mountain. I stand at the station ticket counter with my bags beside me where Dracul left them. I hear the Mercedes driving away. At my window in the Orient Express I watch the day melt into twilight, then into darkness.

As I did years ago I rent a room in the Sixth Arrondissement. At outdoor tables I sip coffee and study faces seeking anyone I might recognize. I rummage through my memory for faces and names. Brendan of course who turned out to be more adventurous than I thought, how does he look today? Bigboned, has he put on weight and settled in with a stout Dutch milkmaid? Dominique, to whom I gave a dress and a smock when I was packing my suitcases, Joe from Ypsilanti practicing on his guitar, Jean-Pierre, Lars, others who might remember me. I scan the faces of passersby. At dusk I wander to the Seine. Two young men pick at their guitars, young and they look it, as our crowd must have. They are Jerry's generation. Absent well over a decade, I've lost my connection to this city, my favorite, with familiar streets and buildings, hotels, produce stands, book stands side by side along the green Seine, the Louvre, the city where I once came to find freedom, where I'm now a tourist like any other.

I urge myself to write Vasile a note thanking him for our years together. My persistent procrastination in letterwriting reminds me I'm temperamentally unreliable, given to sudden enthusiasms and equally sudden retreats into myself. Never having gotten a reply to my letter from his castle years ago, at intervals I wonder if it vanished in one of the postal systems it passed through, or if my sister threw it away, perhaps unopened, still peeved at me, holding a grudge uncharacteristic of her, as if that matters now! I could have followed up with other letters, had considered writing her and Marlon again, many times. The past returns as present. I know what I want, to reclaim a home no longer mine, rejoin a family who can refuse to accept among them a deserter in disgrace. In my Paris room my mind prances through New York, reviving Eleanor and Marlon, now like me entering middleage, Jeremiah resembling the small boy in my memory morphed into the handsome young stranger. A flickering double image. Hope tempts me to override my fear they'll reject me. Wisdom urges, accept your new reality. You're alone in the world. Runaway hope breeds illusions capable of outshining reality. I ponder tactics. If I return home now, Jeremiah is likely still away on his travels with a young woman too assertive for his gentler nature but who can enable him to forget me, and his absence will help me postpone the ultimate necessity of divulging our encounter to some later time when, after winning the family's acceptance, I again become a real Emily to them, not a ghost: a risky scenario. I could undermine myself with a slipped word, a guilty look. Oh, the intricacies of hope! The traps of selfishness! At my window I contemplate walls and rooftops. I see the city as Kokoscha might, or Matisse, or Cezanne. Alignments of metal, ceramic tile, wood, redbrick, stone in the cold geometry I chose above my family, my son. a decision correct at the time only because bold, spoiled, independent, I betrayed the sister who

wound up bringing up my son. Because I live on whims, I have since my teen scorn of pretentious high society elites, claiming I'm different from the subservient spoiled other girls flouncing in ruffles, frills and furbelows. I defy an often pretentious Procrustean society. Selfindulgence gives me the right. Hovering, transparent in my hotel window, my reflection stares at me. In the window my sad eyes rebuke me. Selfish brat you are, abandoning your boy, then seducing him mere months removed from childhood? Could the window image speak, her words would scathe my flesh: Emily, you like your babies fully grown and primed to serve your evil fantasies. Wherever in our social circles I may venture whispers will follow: a woman your age having a fling with a teenager— a scandal to set tongues wagging, as they say, yet not comparable to the scorn for a mother seducing her son! Damn that mute reflected face! Let the social elites, the hoi polloi, the lowest rabble condemn that face, those empty features, that mindless image on glass I can turn away from. Elsewhere in another place and time, condemnation awaits me in judgment fair and merciless. I'll postpone judgment as long as I can.

Where's my delectable sense of irony gone? Dare I turn my sarcasm against myself? My window image brightens as dusk darkens the sky. You are not me, I inform it. I see youth lingering in those features, hope straining in those eyes. An illusion. You've never acted your age. You ran from your baby son as if tossing away a doll you were tired of. You had a quest, or convinced a sophisticated count you had one, while you played your part unaware that it was more a stage performance than a spiritual search, a pose of high seriousness, accomplishment... Doubt hasn't left me. Dreading selfdelusion I continue succumbing to it.

Gossip columns and TV celebrity shows would feast on our scandalous story. They who were once my family have moved on without me. Haughty, careless, having isolated myself from my sister, from the father of my child, finally from my own child, I've harmed them enough. Time to accept my exile, wherever it should take me, not New York, nowhere I'd risk running into family or former friends. Free to go where I want, live wherever I choose, do what I please, I don't feel free. I need a sprawling American city, Chicago, Los Angeles, where I can vanish into the crowd. The wise course.

Primeval instinct urges me to return home. Threatens to overwhelm my good sense. An ocean voyage should give me time to prepare myself to confront my kin, brace myself against their onslaught. If I fail to win mercy I can leave before Jeremiah returns from his travels. Perhaps with the acquiescence of Eleanor and Marlon I can become his crazy aunt and our old deception will continue, enabling him to view me with distaste to spare him the torment of knowing he Biblically knew his mother. For his benefit they may go along. Our family is adept at deception. I can live another false life. Indeed embrace it! What have I to lose? Nothing but my final shreds of selfrespect. Well, dears, they are mine to dispose of. The next morning, assuring myself I'm being rational and destiny is best met than avoided, I purchase a steamship ticket to New York.

About the Author:

Don Dussault lives in the San Francisco Bay Area. His history includes a BA and MA in English literature and postgrad study in linguistics. His work appears in several literary publications, a few of which are excerpted on his website, presently under construction at https://dondussault.net/ He's wrapping up a multivoiced saga of a dysfunctional family.

ALL OF NEPTUNE'S OCEANS
by Rina Sclove

Her hands are the only part of her that isn't scarred.

Everything else is marked, claimed, her skin varying shades of angry red and blistering purple, puckered and dry and stretched out too far. She feels like a drawing done by a toddler, scribbled on with ragged lines and no care, hung on the wall and left to bleed.

She is paper thin, she thinks. Translucent.

It is the scars she hates the most, more than the bruises. The bruises change, shifting in color and form and, sometimes, away. They are proof that there is still blood trapped beneath the surface of her skin, that things are still forming. That they still can. She lifts a shaking hand to her cheek and holds it there, as if somehow she could capture a little bit of its magic. It stings at the touch, and she treasures that, too. Pain, she knows, is the body's way of screaming, of saying *you cannot touch me* and *I will resist you*. She lets her bruises sing.

Her hands, though. They are unmarred, smooth. She almost remembers the way pebbles felt in her hand, glistening from the stream and cold in her palm. She used to collect them, taking all of the perfect things and tucking them away in her pockets. Her hands feel like them now, she thinks, guesses. Not knowing, never knowing.

Sometimes, she looks at her unblemished hands and lets herself believe that they are still hers.

She's quick to remember, though, that they aren't. Once, there was a time when being quick meant racing her sister to the swingset and the speed at which her hand was lifted in math class, that sometimes it still means the days when she was still lightning.

This is a different kind of quick. It is a flinch, the crease between this world and the next, the scars that sit near the cavity where her heart used to be. Is, she reminds herself. Is.

Her hands don't belong to her, though. Not anymore, maybe not ever. It is the price of being a body without a soul, she thinks, or maybe of having too much of one, and she lies and tells herself that it doesn't matter which it is.

Once Upon a Time, her hands had not been so smooth. They were rough, calloused. A warrior's hands, she thinks, and for a moment she almost remembers how to smile. Almost.

She used to row, in school. The oars blistered her hands, marks left from the act of pushing forwards. God, she had loved those. Her teammates all used to compare them, trying to see which one of them had worked the hardest, who was willing to pay the highest price. Sometimes she won, sometimes she didn't. But she had owned those blisters, and she was a part of them as much as they were parts of her.

When she enlists in the army, her hands turn rough again, hardened by push ups and the cold, black weight of a gun in her hands. They had to become stronger, still, for her to be able to hold lives in them. And to crush them - well, that was the heaviest weight of all.

They must have seen promise in those hands, though, enough that she was cherry picked for the CIA. And so she trains and trains, lets herself harden. She stiffens her shoulders and tells herself that she is a weapon, a blade, a *fighter*.

All of the training, though, isn't enough. She fails her very first mission. She may be a weapon, but she is one with a beating heart, and it very nearly gets herself killed. Nearly. At any rate, her fingers stutter on the trigger when the time comes, her body wavering as her soul stands deathly still.

She had been ready to kill him. Ready to take a life without a second thought, as if it had belonged to her, but then - but *then*. He lifts his head, just a little, enough for her to see his eyes from underneath the brim of his helmet.

She can't remember what color her own eyes are. She tries and tries, searching for some sort of clarity among the endless hues of gray, but she comes back with nothing. In her dreams, her eyes are rolling blue, like the river she used to row in. Or maybe it is like the stream - she isn't sure. Sometimes they are a sunset, deep oranges and poppy reds, wispy pinks and purple lightning that all come together to bleed liquid gold. It always changes, and for the life of her she cannot remember the way she used to see the world.

Different names for empty craters, she thinks. Or cries. Does she remember how to that?

Could she?

His eyes are brown. Like dirt, like the things we come home to. *Home.* She has brothers there, small, knobbly things with scabbed knees and open hearts, bits of earth behind their ear in the places they never manage to wash. They're waiting for her, she knows, and all of a sudden home is a knife.

His eyes are brown, but there's something more to them - a little bit of light, dancing right in the corner there. Her brothers' are the same. These are a boy's eyes, she knows. She *knows*.

He is only a boy.

She swallows, sets her jaw, and lifts the gun higher. *Stop projecting*, she tells herself, *it is only the sunlight being reflected, can't you see?*

And then another thought - *isn't that all there ever is?*

Her heart beats. Drums. She's on the river again, an oar in her blistered hands. Water sprays her cheeks and for a moment she remembers how to breathe.

What price are you willing to pay? The river whispers, *what cost will you bear?*

She wants to stay, but that is not what the river is - it is pushing forwards, always forwards, and she is back in the desert with a boy with her brother's eyes and a choice in her hands.

There is one more question - the only question, really. She asks it herself. *How much of a soul do you have?* She asks, *too much or too little? How much is your soul worth?*

She doesn't know, can't know, but she understands what those sunlit eyes are worth, and this is how she finds her answer. *Not him*, she tells herself. Not him.

She lowers the gun.

There is a heartbeat, a shaking hand, a gunshot. The bullet enters her leg quickly, just to the side of an artery. It is a bullet, a flinch, the shadow between life and death - it is quick. They say that getting shot feels like burning, like being consumed by a thousand fiery suns. But when the bullet breaks her skin it feels like an answer, like a promise that one day she will cling to this moment and remember what it feels like to burn.

(she doesn't know this, but a few feet away a boy with brown eyes stares at his own trembling hands, at the weapon clutched in them so tightly that his knuckles have turned white. he knows what he's supposed to tell himself: she would have hurt him, if he hadn't done it, hurt his friends, she is *dangerous*. he doesn't think these things. instead he looks at his pale, blood

-stained hands and asks himself a question. *how much is your soul worth?* he thinks of his mother at home, of how she won't let him sit at the dinner table with so much blood caking his hands. his hands tremble with the weight of the world, and he knows, *he knows* that all of the water in Neptune's great oceans would not be enough to wash away the stain of what he'd done. *less*, the man shudders, *less*.)

They take her prisoner, after that. It is her mind that is valuable to them, the information that they need but what they want - well. They take that too.

I am a weapon, she wills herself, *a blade, a fighter.*

I am not human, she hears, *and metal does not bleed.*

She grits her teeth and shuts her eyes, does everything they told her to do. She bleeds all the same, and somewhere, halfway across the world, the river weeps.

Her captors are fair, as far as captors go. They give for everything they take, a bartering system as old as humanity itself. They carve away her flesh and give her holes where she used to be whole, rob her of breath and give her broken blood cells, shattered lungs and the knowledge that Home is an ache she no longer believes. They take life and give her the space between, the pause between inhaling and ex-haling, between a not-quite hardened heart and a boy with earth-kissed eyes.

In the beginning, she used to laugh, mania-cally, brilliantly, lightning dancing on her tongue. Just to prove that she still could. She did that until she no longer remembered what it was to laugh, until the lightning died and the world forgot how to burn.

Now she is silent, mostly. Her eyes glaze over their shoulders, fixating on the same spot on the wall. Sometimes it is Home, pigtails and freshly-mowed grass, her father's steady hand on her shoulder. Sometimes it is the river, laughter and the things she earned for herself.

Other times she goes to the stream, puts peb-bles in her pockets and thinks of a boy with stars for eyes.

This is the price, she knows, for clean hands and - and for what?

For the sun, she thinks as she traces a finger around the scar that sits where the bullet en-tered her leg and her head and her heart. She feels flames dancing on her fingertips and knows that it is something that they cannot take away. There is a fire that is hers and hers alone, and it is almost enough.

She doesn't speak much anymore, her voice low and croaking, stuck in the back of her throat trying to sing a song whose title she can-not remember. Hope, maybe. She doesn't know.

But there are two words that are never far from the tip of her tongue, and she whispers them day and night, like a prayer. *Too much,* her scars sing, *too much.*

She knows how much of a soul she has, and this, this is the price she is willing to bear to carry the weight of it. *Too much,* she whispers, lets out a breath and knows that it *matters.*

About the Author:

Rina Sclove is currently a junior in high school at Princeton Day School. She lives in Princeton, NJ with her parents, two sisters, and beloved fish, Algae-Won Kenobi. She has previously had work published in Canvas Literary Journal.

NO BETTER REASON THAN THIS

by Torrie Jay White

The cabin smells like my grandfather as a young man. Like my mother's skin in her last days. Like the gunpowder in my father's pistol. Like the earliest parts of my remember life.

—

The key grinds in the lock; the door in its frame. No one has opened it in over a decade. I haven't in three. I put my shoulder into the door, and only then does it give way. It swings open to a pounding dark. Behind me is the pounding sun.

I take a moment, and breathe in the rot. A melee of stench. A whole century of skin and must and moss and mice, bodies rotted fat and round in the walls my grandfather built. I step into the cabin. I've forgotten there is no electricity.

My eyes acclimate, the black becoming a brown haze. I grope my way to the disintegrating curtains, and open them. Outside, I see the lake, the small children I heard when I pulled in. A little boy, with water wings. A little girl, with a fringe on her bathing suit. They're both laughing, both tiny. From the shore, someone splashes them.

I turn my back—I didn't come for the company of strangers—and open more curtains. Let forth whole furies of dust and moths. It looks like rotting snow. I hear, rather than see, the squeak and scamper of mice. Thank god I can't see them. Thirty years ago, forty, they wouldn't have bothered me, but I've gone soft. My grandfather would be disappointed.

I remember. I came for him.

A half century of grime frosts the windows, but the light coming through is getting stronger. It opens the room, and lets me survey the postage stamp of property that is now mine, for not better reason than because everyone else is dead.

The room is a photograph, an almost perfect snapshot of everything I remember. It's become brown and brittle in the years since I was last here, but then, don't photographs? (Didn't I?) Newspapers, once stacked next to my grandfather's armchair, have spilled, their yellowed headlines panicking over events only they remember. My grandmother's umbrella, its nylon worn and chewed, stands in its corner, point held in place by her rubber boots. I shudder. What's made its home inside their toes?

As a child, I saw this room with the narrow specificity of youth: the tiny yellow flowers stitched into my grandfather's arm chair, the oak and iron chest with letters carved into the top, a palm sized cement cat that my grandmother kept on the windowsill. She once told me that the cat's eyes had fallen out, and sent me to the beach to search for them. I feel pebbles between my fingertips, my thick toddler hands trying to coax sight back into her stone sockets.

It comforts me that I remember this room clearly. It means I've done little to tamper with these memories. This half of my inheritance, at least, is still familiar, even after thirty years.

It's the second room, the closed door I'm facing, of which I'm less certain. My memories of the bedroom aren't as solid. Even back then, it was private—my grandparent's room into which I could only be invited—but the past thirty years have blurred what I knew of it. The years rifled through the memories, edited them until I had only fragments of what's behind that door. I don't know which are real, which are created.

I know it's a bedroom. I believe there are gas lamps. I wonder if inside are the cat's blind eyes.

A shiver on my spine betrays me. Decades of disuse have left the cabin cold, an icebox chill preserved between its walls. I run my hand over the gooseflesh to make the pimples disappear. I remind myself that fear can't be placated as easily as cold, but still, I give myself a reason to leave the cabin.

I have a cooler packed with food enough for three days, and an overnight bag packed with clothing enough for seven. I didn't want to be here one night, let alone multiple, but hadn't wanted to admit that to myself. I find crackers and a knife among the dry food. I'll sit outside a few minutes. Eat summer sausage and cheese, like I did as a child. On the grass outside the cabin, I feel the strength of sun. A relentless, beating heat that lends itself only to the lake. If I closed my eyes and dipped my toes in the water, I could be eight years old ago again. Only as heavy as this hot air.

—

My grandfather bought this land in 1921, a small parcel given up for auction by the state. He'd planned to be a logger, like his father, but war came, and in the perverse way the world turns, this secured a kinder life for my grandfather than his father had. He came home from France, got hired as a railway postal clerk, and earned enough money to buy for his leisure a slice of the land that, thirty years earlier, had been his father's labor.

I know this, because I have a both a deed and a letter confirming it. It's what you receive when people die: documents. The deed from a lawyer who handled the deaths of my father, my grandmother, and finally, my mother. The letter from a box marked "FAMILY – DON'T THROW" stored in my mother's hall closet. The box full of the same collection of ephemera and detritus that every family saves, confident that its meaning will remain longer than we do.

The cabin itself wasn't built until 1942. A project my grandfather gave himself and his only son after a work injury earned him a summer away. I know *this* from family lore. Every visit, my grandfather would show me the work of my father's hands, pointing out the nails his boyish fingers had hammered, first haltingly, then competently into place. My father would speak softly at night about sleeping, in the first weeks of that summer, on the ground the cabin sits on.

And herein lies the flaw in our recordkeeping. This land wasn't supposed to pass, as it did, from his mother to my mother to me, but rather from father to grateful son.

—

I finish my snack, and can't think a justification to remain, lazy, in the sun. I haul the cooler to the cabin door, then leave it to circle the building. When I arrived, my eyes and memory colluded to show me only what I remembered, but slowly, I'm beginning to see the decay. Weeds choke the cabin's cinder block base. My grandfather's crude imitation of a lawn has been preserved, but only by a layer of disintegrating pine needles, and, I assumed, the deadening snow that falls each winter. The paint, once red, is chipped and sun-bleached. I'd call it the color of wood, but the wood itself is gray. The windows, dull inside, are covered in spider webbing and leaf debris. The blinds are still closed inside the bedroom windows, and the filth makes them look like eyes gone blind. Again, the cement cat.

Back inside, and again, the darkness assaults me. So does the smell. I place my blue cooler and my purple duffle in the middle of the room. The cabin draws in on itself, suddenly fiercely small. It's as if it knows I've come to colonize its dark corners. It's ghosts crowd me, and again, gooseflesh rises on my arms. From the corner comes a sharp scrabbling. It takes one hysterical second before I remember that ghosts aren't real. That I'm an adult woman, of nerve and flesh and matter, and years enough to know that space can't be occupied by anything invisible. I'm not a child. I can't be taken in by the fears I had when I was one. I close my eyes, and count out my breath

There is a reason that I haven't been here in over thirty years.

I want to run.

I don't let myself.

It takes several minutes, but eventually the tension in my chest eases, and I come back to myself. Grown me. Skeptical me. Middle-aged me who, in a different dimension, lectures young women about the fearlessness of growing old. I put the child away, and demand that she stays hidden. I have work to do.

I carry my bags back out of the cabin. I shouldn't have brought them in in the first place. I'll need the space to separate the detritus from the heirlooms, the valuables, the family relics.

I begin my labor, starting with newspapers, the sun still cool this side of the dirty glass. I unfold each spilled paper, and peel disintegrating pages apart to search for a lost note or piece of marginalia. I feel a small bead of hysteria crystalize, once more in my gut.

—

I am awake.

I go from sleeping to waking so fast the transition is violent. Darkness lies on top of me, a pitch so black I'm blinded. To my right, I hear something—fingers digging in the earth?—and above me, nails scratching the ridged roof. My mind thrashes—where is my mother? where am I?—but my body is paralyzed. Panic. I taste it on my tongue.

I tell myself to lie as still, waiting, listening to these faint noises. They can't be fingers. *They can't be fingers.* They can't be. I want someone to wake beside me, and tell me they're not fingers. Nobody does. There's nobody there. I remain paralyzed, but gradually, my breathing begins to slow. I find I can blink again. The black begins to lighten, and slowly, my reason, hijacked by panic, returns. The stiffness in my bones reminds me that I'm not a child, but that I am lying on a floor. Grandma and grandpa's cabin. My cabin.

I'm the adult I was waiting for.

I sit up, make myself sit up, heat rolling through my body—the indignities of middle womanhood, and of this childish reversion. The sleeping bag I brought from home is too hot for this humidity. Sweat has pooled underneath my breasts and in the crevice of my spine. I unzip myself, pull off my pajamas. Naked, the air becomes comfortable.

I berate myself for this foolishness—acting like a child again, when I haven't even felt *young* in years. I didn't come here for nostalgia, nor to feel like girl again. I stand among the furniture, and still, it hulks like shadowed monsters. Can I be grown here? In this place where I was, most essentially, a child?

I taste the tinny corrosion of rust. The taste of blood. Panic rises in my throat again, my body ready to topple into this abyss of fear. *Stop*, I say out loud. Stop. Go outside. I pulled the curtains down this afternoon, and now I can see the night through the naked panes. It's a pearl, soft and milky. I step out of the cabin, try not to run.

Out here, my fear lessens with the darkness, the moon high and bright above me. The air is same temperature as my body. Bathtub hot. That's what I called this weather when I was a kid. I walk to the lake. The surface is glass, but small lips lap the sand along the shore. I always wanted to swim at night. I used to imagine that I would, when I was older and not scared.

I didn't find anything this afternoon.

I spent the remaining sunlit hours picking through all the physical objects left inside the living room. Searching each newspaper for significance, emptying each drawer, appraising each item, opening each book for something tucked inside, or written on its pages. I even checked a canister of infested four, dumping it outside the cabin to check for something hidden inside—a note? a photograph? What had I expected? A TV detective to come through the trees, and take my rotten flour to a lab for testing?

Nothing. Garbage bags filled with the junk of fettered lifetimes.

I wade into the water, letting the faint ripples nibble my ankles, my calves, my thighs. It's cleansing, after the epic filth of the afternoon. I walk in until the waterline reaches my breasts, and for a moment, the surface tension holds them up. Across the lake, I can see a fire, can hear Hank Williams singing. I'm not alone after all. The water is trying to lift my feet from the sandy lakebed. The night wraps itself around my ears, and its faded sounds are like a lullaby. I could sleep here. Float on my back, and finally rest.

I take one more step, suck in my breath, and plunge my head under. The water runs on my face, cold and bracing. I kick away from shoreline, finding my legs powerful, and my arms long. I dunk again. Here, underneath, all I can hear is the beat of my own heart. I stay below long enough for the melody to turn frantic.

—

It was dark, the night my mother shook me from my sleeping bag. And cold. I remember first her hand on my chest, then her nose in my ear before I realized I was wake. *We have to leave, sweetie. We're going to sleep in the car.*

She nudged me out of my sleeping bag, into my jacket, my limbs wobbling. I'd been sleeping on the floor, my parents on the hide-a-bed couch. She tugged my feet into boots, my head into a hat, and then my body out the door. I thought I heard men's voices. My daddy, and my grandpa.

It was snowing. That I remember well. Sleep-drugged, I thought the snowflakes were the moon, busted open and falling to earth. The cold stung my nostrils and my tongue, smelling sharp and empty, and then I was inside the car, smelling heavy and old. My mother slid me into a seatbelt like she'd slid me out of my sleeping bag.

She took the passenger seat, and I closed my eyes. Dad must be getting our bags, saying goodbye. I didn't say goodbye. It was just Grandpa here. Grandma didn't come in the winter. We didn't usually either. We never left in the dark. I slumped into myself, almost back to sleep.

Then, a blast. Muffled, but loud. Like part of the world, small, but heavy caving in.

I jerked, the way I sometimes did when I dreamed I was falling. Melted snow streamed down the windshield, and down my mother's cheeks. The dashboard lights lit the twin rivers. My father came out of the cabin. He slammed the door so hard it couldn't catch the lock. It bounced, and swung back open.

"Don't."

My father took the driver's seat, breathing heavily and smelling of something I didn't recognize. My mother stayed silent as he shifted gears, staring over my head to find tire tracks in the dark driveway. His eyes gleamed red, light refracting through melting snow. My eyes stayed on the door, watching for my grandfather's hand to reach out and latch it properly.

Three weeks later—snowing again—I heard the same softened blast in my own house. Another part of the world caving in. I was eight.

When my grandmother drove up to the cabin to tell my grandfather, wintering alone like he had since retiring, that his only son, my only father, shot himself, my grandmother found my grandfather dead. Police ruling? Another suicide.

The morning of the funeral, I heard my grandmother tell my mother that it was unusual, wasn't it? For a man to shoot himself in his own chest. *That's not how he did it*, she wept, and from my hiding place, I knew she meant my father.

—

I crash through the thin skin of the water, and in doing so, hear the ghosts of gunshots echoing across decades.

My father killed his father, and then he killed himself.

On the water, the moon breaks into pieces. I am a child again, and I can smell the cold, but I am also an adult, and I repeat these words to myself. *My father killed his father, and then he killed himself*. This much I know is true. The why is what I don't know. What I've been avoiding for thirty-five years. First, by refusing to ask my mother any questions, then by refusing to ask them of myself. Her death snaked his back to me via this cabin. I'd assumed it had been sold or lost to the bank— my mother never mentioned it, nor had my grandma before she died. Then, a week after I buried my mother, there was lawyer, and the will, and the deed, and when I didn't believe him, my father's will, my grandfather's will, my grandmother's will.

"It was always meant to stay in the family," he told me.

You can ban yourself from questions, bury them, braid them with excuses, but that won't get them answered.

My energies crystalize here—*my father killed his father, and then he killed himself*—as I swim back to shore. My naked body is awake, and ready, as I hadn't been when I'd arrived.

I keep a battery operated flood light in my trunk, and when I get back to land, I fish it out. Set it up in the middle of the living room. It does what it's supposed to do, and floods the cabin with light. Translucent spider webs crisscross the closed bedroom door, a thousand tiny "x"s. My brain tries spin the imagine into metaphor here, but I don't let it. I'm done playing the poet, playing the fool. Something specific happened here, something I almost saw. The water made me strong and tall, and, even though what I'm about to do doesn't require either, prepared.

The door handle, at one point brass, is gritty and brittle. I turn it, but the door doesn't move. The wood has expanded, warped. I press first my shoulder, then my hip, then my whole chest into the crosshatching spider webs, and after a few seconds of applied force, it opens with a keening shudder. To my anxious, excited brain, it opens with another gunshot.

The door swings open into the room, smaller than I remember. It reeks. The smell in here is so overpoweringly rotten than I have to suppress gagging. It was what was in the big room, but multiplied. Bloated rodentia, animal piss and droppings, dust and mold, and, a note I didn't catch earlier—rust.

I cup my hands around my nose, and look over the top of my knuckles. A haze hangs in the air, like time suspended and made solid. This room has remained even more immaculately unchanged than the big room. In the middle, the bed my grandparents shared. Flanked by bedside tables. A leg of the left table has buckled, and it's leaning, drunken, against the mattress. On the bedspread, face down, a picture frame; on the wall, a tiny cross -stitching of a bride and groom, faceless and holding hands. Kitschy, except I know my grandmother stitched it herself in the weeks before her wedding.

Elsewhere, mold blooms on the wall, dark patterns scratched into the wood. A small bookshelf with dime store paperbacks—romance, mostly, but a few murder mysteries thrown in for good measure. Many of these, I can see, are shredded, easy bedding for nesting mice. On the very top shelf are three photo albums—two I recognize, one I don't.

These thrill me, but I restrain myself, make myself keep looking. Two photographs still hang, crooked, on the right wall. My father and grandfather in front of the cabin, and my great-grandfather, the lumberjack I never knew, standing before a cart piled with timber. My grandmother's dresser in the corner. Please let it be empty. She spent so little time here after my grandfather's death; I wonder if she had the forethought to clear out the clothing. My throat constricts at the thought of what could have made a home for itself inside my grandmother's sweaters.

This, I stand at the head of bedroom, is where she found my grandfather. This, if they aren't anywhere else, is where I'll find my answers.

I start in the far right corner, deciding to work myself clockwise through the room. It's stupid that I'm doing this in the dark. Already, I'm having to contort my body to keep the single source of light on the small section that I'm searching, but I'm determined. On an elemental level, I'm ready for an answer. For explanation. I run my fingers along the seams of the floorboards, boards my father helped plane. He was gone from my life so early, and in such an overwhelming and frightening way that my memory of him has all but receded. I only remember his face in pictures, and can't even imagine what his voice sounded like. I'm looking for something that would anchor him,

forever, in cruelty and inhumanity, yes, but also in my memory. Because I've spent so many years, my entire adult life and most of my adolescence, actively looking away from him, this hunt is a tribute to him.

I pray I'll see him,

There's nothing of interest on the floor. Dried droppings and tiny spiders curled on their backs, but nothing else. Same with the walls. I'm reaching, I know, to think that I'll find something scrawled on the wood or tucked into the logs, but I look anyway. Why not? Why not. I take the two photographs off the wall, and set them on the bed to look at later. I open each drawer in the dresser. Thank god no clothing. More tiny bones, and underneath the skeletons, dark stains where the animal's body rotted and leaked. I move the dresser, and there's nothing underneath. A small colony of mushrooms growing in the wood.

This whole place will need to be demoed. It's unlivable, unsalvageable. I'd only learned that this was part of my inheritance a month ago, and hadn't yet thought about what I would *do* with the place after I ransacked it. Turning it back into a summer home was never going to be the option.

To the bookshelf. I pull each book out gingerly, each coughing dried and dusty rot. My eyes water, and my nose stings. One book yields a bookmark—"A book is a friend you carry in your pocket." Another a grocery list. But nothing more. Emptied, I search the wood for holes or chips. Did the bullet leave my grandfather's chest? Did it mark this room somehow?

I empty the drawers in the bedside tables. Use my bare fingers to search the dark undersides of the furniture. I press my toes along the length of each floorboard, waiting for one to creak or lift open. I open each picture frame and look for an inscription. Blank. Thumb through all three photo albums—my father with a hammer, my grandparents on their wedding day, crooked landscapes, me holding a fish. I shine my floodlight underneath the bed. I tear back the bedclothes. I find a knife. I tear open the bed.

—

Feathers, like moonlight, like snow, fall. I am sitting in the middle of the room, in the middle of what, thirty minutes ago, had been the bed. I brush clumped down from the floor in front of me. There's a dark stain spooling out towards the wall. The shadow of blood? Of a decayed body? I'm grasping. It's just filth. It's all filth. I'm covered in it. The cabin is covered in it. Whatever I'd hoped to find is buried in it.

Filth.

I stand up, brush down as best I can out of my hair and clothes. The weight that a lifetime of accumulated questions bears hard on my shoulders. I feel my years.

Two bullets. I heard both of them. *Bshoom. Bshoom.* That's how they line up in my childhood. One shot. Two shot. Then the emptying echo.

I pick up the floodlight, and carry it outside. I walk the perimeter of the cabin. This heirloom of our family. This archive of our neglected rot, our shed skin, our buried sins.

It's small, really.

In the predawn black, I pack the few things I brought.

—

I light a match.

Then a second.

Then a third.

My car is running behind me, my headlights already facing out, towards the road. I throw a fourth match through the open door.

After I packed, I blanketed the floor in those fragile newspapers. I see sparks snap against the black. I add another match. Another. My hands are trembling. One catches a single pine needle, tracing its skeleton in red. A flame

cracks as it catches oxygen. Carbon. I see the dark print on the newspaper. Then I hear a roar.

Eight seconds later, a wall.

It takes.

I leap backwards. The door is pushed, smashed shut from the inside.

Already, the heat is scalding, but I stand for a second beside my car and watch. The cabin has eyes. Red and rolling, white, orange with the flames. It's awake. Alive. It makes another groaning sigh, the flames greedy for the brittle wood.

I take the driver's seat, hands still shaking, and find the grooves that my grandfather's wheels ground into place. I maneuver slow down the logging road. The cabin is still in my mirror. It's a riot. I can still see its structure, like bones, but even they are crumbling now. Melting.

I reach the road, and one last time, I turn. The patterns in the flame shift. The pyre rises, a tongue of flame lashing against a sky that's lost all its stars. It falls, and I hear a scream so unworldly I believe, for a moment, that it must be human.

About the Author:

Torrie Jay White is a writer who uses her work to understand identity, pain, and our place within the world. Her short fiction has been appeared in fields, Litro, and Rock & Sling magazines, and she is finishing her first novel. Born and raised in Minnesota's Twin Cities, she now lives in the Washington D.C. area. torriejaywhite.com

ENCOUNTERS MAY BE PREDICTED

by Paul Perilli

Back then, whenever I was looking for something good to read, I went to Spoonbill & Sugartown over on Bedford Ave. There was always plenty to choose from and I spent a lot of time picking at the paperbacks and rows of magazines. That afternoon I met an old friend, Eugene, a clarinet player. He asked me what I was doing around the neighborhood when I'd moved out of it five years ago?

Taking a walk, I said, and it's ending up being longer than I was expecting. They usually are. But to be honest, I still like it around here. This bookstore's still one of my favorites.

Mine too, so I understand, Eugene said. I'm walking off the gig I had last night. How about we go to Teddy's and have a brew? Catch up on things.

We went to Teddy's, took a booth by the windows and ordered pints from the waitress.

I'd been hoping to run into someone I knew. It was one of those days I thought I might. I've noticed when I feel something like that's going to happen, sure enough it does.

Eugene said, You really thought you were going to run into me?

Not you specifically, I explained. Someone though. Anyone I haven't seen for a while. Not that you're anyone. We went through too much to call you anyone. I used my fingers to

hang quotes around that last word. I'm glad you came along. I never forgot the time you let me stay in your place for two months when you went to France and I played house with your neighbor Mo. You know what I mean?

I'm not so sure you weren't thinking of me.

You're not?

No. I think you came over here knowing exactly what would happen when you headed this way.

I found it encouraging there might be a plan out there that determined chance meetings like these, which I guess wouldn't make them chance at all.

Now that you say it, this happened to me another time when I was in Mexico. It was maybe the only time I'd been out of the country when it did.

I was doing research for a project that gave me money to go down there and travel around. The first time that had happened, someone paying for something I wanted to do and would have spent my own money on. Anyway, I needed to be alone to take in as much I could, fill notebooks with observations, take pictures. Just look around. It was really great.

Four of those days I spent in Oaxaca hanging around the cafes on the zocolo. Most of the time I went to the one right around the corner from my hotel. The Del Jardin. It had the most relaxed atmosphere and interesting people. One afternoon I met a couple there from Florida, a German named Jergens. His wife Judy had a southern accent. They were buying objects in the villages to bring back to sell in their shop in Miami.

That's Jergens' business, Judy said with the toss of a hand. I got the feeling she didn't have anything to do with it.

Later in the conversation she told a story about something she saw earlier in the morning. She was out alone, without Jergens. He was still in bed and she didn't feel like sitting around waiting for him to get up and get ready. She went for coffee and a roll and was just finishing up when behind her a pigeon plopped on the plate of eggs a waiter had just set down in front of a French guy. Landed dead center, was how she described it.

The guy wasn't laughing. His wife was though, and she called for the waiter. The waiter took his plate and brought back another right away. He came with it so fast Judy wondered if they'd made him a new one or just spooned off the bad parts and scraped the rest onto another dish.

They'd only do that in New York, I told her.

Right after I said that Judy noticed the sudden change of mood that came over me. She located the position of my eyes. There was a woman standing on the corner across the street from us chatting with another woman. Her name was Andrea. Years back I'd worked with her at a university. She'd introduced me to my first wife and I always regretted not trying to get something going with her before then. Well, my ex and her had a falling out and I wanted to avoid any conversation that might have come up about it.

You know her don't you, Judy said without any hesitation. She didn't miss anything. I might have been gazing into deep space. But she knew it was something more. And I'd been having the feeling I'd run into someone from my past. I didn't know why. And I did.

Why don't you go over there and say hello. You want to. I can tell. I'll go over there for you. Why not? You're down here alone. I'll say the man over there wants to talk to you. He knows you.

Don't do that, please, I said.

Can't you see that's why you're traveling alone, she said. You're afraid of women. You have to come out of that shell sometime so why not now?

Meanwhile, Jergens is staying out of this. Lighting up a cigarette right after finishing another.

Not saying hello to Andrea was a relief. And after that I avoided the Del Jardin, and Judy and Jergens.

I suppose you regret doing that, Eugene said. A swift wave of a hand got the attention of the waitress and the order of two more pints.

Not at all, I said. The next night I spotted Judy and Jergens sitting with Andrea and her travel companion. I could feel Judy's eyes wandering around looking for me. Later on, when I was sitting at another café, I saw the four of them walking together. Thankfully it was time to move on to the next place.

Eugene was staring at the television hanging above the bar. Into the uncomfortable gap, I said, Do you think they're all friends now?

Do you? Does it matter? Eugene said.

Maybe these coincidences aren't all we're making them out to be, I said.

Or maybe it was one of those special moments we were talking about, Eugene said. That there's a power in us that knows more than we do, than we want to or try to. We're connected to something deeper that we don't tap into much since we walk around in a daze most of the time. Something did come to me while I was listening to you.

Do you think Andrea had a feeling like that, thought she was going to run into someone she knew? Is that what you were thinking?

Eugene said, Do you remember Beth Babson?

Of course. How could I forget her. She was part of that group we knew when we all just moved here.

I know you liked her, Eugene said. Without any hesitation he added, I'm going to tell you something I probably shouldn't. Out of all of us, she liked me the most. She was always looking for ways to be with me, to go where I was going, even though she was living with Kevin all those years and it wasn't wise for us to be seen together.

I didn't know that. The second-man-in role, a tough spot. My voice trailed off. It sounded like one of those experiences you never forget and don't want to. Someone you thought you weren't supposed to be with at the time only to realize later it was exactly what you should have been doing.

I thought she eventually wanted to marry Kevin so I never tried to turn what was going on between us my way. Or that's what I wanted to believe. I wasn't with anyone special. I was willing to let her sweep me along if she wanted to. We had a freaking blast together! Everywhere we went, restaurants, bars, museums, all of it on the sly. Once we decided to take two days off from our jobs and go to Montauk. It was July. She gave Kevin some excuse about going there with a friend to help her get over a bad breakup.

We took the jitney. Which was risky if you think about it. Someone might have been on it that we knew. Beautiful weather was forecast and the bus was packed. I had the inside seat and Beth the aisle. The woman sitting across from her, a saleswoman we'd find out, snagged Beth in a conversation she didn't want to be in.

Turn my way and talk to me, I whispered in her ear.

That's what she did. Leaned into me, put a hand on my arm and talked about our hotel.

It wasn't going to be anything special, but it guaranteed three nights together. I'd made the reservations at my place before we left. When we were there Beth remembered she had to call her office to tell them she wasn't going to be in. She hung up the phone and said, Phew, I didn't have to talk to my boss. Her assistant said she had an emergency and wouldn't be back until Monday. That was easier than I thought it would be.

Are you mad I didn't get us a hotel on Old Montauk Highway? I said. The only rooms left were four-hundred dollars a night.

Ours turned out to be a pretty bland place. But it was quiet and away from the main strip, and that's what we were looking for.

The hotel manager, a guy with arthritis and a bent back, told us our room wouldn't be ready for a couple of hours.

There were a few chairs around a table and we sat there waiting for a couple of slackers to get all of their things out of our room and packed into their car, and then for the maid to tidy it up.

We stayed inside the rest of the afternoon. We were in love. That's why we went there. To hook up as much as we could.

The next afternoon we went to a fish house in Montauk center and ate steamed lobsters. We had a table by the windows and took our time, eating slow. We were talking about going to the beach when we were done when all of a sudden Beth got the look of a cornered cat trying to find a way out of the place.

Oh no, it's her.

A tall woman dressed in tan slacks and a white blouse had just come in. She had an air of importance, as if everyone wanted her attention.

Who?

My boss.

What's she doing here?

That's what I'm asking myself.

Maybe she won't see you.

No chance of that. Her boss came over to our table, to reprimand Beth was my assumption. But instead of that, she smiled and winked at her.

If you don't tell anyone, I won't either, she said. She went on over to a table in the back where a guy with curly black hair and a plaid shirt was sitting.

Well, you know, until then I'd been expecting to run into someone we knew. To get caught in our game. Seeing Beth's boss and having her in the same situation made me relax for the first time since we'd left New York.

Later on, her boss' wink and smile became a joke. It reminded us of the good time we were having. But once we were back in the city Beth started disengaging from me. We still talked on the phone and met in secret. Still winked and smiled in a joking way, but something had changed. I didn't want to ask her what it was. I was afraid she might tell me something that would mean the end of us.

I said, People never ask the questions they should ask for that reason. They fear the answer might be the one they know but want to keep pretending isn't true.

I started seeing someone else. Her name was Anne. Beth and I were still in touch. But it was obvious she wasn't leaving Kevin. Anne and I decided to go to Paris. I didn't tell Beth I was going. I hadn't told her anything about my new relationship. I wanted to leave room for her. I was willing to give her more time. We stayed in a small hotel near San Michelle. A quiet place, not too expensive, with rooms that looked out at the square. After four days we went south to Biarritz, then to San Sebastian and Bilbao, then back to Paris. We had three more nights at the hotel in San Michelle.

The first morning we went down to the complimentary breakfast. I'd been having a strange feeling since we got back from the south. Then I saw what it was. Beth came in the door with a guy I didn't know. She was trying to look the other way. When she saw I noticed her she smiled at me and winked. That's when I remembered I'd told her I stayed in that hotel with an old girlfriend.

I didn't say anything to Anne. Though the look she gave me wondered if I'd seen a ghost. Fortunately, I didn't see Beth at the hotel the next two days. And I haven't run into her since then.

You mean you haven't run into her until now. I looked past Eugene and his head made a slow turn that way.

About the Author

Paul Perilli's fiction 'Summary Report to the Committee' appears in Overland's False Documents issue. His story 'Orwell's Year' appears as a chapbook from Blue Cubicle Press. He's currently working on a novel about the 2008-2009 financial crash titled SEVEN SEVEN SEVEN. He lives in Brooklyn, NY.

THE WALL BETWEEN US
by John C. Weill

We walked with the wall between us, just as Robert Frost described.

We picked up the stones, each of them still cold from the winter.

I stopped a moment to slip on leather gloves. He pulled on cotton, the kind you buy stapled together three pairs in a package. Sun had barely risen. I looked down the length of the wall to where it traveled on flat ground as far as the eye could see, rocks fallen on both sides. Then the wall and fallen rocks disappeared in the dips and the rolling hills.

"You know, this is the only time we see each other," I said. "When we repair this wall."

"Our dads built it. I feel like it's an obligation," he said.

We continued another ten-feet, bent over at the same time like bobbing oil rigs, picked up rocks and simultaneously placed them with a clack on the wall. We must be a sight, I thought, him short and squat like a Rhino, me tall and gangly like a Giraffe.

"Robert Frost wondered why neighbors need a wall," I said. "It only separated his apple orchard from the neighbor's pines."

He was quiet for another twenty steps. Then down we went, bobbing once and placing rocks on the wall. "But the neighbor told him good fences make good neighbors... and that's probably true," he surmised. "I've read stories about people actually building room additions that straddle a neighbor's property."

I chuckled then swung my arm across the vast open spaces of rolling green hills and trees, a distant pond whose surface was freckled with black birds, and two modest homes – his and mine – both at least four acres apart on either side of the wall. "Hardly a chance of that," I said. "So it only comes down to wanting to mark our territory."

He had kept walking, kneeled and picked up a stone. "Beats peeing," he said laughing.

I looked at him oddly.

"Marking territory... Peeing..." he said.

"I got it."

I liked him. His name was Paul. His father used to come over with him to our house for dinner now and then. His wife had died when Paul was young. Our parents built the wall because at one time my father kept cows. Today there were no cows on the property. I was a suburbanite really, having lived elsewhere for twenty years until my father died. Having inherited the property and the back taxes, I returned. My modern furniture, even some Ikea were not in sync with the rustic cabin-like home I now inhabited. But the open fields and hundreds of huge trees on my twenty-six acres were true markers of the seasons. In the fall the leaves changed to bright orange, red and yellow. They dropped like the hands of giants on the fields until the trees were bones. Then the snow came and the world slowly turned white.

The snow went on for miles. As had the bright fall leaves. Our properties provided endless views, endless solitude and endless quiet. Especially at night when stars filled the sky like glitter tossed from an airplane. Although Paul lived close to me by the standards of our area, my other neighbors were more than a quarter of a mile away. From my kitchen sink window I could see their homes like little toys in the fields and I could see the chimneys puff tiny clouds in winter. None of them had a wall.

"We're the only ones around having to do this," I remarked, as we bent over, picked up big stones then placed them on the wall.

'Clack-clack'. We did not place them at exactly the same time.

"I know you want me to say let's take the wall down," he remarked. "But I don't want to. I wouldn't know what to do with all the stones and I don't want to have wasted my dad's time."

Paul's father and my father had spent four years building the wall, then as Robert Frost had said, mending wall. They mended twice a year after winter frost. They spent hours walking the wall, talking and sipping coffee now and then, even drinking a beer or two at the end. His father was the first to show his respects at my father's funeral. So maybe it's true, good fences – or walls - make good neighbors.

We walked until dusk. We finished our task then opened two beers and sat on the wall we had just mended. Our legs, without thinking, dangled on his side. We clicked our bottles. The day was done.

About the Author:

John C. Weil lives in La Jolla, California. He graduated San Diego State University with a Masters in Literature and Creative Writing. He has been the Managing Editor of two newspapers and a long term Chief of Staff for a U.S. Congressman and a County Supervisor. He has published in both national and local magazines and newspapers and his stories and poems have appeared in literary magazines throughout the country and abroad. He is currently working on both a book of short stories and a novel.

THE VEIL OF JUDGMENT
by Pauline Duchesneau

The slam of the heavy steel door and the mechanized latching of innumerable locks dropped lead into my gut. I'd tried and failed to prepare for this moment. I couldn't tell if my poker face held. His was stone. The piercing ice blue eyes incinerated my confidence. I silenced the words forming in my mind before they induced panic.

Attempting to smile, I moved forward. "Hello. I'm Walter Ingraham, the writer. Thank you for agreeing to meet with me."

"I know who you are. Don't waste our time. The clock's ticking."

The grating of the chair I slid out from the table raised hairs on my arms. Fumbling with the embarrassing mess the disgruntled guards left when they searched my briefcase, I retrieved a notepad, pen, and recorder. I wiped my brow with a folded handkerchief.

"Ok, I'm ready." If that were possible. I wished the table wasn't so narrow.

"The first wasn't as life-changing as you might think."

He watched me for a reaction. There was no escape from his unnerving stare.

"We have a different understanding of reality, you and me. Crazy you call me? When one willingly accepts the limitation of five senses as the total of human perception, well—pffft…"

He leaned back in his chair and folded his arms. Just when I thought he wouldn't continue, he lurched forward, and I startled.

"When did you decide with certainty that you knew The Truth? That things are the way they are, and there's no other view. See now? You're all set. Just keep calling me crazy. You'll feel better.

Or…think about it. Could be worth forfeiting a little sleep.

We're not so different. Perspectives can change everything. Everyone's capable of anything given the right circumstance. And if it's only circumstance determining whether I did it and you didn't, then *inside* we are no different at all. Deal with that.

She was old, sad, alone and hurting inside and out. The darkness spread out from her and hung in a miserable, tormenting cloud of malice. I watched its talons tear at her soul. She stared at me in recognition though we'd never seen each other before. The look pleaded for help. A lifetime of pain hit me with one word before she directed her motorized wheelchair into the alley and I knew I could not deny her.

"Please."

I understood exactly what she meant and the level of her desperation. She lacked the ability to free herself. She depended on me. I followed her. I felt her anguish. She stopped her chair, still facing away from me.

Do it now, I could hear her beg in my mind, and it broke my heart.

I took the blade from my pocket, flipped it open, and granted her request. She sank into herself. Her head fell back. One last connection radiated thanks, and her shadow dispersed. Peace replaced misery. I'll never forget that look. And I'll never regret helping her.

I stopped keeping track of them all. They were much the same, shrouded by horrific black clouds. The cliché can't be accidental. The blackness is unlike any other: impenetrable, seething, and indomitable. It's more deadly than the fastest-growing cancer and viciously contagious. I might pass the optimistic ones on the street one day and note their determination. The next day, they are overwrought and looking for me with those pleading eyes.

Their relief propelled the mission as I honed my skills over time. I learned to leave no trace of my presence. The afflicted took an active role by retreating to remote places. For the sake of dignity, I worked quickly and didn't linger. Their gratitude spurred motivation. I spread the gift of liberation and felt elated. Don't look at me like that. No, it wasn't about power, not an adrenaline rush, no bloodlust or morbid fascination. Simply my purpose.

I didn't choose the course, but I accepted it. Compassion drove me, and I understood this awareness was rare. These pitiful souls were stuck in a society that perpetuated, if not created, their condition. You've seen it—the mire of worry and despair fed by sensationalism, the toxicity of pervasive negativity and isolation. I never encountered someone needing my help who was not alone.

My services were in high demand. Sometimes I released six or eight a night. And then I knew it was time to move to another city. I hated to leave the others still seeking my help, but they were everywhere. And to serve the most, I needed to be careful. The method worked for a while until that cop caught me by chance. And now *he's* called a hero. How's that for irony?

Now, perhaps you have misconceptions. My reasoning may not be easy to accept. And then we're back to the crazy proclamation. You think you must dismiss my story as the raving of a lunatic mind."

He leaned across the table, straining against the manacles toward me.

"But it's been hard to ignore your soul's message as we've talked today, Walter. I'm genuinely moved by your pain. When your desperation peaks, you'll seek ability like mine. For now, if you can look beyond the traditional, the learned, the commonly perceived *acceptable*... if you can let down the veil of judgment..."

The tension in his face relaxed, and his head tilted. I felt his gaze pass through me. His next words were no more than breath.

"What a rare shift of fate...You see as I do."

The pen slid from my hand. Its clang on the cold metal table echoed.

About the Author:

Pauline Duchesneau writes in rural central Maine with an adorable beagle curled by her side who listens with angelic patience to every word. Her work appeared in Yellow Mama and Dime Show Review and is forthcoming in Riggwelter. She is working on her first novel and is ever grateful to her soulmate wife who shares the vision.

WHAT DID YOU SEE?

by Joel Worford

It's eleven P.M. and your hand is on your belt. You don't see me. There are no streetlights in this neighborhood, so at first, you don't see me. Or her.

Your friends are with you. Sam has two daughters. His oldest headed for college before you put your uniforms on this morning. First year, golden hair—like her mother's. You still call her 'princess,' like you did when she was little. Pink cheeks and laughter at the dinner table. Your son is going to miss her when she's gone. Good folks—practically, family.

Jacob, you've known since high school. All those days ago, this was the dream. Class clowns. High school ruffians, but this was the dream. Shoot the bad guys. Stop the crooks. Cuff the criminals. Justice. Democracy. Good. Evil. This was the dream.

It's eleven P.M. on a Tuesday. The best time to fuck when you're in high school. Too late, everybody's asleep. Too early, no danger in the dark.

She and I met the week before prom. Brown eyes, freckled cheeks, real beauty. Last minute, scrambling. Will you? Yes. Dinner, dancing, stars. Best night of my life? She agrees. More dinners, more stars. True love. Four months later—fucking in the dark.

Suburbs, tree, cul-de-sac. The usual spot. Eleven P.M. on a Tuesday.

Who knows who called? Must've been one of the neighbors. Up for a late night snack. Or a late night piss. Who knows? Saw two kids fucking. Divorced? Lonely? Bitter? Whatever. Sees two kids fucking. Calls you.

You get the call. You're here but you don't see us. You're wasting your time. Should be downtown, getting the bad guys. Two kids fucking. This isn't the dream. Two kids fucking. No bad guys. High school ruffians, at best. No good. No evil. Just kids.

You're about to leave and I'm about to come.

"Guys, let's get out of here."

You all turn around. I finish.

"Wait, I heard something."

You all turn around. It's a miracle, Jacob's hearing. After all those concerts. Screamo, metal, punk. High school scene. Hundreds of bands. No earplugs. Still hears. It's a miracle.

Strain to look.

There are no streetlights in this

neighborhood, so at first, you don't see me. I see you. As does she. She's scared, I'm not. Just kids fucking. No bad guys. No crooks. No evil. Just kids fucking. High school ruffians, at worst. No need to escalate. Slap on the wrist. Go home.

"Over there."

Flashlights. Squinted eyes. Here we are. I'm pulling my pants up. She's fixing her dress. You're approaching. She's embarrassed. She's scared. I'm nervous.

Remember, just kids fucking.

No need to escalate. Slap on the wrist. Go home.

The look on your face. I'll never forget.

Surprise? More complicated than that. Suspicious? Not quite. Excitement? Not only. Combine the three. There it is.

"You kids can't be out here tonight."

Slap on the wrist? Check. Apologies? Check. Explanations?

"Just two kids fucking."

"Ah."

Awkward silence. 'Go Home,' pending.

There's a pause. You're staring at me. You're thinking about those bad guys downtown. Those crooks. Those criminals. I look like one of them. You're thinking about justice. Democracy. Good. Evil. This is your chance.

"Can I see your IDs?"

Your friends are wondering what you're doing. They've seen the news. They don't say anything. You're the boss.

Idenitification? Check. You're talking to her.

"What's your relationship to him?" You're pointing at me.

"He's my boyfriend." Her voice is weak.

You pause again. You look her up and

down. Pretty girl. Pink skirt. Tall boots. Well dressed. Todd's kid? That's right. Good family. Good genes.

You look me up and down.

Nappy hair. Crooked mouth. Ashy knees. White tee. Whose kid? Don't know.

You look at her again.

Pretty girl. Lots of options. Why him? Seems suspicious.

"IDs look fine."

'Go home,' pending.

"We're going to need to search you."

'Go home,' vanishing.

Explanation?

"This is unusual, you see?"

Unusual.

Your friends look worried. They've been online. So have you. Don't want to be trending. Make it seem fair. You point at her.

"We'll search you first."

She's looking at me. Frightened eyes. You're moving towards her. I move towards her.

"Stay where you are."

I stay where I am.

"Wait..."

You don't wait. Your hands are on her. She's crying now. You're moving fast. She's not the one you want. Just for pretense. She's crying. I'm trapped.

I've seen the news. I've been online. I'm frustrated. I'm angry. You're finishing up. She's crying. Finishing up. Hand on her leg. Now I'm yelling.

I'm yelling. They're yelling. You're yelling. I'm blind.

Hands on me. I'm blind. She's crying. You're

yelling. I'm struggling. Jerk my arm. You watch it move.

You see something. You reach for your belt. I know what you see.

You see Sam and his two daughters. You see Jacob moshing beside you. You see your wife crying in bed. You see your spot empty. You see your son graduating high school. You see your seat empty. You see every bad guy you've ever stopped. You see all the criminals downtown. You see their arms jerk back. You see my arm jerk back. You see it reaching for something. You see something.

Yelling everywhere. You swing your arm. A crack. Silence.

She's sobbing. She's screaming. They're quiet. They've seen the news. I'm down. Still conscious. Done yelling.

Face to ground. Handcuffs.

"You have the right to remain silent."

Exercise my right.

You're moving. He's moving. I'm moving. Sam stays. She's screaming. Distant screams.

Door opens. Head down. Backseat. You're driving. Jacob passenger. No conversation. Long silence.

Warm blood. Stained Tee. Matted hair.

Can you see?

Scared Mom, worried Dad, no sleep.

Can you see?

Honor roll. Starting forward. Straight As.

Can you see?

Horny Teens. Starry night. Eleven P.M.

Can you see?

Scared girl. Frightened boy. Two kids.

Can you see? What did you see?

Nappy hair. Crooked mouth. Ashy knees.

What did you see?

Pretty girl. Ebony boy. Probability.

What did you see?

Hand jerk. Dead friends. Orphaned Son.

What did you see?

Good. Evil. Justice. Crooks.

What did you see?

About the Author:

Joel Worford is a writer and musician from Richmond, VA. His short fiction appears in the 2017 edition of Good Works Review as well as the 2018 relaunch of Random Sample Review. Joel also writes music reviews and feature articles for The Auricular, a Richmond music magazine covering local artists and venues."

THE KILLING OF AN ARDENT APPRENTICE
by Sana Mojdeh

A Muffin Man is a mute, a filler, a nodder.

A Muffin Man is an irrelevant, in most cases unfocused subject in the background of the frame who nods once in a while. Nodders nod against each other, mindful of a nonexistent conversation. But often, their engaged commitment makes them believe they are the

leads. The Muffin Man's presence in the frame is insignificant yet essential for the scene as it makes the scene realistic. Under no circumstances does it convey meaning for the narrative or add truth to the totality of the plot or even the scene.

Muffin men are to be forgotten.

Emily dropped me off at the airport at exactly noon, knowing well that she would miss the bi-weekly meeting with her thesis supervisor. I slipped the envelope across the blazing dashboard, "This is the least I owe you and the other two grads... I forgot their names." It isn't much, but what is left of the second mortgage I cashed out three years ago.

We said goodbye in her Subaru '93, and she drove on before I entered the terminal. She didn't cry, didn't linger in the hug. I admire her lack of melodrama. I wish I had met her sooner.

Now I'm surrounded by a trio of aliens in front of me, a woman to my right, and a man to the left.

The aliens stare at me. I can only see the top halves of their heads. I imagine behind the three seats in front, one bizarre body is attached to the three heads. Huge black eyes cover their wooly faces. The bottom halves are masked behind the headrests. The aliens resemble those in cult horror flicks of the '80s with cheap makeup.

I shut my eyes. Something on my seat has been bothering me since the plane's delay was announced, like a seatbelt buckle or a strap, or crumpled lining on the seat. I reach under my buttocks... nothing.

I open my eyes in hope of seeing the runway this time, but I can barely see a slice of it behind the unattached jet bridge. If I lean against the woman seated on my right once more, I bet she will snap. She hasn't complained or even muttered, and to be fair, she did offer her seat when I arrived. During my years of assistant professorship at the university, I would prefer window seats flying to conferences. Now, I don't care where I sit. What bugs me is that I don't recall when this disinterest surfaced.

For the past half hour, my shoulder harassed hers. I stretch my neck again to glimpse out of the window. I just want to see the runway. I feel seeing it would give me a sense of accomplishment—that, despite this *status quo*, the tires are gradually, perhaps imperceptibly, crawling along the scorched asphalt towards the runway. Then the plane will taxi and take me off this land for one last time.

Tilted down, her head is as still as the cabin we are all bound in. On her lap rests a napkin. She is writing or doodling or maybe drawing hash marks counting my awkward impositions. *You have bugged me thirty-three times!* I imagine her confronting me. *What the hell is wrong with you?*

I will continue until I can see the runway, as long as her plain face shows no discomfort.

Why is no truck coming to tow the jet bridge away?

A crunching noise comes from the aisle seat on my left. Baby-faced Eric in his fifties opens another packet of wasabi green peas to renew the *loop*: peas crunched with ferocity (I almost hear his jaw begging for mercy), fingers wiped with the wet towel the flight attendant brought earlier, then he browses film thumbnails on the touchscreen display in front. Earlier, he introduced himself to me with the cheerfulness of Tom Sawyer.

Unlike the woman's neutral mien, his face is animated. Like her, he wears a pair of bifocals—something concomitant with their age, I suppose. Both engage in what they are doing with constancy.

The three aliens in front have lost their comic effect. Their now serious, all but menacing stare meshes with the sudden cold current of air circulating through the cabin. The AC is now on full blast to ease the August heat.

I look to my right. What I see outside—a dancing heat-shimmer on the wing out of the window—contradicts the cold curling up my palms and toes. A strange composition; I don't know which one is real.

"Do you know a good film?" Eric turns to me with a German or an Austrian accent. I

shake my head. He kind of leans against me to ask the woman. She too shakes her head without turning.

I doubt his question will be the end of our interaction before we land in Zürich—if we ever do. This delay feels longer than half hour, certainly longer than anything I have ever experienced; even longer than that six-hour wait for my connection in Madrid eight years ago. I was younger and tireless. I would stand up from the terminal seat to stretch my legs, walking between the gates; or I would go back to the shops for a beer. I had options right there, so it didn't even cross my mind to visit the city. Now, I can do none of that... *is this wait troubling because I can't stand up? Because I can't see the runaway?*

I resist thinking about *the thing* under my butt because when I don't resist, it lurks, or I imagine so.

"Summer vacation?" Eric asks in a forceful tone.

I want him to leave me alone. The truth will make him uneasy enough. I open my eyes facing him so he can take a good look. He sounds clueless.

"Yes, I'm *the guy*." It takes a minute or two for some people. I wait. He too waits, baffled.

"Strasbourg?" I give him time. "The Court of Human Rights? The three-year battle?"

He has no idea who I am. Perhaps it's the bushy beard I shaved last month. My neck hurts. I give up. "I'm heading to this clinic in Forch for an assisted suicide."

"Forch?" he replies at once. "Outside Zürich?"

I nod. He seems more amazed by the fact I know the village than with the other keywords I just uttered. Other than Emily and outside the context of the court, Eric is the second person with whom I personally share my intention.

*   *   *

I used to stick to my bed for hours, sloth-like. One morning I felt hundreds of pencils poking me. I read an article on my tablet about this European clinic which provides suicide assistance not only to terminally ill people but also in cases of severe chronic depression. Electricity rushed through my loins, awaking dull muscles.

As far as the university was concerned, I'd been out of the country on a sabbatical, researching. I spent most days miserable in my bed, logically and systematically searching for a reason not to end my life. The ecstasy on reading the article pushed me out of bed under the shower, then behind my desk to email the clinic. Washing the mold off the coffee pot was too much, so I strolled out to the local café.

Days later I received the reply that unless an applicant can provide records of unsuccessful in-house treatment, the clinic would reject the application. I obviously couldn't provide such supporting documents. I'd never been an inpatient.

I had tried a number of psychiatrists in the past. They were unanimously unable to recognize the severity of my case, much less refer me to a mental institution. I knew had I told them I wanted to kill myself they could have put me in a ward. I didn't tell them.

"Honestly, you look fine to me," one of them said after I spent an hour reasoning with them on the high concepts of life and death. "Take a long vacation and let's meet afterwards," another one suggested.

I understand why they wouldn't take me seriously: instead of typical sessions of cognitive therapy or psychoanalysis, I would turn the table to one-on-one philosophical debates, rationalizing the absurdity of life with such tenacity on my side. Being an academic, naturally I would approach the conversations methodically which, in turn, would push them to see me as a bored egomaniac—a persona from which I was far removed.

I merely wished one of them would prove me wrong by rejecting my logic. Anyway, they treated my case at face value. I believe this is why I thought no one else could see through me either, although I had never shared my thoughts with colleagues or friends outside the university, not even my brother. All they could see was a masquerade of a bourgeois assistant prof.

* * *

"Schön! Forch is beautiful. Small but beautiful," Eric says, wiping his fingers first to browse the film thumbnails on the display for the tenth time!

His naïve but transparent reaction, unlike anything I have experienced with the psychiatrists and the clinic, breeds a sense of acknowledgement which I'm tempted to examine further: "I don't work in the clinic. I'm not a *clinician*," I say, "I'm going there to end my life."

"You don't look like someone who works there anyway." He holds up the packet in my face. "Green peas?"

Once I pass, he leans further against me with a stretched arm, "Evia, green peas?" I take advantage of this domino effect to lean on her again... I can't see the runway.

She shakes her head, still occupied with her napkin project. I assume they exchanged names before I got to my seat. Eric must've started it all. I wouldn't be surprised had he—in a matter of minutes—shared with Evia his most vivid memories; like how he once pranked his second-grade teacher, Miss Mitchell of Scottish descent.

"I discovered *these* here in your city," Eric points to the packets of wasabi green peas he stashed in the seat pocket, "Lecker... Tasty! Can't get enough."

One of the aliens' head slithers along the headrest and stops. Creepy. I want to turn back to see who else or what else is behind me, but I don't.

Before I realize, I tell Eric, "And I'm not terminally ill."

Chomping on peas, he can't hear my quiet confession. It reminds me of one April afternoon—prior to my discovery of the clinic—when I finally decided to ask my brother to meet me. I wanted to open up about the void inside. Although we had never been brotherly close even in our teenage years—as *she-is-my-first* close; brothers tell each other these kind of stuff. I thought it was time to confide in someone. I couldn't think of anybody else.

I didn't mind his suggestion to meet at the greyhound racetrack he often visits on Saturdays. He could have suggested the pub close by, the Faculty Cafeteria, or even by the dumpster right in the middle of that filthy alley behind my apartment, and I still would have said *fine*.

We grabbed a couple of Budweisers at the edge of the balcony, overlooking the muzzled greyhounds behind the closed gates. My brother told me he'd been saving to take his family to the Caribbean for Christmas. I stopped listening when he reached "and for next Christmas, I'm thinking…"

As the gates opened, a buzz resonated behind us like a tsunami hurling me beneath the tide. Turning back, I heard whistling and cheering and shouting. I envied the audience for whom the universe was reduced to that very racetrack. I kept silent and observed my brother watching the race closely. Following the greyhounds with his eyes, he gawked under his puckered forehead for seconds, then squinted for the rest of the race. I assumed I lost his bet.

During the break, he kept on about the management role he had been promoted to in the consulting firm. He spoke of an opportunity to *fuck their new client* (figuratively or literally I don't know). Then he asked how I'd been lately—a rhetorical question, as he was then clueless about my situation. Just before I shared the burden on my shoulders, I wondered what good such an abrupt revelation might bring us. How could I reveal the absurdity I breathe every day amid his fever for beer and betting? My words would've vanished in his hectic world much like my voice would've died in the hubbub as the greyhounds raced for another round.

I said goodbye and walked up the balcony stairs, pushing against the masses.

* * *

Eric touches a thumbnail on the display to read a film's synopsis. Another page pops up. Then he returns to the main page; then, another synopsis, another loop. Greasy green peas slip out of his mouth. *Maybe one or two slipped under my butt too, and that's what has been annoying me.*

I search the seat cushion, imagining objects and trying to keep my quirky movements to a minimum. My right arm should only touch Evia when I try to see the runway—otherwise it's a waste! I can't see how many hash marks I have now made on her napkin. This stupid position hurts my elbow, looking as if I'm giving myself a rectal exam. I rest my palms between my thighs anyway. The cold in the cabin is getting intolerable.

"Are you in the film industry?" I ask him. My question doesn't come out as sarcastic as I wanted it to be.

"No," Eric says. "I'm a therapist with the Polizei Zürich."

How I wish I could grab the packet out of his hand and throw it away, maybe at the aliens… *My god! How many more packets has he got?* I'm desperate to break Eric's loop. I want him to stop touching the display.

"Are *you* in the movie business?" he asks.

I shake my head.

"You got a moving city. I think six days didn't do the justice here."

"You flew in six days ago?" I ask.

"Same airline; although the flight was a bit—"

"So you already know all the films available on this flight, right?"

"It was a week ago," he wipes his fingers. "Maybe they added new ones."

Moving city… I'm unsure whether he meant the city is exciting or whether something got lost in translation; maybe he wanted to complain that everything in this jam-packed city ceaselessly moves…

Another announcement apologizes for the delay. With each announcement, Eric's display freezes. When it is over, the film menu jumps back to the front page.

"Do you know this thriller with this man trying to escape the building?" Eric asks, but he doesn't wait for my answer, as though he has learned by now that I would probably shake my head. He bends over me again, "Evia, you know that one? It's a—what do you call it?" he looks at me, waiting for my contribution, "New release," he figures out himself.

The jet bridge is still blocking my view.

Evia doesn't know the film. She spreads her blanket across her lap before returning to her project. Now I can see the napkin—the sketch of a face. I can't see the details.

"What about the other one? They filmed the fight scene here in your city," Eric tells me. "Somewhere in Old Town inside that famous bakery."

I let him know I never heard of that place.

*   *   *

I bet Eric would dig *my* thriller—the nerve-wracking game I got myself and Emily into with the clinic.

Two weeks after my rejection, I emailed them with the subject line *Appealing a decision.* They declined: "This is not a decision made in a court of law." I sent thirteen more emails before they agreed to listen to me.

The night before the first call lasted long, humid, and quiet. It was two hours past midnight when I hallucinated a circle of -suited-up decision makers at the far end, around a giant table. They put the spotlight on me for hours. My hands cuffed behind me, I saw the grim faces of *the committee.* I imagined them questioning every decision I had ever made.

Later, behind my desk, I drew a mind map, trying to include every possible subject over which our conversation might pass—every plausible scenario. Then, for each branch of the map, I devised a series of questions the committee would most likely ask. I dozed off once or twice, but the result were perfect.

By the time I had answered all three hundred questions in my sixty-five scenarios, I could hear the elevator now running up and down behind my apartment wall. Another day had started for my neighbours. A wide plain of vanilla light crept up over the desk, onto my laptop, then onto the wall. I turned back and, through the window, saw a scene to which I'd become a stranger long since. Ever since I had joined the university ten years ago (and even during my graduate study before then), I never had to wake up early in the morning. The classes I took as a student, the classes I taught, all were incidentally scheduled for afternoons or early evenings. As for the rest, I could research any time, day or night.

Two hours later, I had a mug of fresh coffee in my hand, waiting for the call in the bedroom I'd cleaned up, an eerie feeling swirling in my chest—sleepless and hyped simultaneously. I don't know why I had vacuumed the room or dumped the filthy pile of clothes in the hamper. Perhaps because I imagined one of them would request a video tour of the apartment... *Sorry, we cannot help you die, your place looks like shit!*

The call ended before it even got started. An intern with a flat voice needed some basic info to create a dossier. Then he said the clinic would contact me in a week to set up an interview. I hung up and blacked out on my bed.

The interview was then scheduled for two months later. I read the five-page document attached to the email. The bureaucratic nonsense enraged me into punching the bedroom wall. The pain burned up in my bones like bubbles in boiling water as I walked to the nearby ER downtown.

On my way, I did nothing but curse the clinic... *two months? Why should THEY decide when I die?*

Walking back with a cast on my hand, however, I embraced the fact that I could use this time to map out a convincing strategy to further prepare for the interview. I also stopped by the hardware store and bought a few wire-nuts to cover the exposed wires I'd found in the bedroom wall. The guy working in the store asked whether I had a color preference for the wire-nuts!

Having planned my strategy two weeks into the practice period, I asked three top second-year graduate students I knew to meet me at the café. They had no reason not to. In jest, they knew me as a *sane one* among the professors. Our encounters had always been rational and honest, if not amusing. Besides, I had awarded them generous grades in Sociology of Mental Health. In fact, I passed everyone in that class with an A. That was the time I was thrown into apathy, slowly, steadily.

They seemed surprised to see me back in the country in the middle of my sabbatical, especially Emily, the sharpest one. She suspected I was up to something.

I told them I'd been flirting with the idea of a consulting startup for which I must conduct a team simulation first. This funded simulation would take several sessions and consist of three judges (the committee) set against an applicant of euthanasia played by myself. The committee should work coherently through sessions to question the motives of the applicant, then analyze the result during recess days in order to throw back a stronger case. They would have to hit the applicant left and right with tough questions. They must push the applicant to the edge. In the end, either the applicant would emerge completely vindicated, or the judges would reject the application.

Emily's topaz eyes remained calm and curious. The other two grads held each other's stare just like some of my undergraduate students as I announce a pop quiz in class.

As long as they keep the matter secret from the department, I promised them top grades in Sociology of Ethics II which they ought to take the following spring. I told them it is *bad faith* for professors to practice private business. Of course, there wouldn't be a next spring should the odds be in my favor in the interview with the clinic.

"I don't wish to pry into your schedule," I said politely, "but you could really benefit from this."

I saw doubt in their dull faces, but not in Emily's. I asked them to lean closer (as if we were in some sort of spy drama). "I will give you each two percent in shares."

In the heat of the moment, lie after lie spewed out of my mouth mindlessly. One after another, they energized me. I was born that afternoon in the middle of the café. When the grads gave the green light, we got carrot cake slices and carried on, babbling on about god knows what for another half hour—subjects I'd never imagined showing an interest in or even deliberately listening to in hundred years... about the tasteless music usually played at the faculty cafeteria (which I haven't had noticed).

I kept up with my sincere bullshitting just for the sake of the conversation. *How liberating!*

We rehearsed every other day for six weeks, taking the matter seriously. They would step into the café, eyes lit up, dressed up like some interns working their butts off for a big-shot partner at a multinational law firm. All three would come prepared after surfing the web all night long—*Euthanasia laws in Europe* or *How to become a lawyer for dummies*, I'd think. They slipped away from the grad school duties. I kept my mouth shut. Who I was to blame? It wasn't my fault that they found my project enticing. If anything, I brought them adventure.

The sessions became freak shows with our heated arguments and Socratic dialogues. One time, in the course of my defense, I got unprecedently irrational under pressure. "You don't know how to run a clinic!" I blasted at the committee. "Go fuck yourselves!" The whole café turned to us. I expected an instant rejection by the committee; instead, Emily replied, "You do realize you don't need us to kill you, right? You can do it yourself."

That was one critical yet simple comment about which I hadn't thought. *What if the committee asked me that?* We all high-fived in sheer joy, having found a loophole, like a sports team on the verge of glorious victory. The barista refused our order of four caramel macchiato.

The practice became exhausting when we transferred to having them in my apartment. I was ready. Apparently, too much excitement can throw you in the ER bed. The grads waited outside the room while I had the interview, together with the IV. Emily brought in some mango juice and tiptoed out.

* * *

I hadn't kill myself yet because I don't want to die alone. I could've done it on any Saturday at the racetrack. The presence of others is not enough. I want them to look at me when paralysis twists up in my bones. I want them to look at me the way my brother used to look at the greyhounds racing.

Evia has slowed her pace. She is adding details to the face. I don't know how she manages to keep her hand steady in this cold.

The thing under me is now crawling. Maybe it is not on the seat but under my skin.

One of the aliens in front stretches her arms. I wonder why all three girls have identical topsy-turvy ponytails and why they wear their sunglasses on the back of their heads. The sunglasses sit looking ridiculous on their ponytail ties. The ponytails become the hairy trunk noses of hairy faces... I want to tap one of the girls on the shoulder to tell her she and her friends resemble a trio of aliens from a retro horror flick, at least, from where I sit... *but that's absurd.*

Something is wrong with Eric. He has paused browsing the thumbnails with his greasy finger resting on the display. The munching too has stopped. His mind rambles elsewhere. I can see his loop is broken, but the suspension irks me.

"Best banana muffin ever!" he says without turning. "How come you don't know that bakery?"

I tell him I don't even know the intersection. Only when I utter it, I realize it sounds moronic for some reason.

"I was waiting for my muffin when the crew came inside," he says with a grit. "They filmed the fight with four cameras. Huge cameras." His hands spread out all the way to my mouth, Eric tries to carefully show how massive the cameras were. His eager gesture pushes me to the right, giving me another chance to lean against silent Evia...

That fucking jet bridge!

"Took them three hours to set up everything. I watched. My wife was pissed at the hotel waiting for me." He describes how the lighting crew mounted up and tested the LEDs and reflectors and dimmers and diffusers in such details that I can't imagine even the actual lighting supervisor could explain it all so thoroughly.

"They gave me a part on the spot," he chuckles. "I had to buy a bag of muffins and leave."

"The Muffin Man!" I mutter.

"I asked them about the dialogue with the barista," Eric says. "They said we can *mouth* something, anything. Really doesn't matter what."

Facing me, he forgets about the thumbnails on the display.

"It was a stressful situation. I was just talking to the barista before they arrived, but-"

The captain apologizes. We won't be going anywhere soon. The passengers' humming fades shortly. My hands stay warm under my buttocks. I'm losing sensation in them.

"But when there are eyes on you under so much light, it's different," Eric says, somewhat troubled with the memory. "I screwed up. They got twenty takes just because I couldn't mouth. I kept picturing --them ---watching me. I would see myself and freeze like a mannequin."

I know the feeling—the gaze.

"The director herself handed me a muffin. She tried to calm me down," he chuckles again. "A blockbuster's director was talking to me. They don't do that. They don't talk to a nobody on the set. I almost fainted during the next take."

* * *

I fainted too, after the interview. Good thing I was already in the ER bed! I hardly recognized the voices of the committee—they were exactly as I had imagined for so long. They rejected my case on the basis of lacking evidence for the need of euthanasia.

When I regained consciousness in the morning, the grads were gone. None of them replied to my messages until I learned the department now gathered I had lied about my sabbatical.

After a week of silence, Emily reached out to me, distressed with her academic status. The department had cornered all three grads and got them to tattle on me. They got furious that I had lied about the Sabbatical. I didn't have the mind and time to waste on the hearing. On the phone and without a fuss, I accepted the one-year suspension. Emily and the other two got no-pay suspensions for a semester.

I sensed a reason for Emily's return: she was hooked on the project. Her eyes begged for more excitement. I told her the truth. For about a week, Emily would stay in my apartment until late googling international lawyers to fight back the clinic.

"What about Amnesty International?" She joked one night sunken in the couch, holding an extra-large Pepperoni pizza slice. "It's your *right* to kill yourself after all."

"You see the guy in the phone booth in the background?" I paused the film we were watching. "You know what they call him in the film industry?"

"*The guy in the phone booth in the background.*"

"The Muffin Man."

"Because he is chubby?"

"Because he is irrelevant."

"Why *muffin* then?" Emily faced me. "Can you even pay a top-notch lawyer?"

"I will apply for a second mortgage."

For the next three years, I fought for my death. She fought for me like Joan of Arc fighting for Henry VI. I couldn't do it without her. With the time Emily put into the project, she could have probably earned two PhDs and three postdocs. We would go jogging in the mornings we had to meet the lawyers she'd found herself.

I still don't know how she gathered the money to fly with the lawyers and me to Strasbourg four times. I recognized her one late night in downtown, waving down a Bentley... that's all I saw. I dashed to the nearest bar and drank myself to death. I dozed off for two days in my bedroom. Emily had left thirty-two messages on my phone.

When I opened the door, I saw two Emilys. Each slapped me once. Then they dragged me downstairs right into their Subaru. I sat too hungover to realize the direction she was driving and barfed out of the window every other time she turned right. I swear she turned right at least fifty times!

A careless weekend in a quiet mansion too quiet and white to be real. For most of the time, we found ourselves drawn onto the marble terrace overshadowed by oceanside red cedars. I couldn't take my eyes off the cliffs. Pure oxygen tranquilized us on beanbags. She said she had been babysitting for the owner and he had let her stay. Apart from that exchange, we didn't speak a word.

The lawyers took my case to the Swiss Federal Supreme Court and they pushed it to European Court of Human Rights in Strasbourg to mediate between Canada and Switzerland. For about a year, the representatives of the clinic would go ballistic amidst the camera flashes in front of the court. They thought the whole case was absurd to begin with. I guess they only cooled down when they realized the power of the publicity of the case for the clinic. The sides eventually shook off the rage they carried for each other.

We both won.

The morning the court's judgment was read, the verdict concluded the best years of my life.

* * *

Evia is done sketching the face. She hands me the napkin.

"Isn't my wife a great sketcher?" Eric says in awe. "She recently got a one-year contract with the Polizei as a forensic artist."

This ugly-ass face is mine? I wonder.

All the displays freeze for the announcement. Eric stands up. "I will get blankets."

Finally, I have enough room to properly search for whatever the hell it is under my buttocks.

Evia slides down the window shade. When Eric returns, I will listen to him talking about the faith of the Muffin Man. I tap one of the aliens on the shoulder.

About the Author:

Sana Mojdeh lives and works in Toronto. His recent work (M2K) is forthcoming in On Spec Magzine. He is currently working on his debut novel.

WILL I DIE OF HEAT STROKE?
by Ruth Deming

My metallic gray Nissan with its red racing stripe sped confidently into the parking lot of Staples, a seven-minute drive from home. Friendly Dave installed an anti-virus protector onto my laptop.

Back to the car I went, gently placing the encased laptop onto the back seat. I slid in the front, and turned the key in the ignition. Silence. Not a sound. As quiet as a winter snowfall. I tried once more. Nothing. Nada.

"Why didn't you call me?" asked my boyfriend Scott later on. "You know I'd do anything for my Ruthie."

I had absolutely no answer for him.

All I knew was that I would walk home. It couldn't be all that far. A forty-five-minute walk perhaps. After all it was only a seven-minute drive to get there.

With insulin-dependent diabetes, I knew I must fill up on food during the walk home so I wouldn't go "low" and pass out.

Dunkin' Donuts, with its warm brown and pink colors, is right there in the parking lot.

Walking into DD, I felt the cool of the air-conditioning on this hot July day. Studying the menu on the wall, I ordered something that wouldn't be too sweet. A buttered croissant was the perfect choice. When I sat down to eat, unwrapping the tissue paper, I realized we were in a blistering heat wave here in suburban Philadelphia. Luckily I was wearing shorts and a tank top.

Let's back up a moment. In 2011 I had a kidney transplant. Sixteen and a half years on lithium for bipolar disorder had ruined my kidneys, both of them. My oft-estranged married daughter Sarah Lynn donated her kidney to me. Ah, she really loved me.

I was not going to sacrifice her 38-year-old kidney. I was not going to die of heat stroke on busy Terwood Road, crumpled up on the sidewalk like a dead mouse.

My immunosuppressants are two: Prednisone and Tacrolimus. How fortunate I was to take these meds. Prednisone was invented by Arthur Nobile in 1950 and sold through various drug companies. Today its generic version is incredibly cheap.

Tacrolimus was discovered in 1987, when I was a young lass of 42, working as a psychotherapist in Bristol, Pennsylvania. Few people knew I had bipolar disorder. And I certainly had no inkling that one day I'd be knocking on the door of Tacrolimus to save me.

Or that, in a twist of fate, my bipolar disorder would vanish, like a helium balloon disappearing in the clouds.

As I sat munching on the buttered croissant and sipping on ice-cold water, I planned my route home. Straight all the way down Terwood Road.

I put on my blue long-sleeved shirt to shield me from the sun. Normally I wear sunscreen since a small percentage of transplantees develop skin cancer. Not me. I would walk in the shade at a brisk pace.

Out of the air-conditioned doughnut shop I came, bursting into the inferno of the day.

"You can do it," I said to myself. My body remained cool from the A/C for less than five minutes. It was eleven a.m. The sun shone with a malevolence as if it would burn me alive like Joan of Arc.

And what was this fairy-tale that I'd be home in forty-five minutes?

A stillness prevailed over me. My wandering mind never wandered. All I thought of was the next step ahead of me.

Damn! My shoelace was loose. I had bought a pair of cheap black sneakers at the mall and had painted them – yellow, blue, red, and gold – and stooped down to tie them in double-knots. How vulnerable I felt as the traffic whizzed by.

Onward I marched. What if I panic, I thought, and fall down in a faint.

What if a car careens off the road and kills me. Well, at least they would know the identity of the dead: a tiny – four-foot nine - 72-year-old woman.

My gray canvas backpack was securely attached to my back. My driver's license would identify me. My hair was blonde on the license photo, unlike now, when it's a lovely fake red. About two-hundred people would mourn my death – I was the founder and director of New Directions, a support group for people with depression, bipolar disorder and their loved ones. My kids knew what to do with my lifeless body: cremate me and toss my ashes into the Pennypack Creek.

Step lightly. Step lightly. There on the right was Old Tyme Burgers and Shakes. The last time I was there I'd ordered a cheeseburger and fries and glass of iced cold water.

"How is it?" Julie had asked.

"Oh, it's delicious," I said, swiveling on my stool with the red cushion.

Step lightly. Step lightly. I thought of hitch-hiking the rest of the way home. Not a good idea. When I attended Goddard College in Plainfield, Vermont, I'd hitched and a dirty old man with tufts of nose hair had picked me up. I knew if I needed to, I could open the door and roll out. This was no Ted Bundy, serial killer, who popped his victims in his van with no door handles.

Step lightly. Step lightly.

Off to the right was the office of my nephrologist, voted "Best Doctor" in Philadelphia by his peers.

"Why?" I asked the slightly balding Dr. Ghantous.

"They say I spend a lot of time with my patients."

He would always tell me the creatinine level of my new kidney. "Point seven or point eight," he'd say.

"That's excellent," he'd tell me in his slight Lebanese accent. He always boosted my self-esteem when I left his office and drove home, a quick five minutes away. I rarely veer far from home.

My shadow on the sidewalk revealed my uneven shoulders. A reminder of an operation the same year as my kidney transplant for my devilishly painful sciatica, an unstoppable pain, both day and night, that ran from the toes on my left foot all the way up to my left buttock.

Thankfully my plantar fasciitis had finally gone away. Exercises I did every morning did no good and made the bottom of my left foot ache even worse. Were the opposite sides of my foot engaged in a boxing match?

My whole health history revealed on this walk home.

When I walked the slight breeze I created cooled me off a bit. Not so when I waited to cross a busy street. The seconds ticked off as I waited for the light to change. I'd touch my toes to keep up my momentum.

The sun seemed to drain the life from me. Was my blood thick and viscous? Desperately, I wanted to run, like I did as a kid. Seventy-two isn't terribly old but my legs and a foot whose bones, two years ago, had literally broken in several places would not bow to my wishes.

Walk spritely. Walk spritely.

One fear was left as I neared my yellow house on Cowbell Road. My three-bedroom house where I lived alone - now that my two children were on their own - was at the top of a hill. Whatever energy I had left would require a massive effort to make it to the top of the hill.

Looking at my colorful sneakers, I bounded up the hill. There was Sean's mail truck parked in its usual spot. Did I care? There was my favorite house made of warm brown wood and the tall ornamental grasses on the lawn. Did I care?

Finally I burst through the church-red door into my house. Thank God I was home. I turned up the A/C, went into the kitchen and splashed cold water on my face.

The clock over the sink read 1:30. It had taken two whole hours to walk home.

On my white Ikea shelves, I chose a tall glass, stuck it under the water dispenser on the outside of the fridge, and listened as cold water splashed into the glass, like Niagara Falls. I took small sips, gasping with relief at each swallow.

Sitting on the stairs, I carefully removed each sneaker.

"Yow!" I cried out in pain. My sweaty feet stuck to the sneakers I had worn without socks.

"Yow!" I hollered again. A blister had formed beneath my right toe.

Bent over double, I limped into my bedroom, fell on my face on the mattress and slept for an entire hour.

Not bad for a woman of seventy-two.

About the Author:

Ruth Z. Deming is a poet and short story writer who lives in Willow Grove, PA, a suburb of Philadelphia. Her works have been published in Mad Swirl, Literary Yard, Scarlet Leaf Review and other writing venues. She runs New Directions, a support group for people with depression, bipolar disorder and their loved ones. "Yes I Can: My Bipolar Journey" details her triumph over bipolar disorder. A mental health advocate, she educates the public about this treatable illness.

FLIPPING THE TORTILLA
by Anita Haas

"You have lived here in Madrid for twelve years?" Cheryl eyed Peggy, challenge in her tone. "And married to a Spaniard? You must be an expert on the culture by now."

"Well …" Peggy's cheeks started to burn.

"Can you cook Spanish food? Spaniards are so proud of their cuisine!"

"I …"

Elaine interrupted them, "Peggy makes a killer *tortilla de patatas,* the famous Spanish omelette."

Peggy turned to Elaine, "No. That was …" she was going to say "my mother-in-law's", but Elaine winked, and raised her voice, "The best *tortilla* I've ever tasted! Even better than …"

Cheryl cut her off, "Bet mine's better."

Peggy and Elaine caught Cheryl's smug grin. What was up with her? Why always so competitive? Cheryl boasted about the gifts her students showered her with, their raving feedback on her classes and the high grades she had gotten in university. She moved her tall, slim body like a dancer, and glossy, dark locks framed a face that tricked you into believing you were looking at the cover of *Vogue* magazine. Listening to her and looking at her always left Peggy feeling like a loser.

"That's settled then." announced their boss, Adam, in his business-like voice from the other side of the cramped teacher's room. "Peggy and Cheryl bring the *tortillas,* Elaine and Cecil bring scones or Yorkshire pudding." He deliberately mispronounced scones, "Jackie, bring something Irish. Potatoes. Virginia, you can bring poutine!" He waved his hand around in a circle, "Everybody bring something typical from your country, and I'll supply the Thanksgiving turkey and fixings. Ok, back to work, or as the Spanish say, *Manos a la obra.* Hands on the job!"

That night Peggy was telling César about her boss's plans for the upcoming dinner. "Somehow, Cheryl and I got roped into bringing Spanish food. Probably because we're the only ones married to Spaniards."

César's eyes glittered as he pictured the plethora of palate pleasers his country had to offer, "You could take *lomo, morcón* … remember the first time you tried *morcón?*"

"*Cariño!* Remember, there are a lot of vegetarians …"

"Oh right. *Imbéciles.*" He shook his head.

"And Cecil is a vegan."

"Oh, *pobrecito.* I've heard of that … something like a diabetic, right?"

Peggy sighed. She had explained that one time too many.

"These people … they just have to open their minds. If these vegetarians just tried some good *jamon de jabugo,* they would give up vegetables forever!"

Peggy smiled. They knew a few Spanish vegetarians who treated ham as an honorary vegetable. "Vegetarian, but not stupid." they said.

"These ones are different. Thery are foreigners, *guiris*. Don't you remember my hen party?"

"Oh." César's shoulders slumped as the memory struggled to form itself in his mind.

But Peggy remembered. She had been drowning in work, so César had gallantly offered to do the shopping, and then disappear with his best friend Antonio. "Oh thank you, *cariño*, but remember... we are a group of *guiri* ladies. We like our vegetables."

"*Si. Si.* Don't worry. Leave it to me."

When she arrived that evening after work, she saw the dining room table pushed against the wall. Wax paper packages waited neatly on china plates. Cured aromas tickled her nostrils as she peeked into each one in an escalating search for green. Just enough time remained to toss a few salads and slice some broccoli and cauliflower for dipping. But the packages only contained several varieties of prepared pig; *chorizo* from Pamplona, *butifarra* from Catalonia, *jamón de bellota*, *lomo*, *morcón*, and *salchichón*. Behind them she discovered some *cecina*, cured horse meat from León, and several fragrant cheeses ranging from tingly *cabrales* from Asturias, tangy manchego from Castilla, and *casar*, the stinky-feet cheese from Extremadura, along with several long crunchy sticks of bread. He had spent a fortune!

"César!" Peggy panicked as she spotted him grab his jacket and head for the door. He smiled proudly, trying out a new American expression he had recently picked up, "Not a bad spread, eh?"

"Where are the vegetables?"

"Oh that," he shrugged on his jacket, "There wasn't time. They were closed when I got there, but don't worry, there is so much more better stuff for them to eat."

I told you! I told you! She fumed to herself, but it wasn't worth an argument. *Let's just hope the ladies aren't very hungry.* She found a can of olives and a jar of asparagus in the back of the kitchen cupboard, then scraped and sliced a lonely dried up carrot into eight strips. That would have to do.

Two hours later, Peggy was laughing and sipping wine with her female friends and colleagues, all teachers at her language school. The bowl of olives was empty, the plates of asparagus and carrot picked clean, and not a crumb of bread remained, but a dozen plates, like open hands, held the sweating delicacies her future husband had provided.

"Okay, okay. You have repeated that story a hundred times."

"Then, remember it!"

"There are more then just cold meats in Spanish cuisine. There is fish, shellfish, shrimp, prawns, mussels, ..."

"Yes dear," she changed her tone, and hugged him before he worked himself into a food fit. "I love them all. But this time it has to be *tortilla*."

"Well, that's easy then. We'll get *mamá* to make it for you. She would be more than happy to."

Peggy pulled back, shocked, "We can't do that! It would be dishonest. I have to make the *tortilla* myself."

Cesar was bored with his wife's hypocritical and impractical American sense of honor. As far as he was concerned honest people were not to be trusted. Let them die of food poisoning then. "*Como quieras.*"

Thanksgiving Thursday loomed seven short days away. Tortilla-making lessons were desperately in order. Doña Pili, Peggy's mother-in-law, obligingly donated her next Saturday morning to the cause.

Unlike other women she knew, Peggy had no gripe with her *suegra* (other than an inability to pronounce her name correctly, and a disconcerting habit of finishing her sentences for her). Cheryl fretted in the teacher's room all day about how her husband, Jesús, was enslaved by his mother. Not only did they have to have lunch at her house every weekend, but he took her shopping, to visit relatives, and to every doctor's appointment. And he never complained. The typical Spanish mama's boy.

"I'm sure she does it on purpose!" Cheryl grumbled one morning at the photocopier, "Invents aches and pains just so she can take him away from me, just like her sister did with Jesus's cousin. And the Christmas holidays are just around the corner! Imagine, we'll have to spend every day with her!"

"Mmmm." Peggy made an effort at sounding sympathetic, "Is she a good cook, at least?"

Cheryl's face brightened, "Oh, yes! Her *cocido* is considered second best in her *pueblo,* and she makes an amazing *tortilla*. Doesn't let me near the kitchen. That's one of the problems I have with Jesús. He says I can't cook."

Peggy recalled that conversation on Saturday in Doña Pili's kitchen, as the older lady gently coaxed her daughter-in-law along in the mysteries of the local cuisine.

"*Es muy fácil*! So easy. Now, remember, Peki. Never use *patatas gallegas*. They are too watery. Good for stews, but you want potatoes for frying. Peel them, and slice them thinly, but not too thin. Also, is best if you use gas stove." She watched the younger woman nod, pity swelling in her heart. This *americanita* tried hard, but she was never going to master the art of *tortilla*-making.

"Then you take two eggs, good ones from the farm, not from those poor caged creatures ..."

"And the onions? Are they sliced thick or thin?" Peggy peeped.

"No self-respecting *tortilla de patatas* has onions! Some people use them to make the tortilla juicy, but if you do it right, it won't be dry."

The potato slices and a pinch of salt joined the beaten eggs and were left to sit. Olive oil was heated, and when it started to crackle, the mixture was spooned into the pan. The next part, knowing when it was solid enough for flipping, was tricky. As the *tortilla* cooked, the comforting smells of egg and potato played in Peggy's memory, scooping up images of her earliest discoveries in this fascinating country. They seduced her back to a summer terrace in Córdoba, flamenco guitar, orange blossoms, red wine, *gazpacho andaluz* and her first *tortilla*.

"Okay," Doña Pili announced, "Time to flip! *Ves*?" she showed her daughter-in-law, "See? It is solid enough now."

"*Sí.*" Peggy lied. The tiny lady reached for a dinner plate with a frail left hand, and with the right agilely slid the round mass onto it. Then *flip*, the pan was over the plate, and *flip*, the plate was over the pan, and the *tortilla* rested placidly in it while firming up its back side.

"See? *Fácil*. Now, your turn." Doña Pili went off to fold laundry so Peggy could work on her *tortilla* alone. Peggy followed the steps one by one, but despite her diligence she miscalculated, and when it came time to flip the *tortilla,* an eggy mess slithered onto the plate.

She presented her creation to César and her father-in-law, Don Eustaquio. (This antiquated use of the titles *don* and *doña* were an affectionate joke César and his siblings had started in adolescence.) The two men tried to be encouraging.

"*Hombre*, not bad for a first try."

"No, no. Shows promise. Just not very hungry today."

And they both reached for their glasses of *tinto con gaseosa* and another helping of salad, an action of particular eloquence, as Peggy knew that if this father and son saw eye to eye on anything, it was on their loathing of vegetables.

"Don't worry, Peggy. You were just nervous with my parents there. You'll see. Tomorrow you'll make a fantastic *tortilla* at home."

But Sunday's *tortilla* was runny and crunchy with eggshell. Monday's *tortilla* was so salty they had to get up to drink water all night. The potatoes in Tuesday's *tortilla* were sliced too thick and wouldn't cook through without burning the eggs. Their stomachs churned a lot that night.

Only two days remained until Thanksgiving.

César, always positive, was starting to sense his patience slip. "*Mira, que eres cabezota!* How stubborn you are! Just let Doña Pili make a *tortilla* for you. Tell your friends you made it. Who cares?"

Despite her sense of honor, Peggy had to admit he was right. She was reminded of the time when he had finally convinced her that she didn't always have to tell her mother the whole truth. "Every week your mother calls to check if you have bought long underwear. Every week you suffer having to tell her not yet. Next time, tell her yes, *mamá*, and that's it!" Peggy gave it a try, grateful that her face could not be seen, *voilá*, her mother never asked about the long johns again. However, thrilled with her daughter's obedience, she found many other objects to replace the long johns with in her repertoire of commands. *Get a new haircut, get a new bed, get a new job.* "Yes, Mom! Yes, Mom!" Peggy trilled call after call. She soon lost track of the fibs.

"Well, there is one more day. I could try again …" she peered at César, fearing his answer.

He shook his head, and ruffled her hair, "Give up. We all have our limits. I won't love you any less. But, *cariño*, you will make me hate *tortilla*!"

"But Cheryl …"

"Cheryl's *tortilla* won't stand up to Doña Pili's in a million years."

It was Thursday evening. They had said good night and happy thanksgiving to the last of the students in the "I Love English" Academy, each gingerly carrying home a complimentary piece of pumpkin pie.

The teachers had overheard some of them laugh while smoking outside. "How can *los americanos* eat sweet vegetables for dessert? Disgusting!" But Adam insisted, "They just need to open their minds."

Adam enlisted his dozen employees to maneuver tables and chairs around in a classroom to accommodate the dinner party.

Peggy cradled a tin foil plate with Doña Pili's *tortilla*, warm as a baby, in her arms. Elaine, eyeing it, approached and hissed in her ear, "I hope you didn't make that yourself."

Peggy peered back at her guiltily. Was this a trick?

"Because I happen to know that Cheryl did not make hers."

Peggy gasped, "Are you sure?"

Elaine crossed her arms over her ample chest and nodded, "Told me herself. *La suegra.*"

Peggy's forehead furled and her lips puckered. She was pretty certain Cheryl's *tortilla* was no match for her *suegra's*, but she didn't know about Cheryl's *suegra's tortilla*!

Within ten minutes they were all standing around the festive table, respectfully listening to Adam drone on about Thanksgiving, gratitude, the trials and tribulations of the past year, and his hopes and plans for the next one. He concluded by saying "As the Spanish say, you have to break some eggs if you want to make *tortilla*." Obedient chuckles followed, "And on that note, might I suggest we start the evening with a glass of wine and a piece of that delicious dish, compliments of our two most integrated *españolas*, Peggy and Cheryl!"

Peggy's stomach pinched as her colleagues descended upon the omelettes. Cheryl was pontificating to the newer, younger teachers about just how a *tortilla* was made and what sensations it should arouse. "And onions! There should definitely be no onions!" Peggy watched Cheryl nibble at a dainty sqaure of her own *tortilla.* Suddenly, her face distrorted. She caught herself in time, but Peggy had seen it. Then she turned to observe the others. Those who had taken Cheryl's squinted at their little squares, turning them over this way and that.

"Didn't you say there shouldn't be onions?" asked Colin, perplexed.

Then, Chloe, genuinely intrigued, added, "Is that vinegar I taste? How original! Too bad I had such a big lunch."

Peggy turned to spy on those indulging in Doña Pili's *tortilla.* Each one hunched their shoulders and turned slightly away from the rest of the group, enjoying a private moment with their *tortillas*, their faces betraying a bliss that was almost indecent.

To no one's great surprise, Cheryl's marriage didn't last much longer. By New Year's Eve Jesús had moved back home with a triumphant *mamá*, Cheryl was planning a new life in L.A., and Peggy and César were toasting Doña Pili with glasses of rosé wine from Navarra over one of that fine *señora's* tasty *tortillas*.

About the Author:

I am a differently-abled Canadian writer and teacher based in Madrid, Spain. I have published books on film, two novelettes, a short story anthology, and articles, poems and fiction in both English and Spanish. I spend my free time enjoying tapas and flamenco with my writer husband and two cats.

STANDOFF AT THE COUNTRY PRIDE MOTEL, STARRING BILLY FITZ
by P. J. Gannon

A few hours after spiking some Afghan smack in Room 5 of the Country Pride Motel, Billy considered introducing a girl into the movie that he was pretending to film. Such a plot development would depart from the original one-man-against-the-world storyline, but he felt that, all things considered, a little female companionship was in order. "Lights, camera, action," he said to himself, as he scooped up his phone off the motel's scuffed nightstand. Better to get a girl now before his wireless provider shut him down next week. He scrolled through a bunch of local Backpage ads—the pickings were slim in his area—and settled on a woman by the name of Dandelion. Full-service and party-friendly. A photo depicted her curvy, bikini-clad body from the neck down (pale as crack, sweet as brandy).

He rang her up and a half hour later she was at Room 5's door, gripping the handlebars of a vintage 1950s Huffy Eldorado bicycle. "Mind if I bring my ride inside?" she asked in a haggard voice. "It might get stolen out here."

He stepped outside and looked around the parking lot to see if anyone was watching. There was no one. "Not a problem."

She rolled in the bike. Her body, compared to the one in the photo, was as flat as plywood,

but he didn't care. He stepped back inside and closed the door behind them. Near the bathroom, she lowered the bike's kickstand, while he undid his belt. "I'll need the paperwork first," she said.

He pulled a money clip from his pocket and counted out four twenties and waved them in the air. She grabbed them as though she feared he might change his mind now that he knew what she really looked like. She counted the bills and, satisfied, opened the lid to a wicker basket that was hanging from her bike's handlebars. She dropped the money inside and pulled out a condom.

"How long you've been shooting up?" she asked Billy. They were sitting on the bug-infested queen-sized bed. He still had his pants around his ankles from the blowjob and was wrapping a tourniquet around her skinny tattooed arm.

"Too depressing to think about," he said.

She picked up the syringe off the bed and aimed it at the wall like a dart. "I'll stab myself. I worked at a farm. With all the training I got, I had no problem going from lines to needles."

"Huh?"

"You know how many fuckin' animals I helped the veterinarian put down?"

He grabbed the syringe from her. "Let me do it."

"Oh, you get off on that, don't you, motherfucker?"

He giggled.

"Stick it to me, baby," she said in jest, spreading her dress-hidden legs.

"Hold still," he ordered, and he tied the tourniquet. Then they heard a gunshot.

"What the fuck was that?" she asked.

Another gunshot. "My ringtone, dummy."

She punched his shoulder. "What kind of sick fuck are you? You scared the shit out of me." The gunshots finally stopped, and she pointed to a blue line near the crease of her arm. "Right there, Billy."

Billy imagined a cameraman zooming in for a close up of the syringe. He guided the needle toward her vein and eased the point into her arm. A few seconds passed—her expression turned from dumb to dumbstruck—and with outstretched arms she fell back on the bed. "Wait for me, Dandelion," he said, undoing the tourniquet. "I'm right behind you."

Before she came knocking on his door, he'd seen her around town a few times. Always alone. Blond stringy hair, a dimpled smile, long stem-like legs that went on forever. One morning, when he was climbing into his F-150 to go to his former nine-to-five gig at the cement plant, he spotted her in front of his neighbor's house, digging through a trash can for five-cent bottle and can deposits, a wobbly shopping cart of recyclables standing beside her. Another time, shortly after losing his driver's license due to another DUI, he was hoofing it home from the Appalachian convenience store, a twelve pack of Rolling Rock in his arms, when she came whipping by like a bullet on her vintage bike. Their paths crossed again one morning. He was taking the bus to another mandatory meeting with his probation officer. She got on at the corner of Chestnut and Lake and sat a few rows in front of him. She was on her phone for the entire ride, talking loudly (the person on the other end must have been hard of hearing). Riders were giving her dirty looks and shouting for her to pipe down. She ignored them.

Months later he was at Oakwood Farm, filling an order for a hundred cinderblocks to be used in the construction of a new hog house. She was at the edge of the cornfield, on her knees, bottle-feeding a drove of sheep. She was wearing an orange dress that when she straightened herself made him think: carrot stick. Her legs were sprouting out of a pair of distressed-leather cowboy boots. She looked no more than 35 years old but like a person whose days were numbered.

Not a word was ever spoken between them until she knocked on Room 5's door, shortly after Billy had checked himself into the Country Pride Motel, his fed-up roommate having finally kicked him out of their two-bedroom apartment for good due to months of unpaid rent.

Hours after shooting up, Billy and Dandelion were lying in bed, passing a bottle of Jack Daniels back and forth, when he said, "I want to be an actor." The words tumbled out like a confession.

"You're handsome enough," she said.

He turned to look at her. Her face, up close, looked surprisingly innocent. "You think?"

"Fuck yeah." She took a swig of the Jack. "You have the greenest eyes I've ever seen. You got a nice smile too." She grabbed his shoulder and squeezed hard. "Your muscles are big!"

"I starred in my high school play," he said proudly.

"You graduate from Mittermann?"

"Uh-huh."

"We called it Shittermann." She cackled like a B-movie villain. "Graduated '03."

"Small world. 2012."

"You're a baby."

"Honestly, I thought we were about the same age."

"A fuckin' bullshitter too." She elbowed him and he smiled.

"You're hogging the bottle," he said. She took another swig, and he ripped it from her hands. "I was planning on going to Hollywood after graduation. Try my hand at a few auditions. I was saving the money." He shrugged and took a drink. "I could still do it, I suppose."

"Let me see you act."

"You kidding?"

"Do something for me. Something from the play."

"Not sure I can."

"Oh, I bet you can."

He paused to remember. He then handed her back the bottle and climbed out of bed. She sat up and fixed her drowsy eyes on him. He rolled his shoulders to loosen up and then his face grew rigid as though his life depended on what he was about to do. "If I profane with my unworthiest hand," he said in a loud authoritarian voice, "this holy shrine, the gentle fine is this: my lips, two blushing pilgrims, ready to stand to smooth that rough touch with a tender kiss." He stopped and shrugged. "Well, there you go," he said meekly. "That was just a sample."

"That was really good."

"You think?"

"Fuck yeah."

"Romeo and Juliet."

"I knew that."

She was bullshitting about knowing the play but he didn't care. "The English teacher shortened the play," he said. "Turned it into a one-act thing. The action took place in a modern-day high school like one of the movie versions released a few years ago. Same premise though."

A cymbal crashed and Billy heard Lil Wayne's voice. "Is that your phone?" he asked.

"If I don't quiet it now, it'll be ringing nonstop." She picked it up off the nightstand and turned it off.

"You're in great demand, huh?" he said, rolling back into bed. He put his lips near her ear, which was studded with many piercings, and whispered, "I can see why."

"I thought about being a veterinarian for a while." She hung her head like a schoolgirl who'd just been scolded.

"That's why you worked at that farm?"

"I guess." She took a swig of Jack and fell back on the bed.

"Why you don't work there no more?"

"They caught me shooting up in the barn."

"You can still be a veterinarian."

"I can't fuckin' deal with no school."

She rolled onto her side, showing him her back. She had a tattoo of a King Cobra running up her spine, the snake's forked tongue licking her neck. She rested the bottle on the worn commercial carpet. She then hiked up her ragged dress and pulled down her torn underwear, her smell reminiscent of the stench from Billy's childhood fishbowl. But that didn't stop him from crawling on top of her. They heard another gunshot. "Who the fuck keeps calling?" she asked.

"My mother."

The next morning, they were all out of smack. "You gonna get some more?" she asked him.

Billy staggered out of the bathroom, a towel wrapped around his lean waist. "If I do, you'll need to give me back my money."

She climbed out of bed, stumbled over to her bike, and pulled the money out of the basket. He got dressed and dialed Room 8. A short while later, a glassy-eyed fiend with frosted hair swaggered into the room. His name was Crow, and he was dangling four $20 Ziploc bags before their hungry eyes. Dandelion paid Crow and, the following afternoon, when she and Billy had finished the smack and were lying in bed, completely spent, and immersed in the sickening silence of the room, she said to him, "My mother died when I was at Mittermann."

"Oh?"

"Yeah. Breast cancer."

"Well, that sucks."

She was staring at the water-stained ceiling. "Worst thing that ever happened to me." She went to take a swig of Jack but the bottle was empty.

"I'm sorry, Dandelion." He reached for her pointed chin and stroked it with his fingertips.

"She was only 39."

"You were close?"

"Like BFFs. We'd wear each other's clothes. Talk about our problems." She turned to him. "Why? You close with your moms? That why she keep calling?"

"I think she wants to be close."

"I'd braid my mother's hair. We'd shop for bathing suits together."

"What's your real name? You mind me asking?"

"Charlene."

"That's a pretty name."

"My mother named me after her cousin who got run over by a tractor before I was born." Charlene picked up the syringe and held it like a pen. "What do you want to do now?"

"I feel like screaming," he said.

"Your real name Billy?"

"Sure is." He grabbed the syringe from her hand. "I hate this."

A cymbal crashed and Lil Wayne's voice let loose. Charlene grabbed her phone from the nightstand and looked at the number. "Maybe I should go back to work."

"No, I don't want that." The phone went quiet.

"Then what am I supposed to do?"

This was the point in Billy's imaginary movie where, if he hadn't introduced Charlene into the film, he'd be returning his mother's phone calls and begging her to send him back to detox. "I've broken my mom's heart too many times, Charlene. She's been crying for years over me and I guess she has every right to. She raised me all by herself."

"Mine too."

"Worked her ass off every day cleaning office buildings so that she could buy me things: video games, Kobe shoes."

"Which buildings?"

"Oh, a lot of them."

"The one at the Triangle Plaza?"

"I think. Probably."

"My moms worked there."

Billy cocked his head. "You shitting me?"

"Nah."

"Well damn."

"She managed the office for a bunch of ungrateful doctors."

"Small world."

"Sometimes I'm glad she's dead though. Not to see me."

Billy's stomach churned and he dragged himself out of bed. "I could go to the liquor store," he said.

She held up the empty bottle. "We're all out of Jack."

"I'm not talking about that." His knapsack was in the corner of the room and he walked over to it and pulled out a pistol: a pearl-handled classic six gun.

"You like guns, huh?"

"When you've been ripped off enough times, you need a friend."

"I've been ripped off enough times and I don't need no friend. Don't tell me you're thinking of . . . ?"

"The old guy practically sleeps behind the register."

"I know. I go there from time to time."

"I've been considering it for a while." A cymbal crashed and Lil Wayne's voice let loose again. "Turn that thing off, will you?" he said.

On the way to Carney's Wine and Spirits, Billy stopped in a small novelty shop called Felix's Assorted Tricks. They sold wigs, posters, magic tricks, sex toys, and other curiosities. The longhaired man behind the counter was busy ringing up a customer so Billy ducked down and turned into an aisle. Halloween had just passed so there were masks hanging on the wall. The prices had been slashed significantly. Not that that would have made any difference, since having spent all his money Billy had no intention of paying for anything. His eyes settled on the Joker mask. *The Dark Knight* was still one of his favorite movies. He glanced at the counter. The longhaired man was gone, probably in the stockroom shelving a shipment of bongs. Billy grabbed the mask and hauled-ass out of the store.

He got to Carney's and looked around the parking lot. He didn't see anyone so he put on the mask and pulled out his pistol. (Another reason he'd decided to rob Carney's—besides the old sleepy cashier—was that he thought it'd be the perfect location for a stickup scene.) He took a deep breath, opened the door, and burst inside. "Everybody to the floor!" he hollered, his pistol pointed at the ceiling. At first, the old sleepy cashier didn't comply. He just groaned as though a fire drill he wanted no part of was about to commence. The two other people in the store—a hipster couple who were in town to hike the scenic mountains—however, immediately dropped to the floor behind a display of Baileys Irish Cream.

Billy lowered his pistol and sauntered over to the register. "I know you have a gun in that draw," he said to the old sleepy cashier. "Don't be a Goddamn fool."

Ole sleepy met his gaze as if to say, Never considered being no fool. Not for one second. He pushed a button or two and the register draw slid open. He stepped aside, as if to say, Help yourself. See if I care.

Billy peered down at the carefully arranged buffet of U.S. currency: some Jacksons but mostly Hamiltons and Lincolns. A few hundred bucks, he surmised, and he leaned over the counter and helped himself to the cash, stuffing the kangaroo pockets of his hoodie.

When he'd cleaned out the register, he turned to the hipsters who were sobbing and yelling: "Please don't kill us! We're engaged! We just found out we're pregnant!" Their blabbering sounded like heavy-metal harmony.

Then ole sleepy, who was still on his feet and calmly paging through an issue of *Sports Illustrated,* without looking up, said, in a tone that should have been reserved for paying customers, "All set now, sir?"

"I think so," Billy said, his face behind the mask wet with perspiration. Billy decided then that it would be the perfect time in his movie to kill everyone in the store. Doing his best

Matt Damon, he earnestly pointed the gun at sleepy. Ole sleepy looked up slowly from an article he had started reading—a story on the untimely death of the Miami Marlins pitching-ace Jose Fernandez—as though the loss of his life was something that he could just shrug off. Billy had never seen such an apathetic look and it made him realize right then and there that he could never kill anyone; he'd just never allowed the kind of sprawling evil needed to lay people to waste to take root in him. "I may let you live," Billy said, lowering the gun, "if you do me a favor."

The hipsters shouted: "Anything! Anything!"

Billy strode over to a shelf of booze and grabbed a liter of Jack Daniels. "Wait a half hour before calling the police."

"We don't have a problem with that!" the female hipster yelled. "We're sure you have valid reasons for doing what you're doing."

"If I hear any kind of siren while I'm making my getaway," Billy continued, "you're all finished. I have a way of finding people. I'll hunt you down. I'll kill you all."

It was a deal the hipsters couldn't refuse, and they seemed honorable enough to abide by it. "Maybe you should get some help," they said. "Did you lose your job or something?" Ole sleepy? No way. He'd call the police as soon as he finished reading the Jose Fernandez story. Not a second later. Either way, Billy didn't give a shit. He stepped out of Carney's and into a crisp cool breeze. His offer was as hollow as his mask and simply a way of saving face for not having the necessary sprawling evil to lay them all to waste.

When he got back to the Country Pride—it was only a few blocks away, still another reason he decided to rob Carney's—the Joker mask in the bottom of a dumpster behind a Gulf station, the liter of Jack already a quarter finished, Charlene was lumbering out of Room 5's bathroom, hunched over like she had a pair of balls that'd been kicked. She saw the Jack and straightened herself. "Don't fuckin' drink it all!" He unscrewed the cap and took another swig, figuring that the way she drank it might be his last. He offered her the bottle. She yanked it out of his hand and eased its neck between her purplish lips.

Billy threw the rest of the cash from the register on the bed ($343) and pulled off his hoodie. "Don't forget. Forty-five dollars of that goes for the room," he said.

She nodded and put the bottle down on the carpet and went to the phone and dialed Room 8. "We got the money now, Crow. Hurry over."

In no time, Crow was haunting their doorway. Billy gave him stink-eye. "I thought you'd be happy to see me," Crow said. Billy didn't respond. Crow stepped into the room and gently closed the door behind him. He pulled ten $20 Ziploc bags from his thrift-shop raincoat and dangled them in the air like a dog trainer promising biscuits to pups. Charlene, who was sitting on the bed, counted out the cash and forked it over.

The next morning, a siren awoke Billy and Charlene. Charlene sat up in bed. "What the fuck's going on, Billy?" Outside, they heard tires skidding. Billy, whose eyes were half open, knew exactly what was going on. He pulled his pistol from underneath his pillow, leapt out of bed, stepped into his jeans, and stomped toward the window. With his finger and thumb, he parted the blinds and peered out the tiny opening like Blackbeard on the lookout for rivals on the high seas.

Outside, in the parking lot, a patrol car was idling. On the road abutting the motel raced another patrol car. It turned sharply into the parking lot and screeched to a halt.

"I wore a mask," he said to Charlene.

"We should have left right away, Billy."

"They can't be coming for me. Maybe they're coming for Crow."

Two police officers jumped out of each car. Then the four of them huddled in the middle of the parking lot like a touch-football team. A minute or so later, they broke huddle and one of the cops—a goateed man whose relaxed gait made Billy think that he was in charge—disappeared inside the motel lobby. He was in there a long time, no doubt chewing on the ear of the front-desk clerk, while the three other cops just waited outside, talking among themselves, toeing the crumbling pavement.

In the meantime, Billy tried reassuring Charlene that the police weren't there for him. "But you don't know that, Billy," she said. "I need to leave. I gotta go."

The goateed cop finally stepped back outside wearing a cocky smile. He strutted across the parking lot as though he were a regular Sherlock Holmes who had just connected the dots. He called another huddle and, a little while later, he and another cop—a man who looked more priest than police—headed for Room 5.

"Shit. They're coming," Billy said, stepping away from the window.

"I told you so," Charlene said, and she picked up the tainted Ziploc bags and ran into the bathroom.

There was a knock on the door. "Police."

Billy heard the toilet flush. He turned toward the door. "Yeah, what do you want?" he asked, putting his finger on the trigger of his gun.

"Is this Heath?" one of the two officers on the other side of the door asked. The officer's voice was sturdy and professional. It probably belonged to the goateed cop.

"No one here by that name," Billy said, inching toward the door.

"Heath *Ledger*," the other officer said, his voice as thin as a child's.

Billy froze. Fuck. Now why did he have to go and use that name when checking in?

"We'd like to talk."

Charlene tiptoed out of the bathroom, rolled into bed, and hid underneath the covers.

"I told you," Billy said, looking through the door's peephole. (The officers had their guns out.) "No one here by that name."

"There was an incident at the liquor store yesterday, Billy Fitz," the goateed cop said.

Shit. They knew who he was. "I wasn't there. Wasn't me."

"Wasn't you what?"

"I don't know what you're talking about."

"Someone saw you headed that way."

"Who said that?"

"You'll find out at your trial, Billy," the thin-voiced cop said.

"No Billy here."

"If you don't let us in, we got the keycard."

"Won't do you no good. I got the chain lock on."

"Then we'll break down the door," the goateed cop said.

There was no way Billy was going back to the county jail.

Charlene popped up from behind the covers. "Billy, just fuckin' let them in!" she hollered.

"You have someone in there with you?"

"I'll tell them you were here with me, Billy," Charlene said in a low voice. "We never left this room. We were together the whole time."

"I'm sure a legal aid attorney can arrange a fair sentencing," the thin-voiced cop said.

Billy pointed his pistol at Charlene.

"What the fuck are you doing?" she yelled.

"Get over here," he said.

She jumped out of bed and threw on her

dress. Then she ran to her bike and climbed on it. "Out my way, Billy," she said, walking with the bike between her legs to the door, her hands gripping the handlebars. "I'm getting the fuck out of here."

When she got near the door, Billy, cringing, put the gun to her head. He hated playing the role of the bad guy, but, again, what choice did he have? Charlene made like a statue. "Do as you're told," he said to her. "Understand?" She looked like she wanted to say something but couldn't.

With his free hand, he undid the chain lock. Then he turned the doorknob and slowly opened the door.

The officers outside looked as though they'd been checkmated. "Now take it easy," the goateed officer said, his wide eyes assessing the situation. "Put the gun down, Billy."

Though Billy would die before he'd hurt Charlene, he said, "If you arrest me, she gets a bullet in the head."

Charlene started crying.

"Billy Fitz . . . Billy," the thin-voiced officer said, shaking his head. "You're a drug addict not a criminal. She tell you to up your game?"

"I didn't tell him shit!" Charlene screamed.

"Are you gonna let us walk out of here?" Billy asked them.

"Charlene, what in God's name are you doing with this loser?" said one of the other two officers. He had a smirk on his face and looked as though he'd grown tired of handcuffing kids for graffiti and was actually enjoying the standoff. "You all trying to get me killed!" she yelled at the officers.

Then the goateed cop said, "One part Dandelion, the other part Billy Fitz, add a dash of junk, and you got yourself a Molotov cocktail."

The fourth officer, who was standing a good twenty feet behind the other officers, had a Band Aid across his nose. He said, "Charlene, I don't know how many times I warned you about turning tricks."

"I know, I know," she cried, hiding her face in her hands.

"Where's your truck, Billy?" the goateed officer asked.

"I ain't got no truck."

"He ain't got no car!" Charlene screamed, tears streaming down her face.

"Now just leave us alone," Billy said, escorting Charlene—her bike still between her legs—out of the room, his eyes on the auto-body shop next door and then back on the four officers. "Stand back," he said.

Charlene, who was now sobbing, lowered her bony ass onto the bicycle seat, and Billy guided her out onto the parking lot like a parent teaching a child how to keep balance without training wheels, his only thought: get as far away from the officers as possible.

He and Charlene got halfway across the lot—he could see a scared and astonished Crow watching them from Room 8's window—when he said to her, "You're doing just fine, Charlene. Don't you worry. I won't hurt you."

"I don't feel fuckin' fine, Billy," she said, her voice trembling.

Then he heard a cymbal crash and Lil's Wayne's voice. Billy remembered his own phone. Shit. He reached inside his pocket to turn it off but heard a gunshot. Charlene screamed, and Billy turned to the officers. The one who seemed to be enjoying the standoff—the one with the smirk on his face—raised his weapon and aimed it at Billy.

Billy heard another gunshot and Charlene screamed again. The smirking officer then fired two shots: one hit Billy square in the shoulder, the other flew by his head.

Charlene hit the pavement. Billy, whose shoulder was burning, dropped the gun, stumbled, and fell too. A few seconds later—their phones having finally shut up—they were surrounded by the officers who were looking down at them as if they were two half gallons of spilt milk.

Billy, whose head was resting on the front wheel of Charlene's Eldorado, craned his neck. Charlene was pinned beneath her bike, her arms outstretched. Her eyes were open, and her head gushing like a cracked pipeline.

"You fuckin' killed her!" the goateed officer yelled at the smirking one, who was smirking no more.

"He took a shot at me! He fired his weapon!"

Good God! Billy thought. What'd he done? He should have let her go!

The goateed cop crouched beside Billy, his face on fire. "Look what you did, Billy! You Goddamn son of a bitch!" He punched Billy in the face again and again and then rolled him onto his side and into a rivulet of Charlene's blood. He handcuffed him.

Wishing for another ending to his movie, Billy started crying. All along, he'd envisioned it as a redemption story—he should have called his mother and gone back into detox—not this, but from the time he'd met Charlene the plot had started turning in weird ways.

The officer with the Band Aid on his nose ran back to the motel. A short while later, he returned gripping a white bed sheet, like a matador a cloth. He draped it over Charlene's body.

She wasn't going to be waking up anytime soon, Billy thought, not like the girl who'd played opposite him in the high school play. God, he wanted to kill himself. But how could he here? "Wait for me," he said to Charlene's covered body. He was right behind her, and for all he knew death would be the ultimate high. There would be no bottles to pass or needles

to prick their skin with. No ugly hollow masks or phony names to hide behind. He'd do his best Romeo, and she'd watch mesmerized and, when he was done and not quite sure of his performance, she'd clap and say, "That was fuckin' good, Billy."

THE END

About the Author

P. J. Gannon's work has appeared in The Alembic, Slow Trains, 2 Bridges Review, Agave Magazine, Gadfly Online, The Talon Magazine, Amarillo Bay Literary Journal, The Blotter Magazine, Anti-Heroin Chic Journal, Across the Margin, Down in the Dirt Magazine, and other journals. He lives in New York City with his wife and is a Columbia University graduate who likes to travel and hike.

GOD'S OWN

by Samuel Buckley

I. Adulthood

Nick's fists thump the counter: come on.

His teeth crush his lips: come on.

His eyes move from the lurid displays set about the windows and shelves to the forbidden library beyond the counter to the flickering LED displays of the tills: oh God, come on.

An intolerable restlessness rises up him like flames up a heretic, and a cold sweaty horror swirls across the floor, forces its way up his nose, crushes his sinuses, screams in the tiny space behind his eardrums: oh Jesus Christ please come on.

The pain starts to smoulder and glow. Under his skinit creeps, making itself known at last in his hysterical whispering: oh come on please. In the white light beyond the pharmacists, a thousand potions and powders sit.

Then at last at last his greedy hand closes over the packet. Oh God thank you. He knows that the lips are waiting, lips that never spurn the kiss, lips that suck and slurp and eat him up and tell him it isn't over till it's over, whatever *it* is – lips that bring a warmth, bring a kind of lessening; lips that want him and only him, and will not share him with anyone or anything.

The pills' first kiss pitches him into an abyss of divine pleasure, flailing after some imagined grail.

But there is something else. Something he wasn't prepared for.

Princess Heather.

II. Childhood

Nick's mother and grandmother are fussing over him.

'Nick will marry Heather, won't you Nick...Nicky?'

Nick shakes his head at them.

'No! What do you mean no? You lurrrrve Heather.'

He shakes his head again.

'It's okay, Nicky,' his mum says. 'You can tell us...granny won't say anything...aw, he's still shaking his head look...Aw, bless... He lurrrves Heather! He lurrrves her!'

'Oh now Celia,' his gran says, 'give the lad a break will you?'

'Nicky Nicky Noo's in lurrrrve.'

They go quiet, his mum and his gran, as Heather bounds in.

'Nicky,' Heather says, 'you're Shrek. That means you have to save the princess.'

His mum giggles and his gran shushes her.

*

'Higher,' Heather says, 'higher, Nicky higher you wuss.'

She rises on the swing and it sings out an unoiled shriek, rises, falls, rises. The wind whistles through the trees and the traffic rumbles and above it all Heather's cry is clear: 'higher, higher, come on...!'

*

The earth oozes dampness, a deep soil-smell; Heather has wrecked her cardigan and muddied her tights and he has gotten his joggers all wet and muddy, and they are in for it from both their mums. Neither care.

III. Adulthood

'What do you mean, you don't carry it?'

His fingers tap at the dashboard, bass-heavy music drowning their voices. Outside, blue lights pulse and recede.

'Mate, listen: I can get you stuff, real good stuff, but it'll take time. My mate...'

'I don't want weed, Dev. I just want a pick-me-up. The stuff I'm talking about, it works for everything. You should look into it yourself to be honest...everyone should...'

'M? Are you serious, mate? Jesus no. But if you want it that badly why don't you just ring and say your back's playing up again?'

'They'll know.'

'Know what?'

'They'll just know.'

'Know *what*, Nick? Look, calm down mate. You're sweating everywhere.'

'It's hot. It's June.'

They drive around, not going anywhere. The blinking movement of the hatchings is hypnotic, soporific – he wonders if he might fly into a trance, his tiredness as good as any narcotic, and just float away – float on the lips, the softly touching lips, the lips dancing upon his expectant mouth, upon his insides, spreading a fathomless warmth, lips smacking rhythmically upon his skin.

Dev pulls the car over, waits. The silent blue strobes of a cop car pass by and recede into the blackness.

Dev sighs: 'Nick, mate, come to think of it I probably can get you some. Just to tide you over. It's nasty stuff but it'll keep you going, ok? Just because it's you and you're my mate. I know a guy who carries it sometimes. Works at the pharmacy.'

He shakes his head and puts the car back into gear.

'I shouldn't,' he says. 'I shouldn't, Nick.'

Nick takes the nineteenth and twentieth pills of the day some of the last left in the pack; Dev shakes his head.

'This is bad, mate,' Dev says. 'You need help.'

Then the lips kiss, the world starts to fuzz, and a coat of gold curls its way around him.

'It's good,' Nick says.

*

'You mate are actually crazy,' someone says to Nick.

'Listen to him Hazza. Nick tell him what you told me. Hazza we got somma Dev's stuff and he's cooked.'

Hazza gazes, nodding with approval.

'Haha, Jamie mate, I swear it looks like you've rubbed soap in his eyes, he's that baked.'

'He is *trippin*, man.'

Hazza puts on a voice before requesting the smouldering stub: 'Nicholas I am shocked and appalled at you sir, and you, James, corrupting him like this. Spoiling the innocents.'

Jamie just says: 'He is teh--*rippin*, mate.'

Hazza: 'A man in the public service. Tut-tut...' and he shakes his head, laughs and draws deeply.

'Teh- *rippin* he is Hazza mate. Didn't I tell you Nick, much better than popping pills isn't it lad? Nick. Nick matey. Nick.'

'He is far from here Jimmy old boy. I think we've killed the poor lad...'

As, in the blueness of the pre-dawn, the milkfloat comes whining up the suburban roads, they sit and smoke and devise plans for the running of the world come Monday morning.

*

He starts the day with the last two doses on his prescription. As he heads to work the pills dissolve and bliss fills him; there is no reversal, no true reversal; there is pattern and patterns need neither reverse nor alter at all...he is crystallised, suspended; even as he minces through the boiling streets, head filled with the smells of meats hanging under the awnings of artisan butchers' stalls, of dubious cheeses, the rank salt of drying fish, clogged drains, bodies, stale booze.

But again, something unexpected—some*one* unexpected—strolls into his buzz.

Professor Heather.

IV. Childhood

Here, in The Spinney, the houses obscured by trees, there is no time to Heather and he, only a gentle changing of the light's quality; when they sit upon a high bough, moss-covered and muddied, the passage of the seconds is marked only by birdsong and breath. Here, in the trees, here, upon the rolling hills that the suburbs gently eat, here, he is free: there is no time, only pattern.

'Dare you to jump,' she says.

'Bog off.'

'Poof, are you actually scared of that drop?'

Her eyes, hazel and sun-crossed, fix him like they always do.

She's right - why is he scared? He drinks a pint of milk a day, after all, for his bones and teeth...and it isn't a long way down.

'You're scared,' she says. 'I can always tell when you are. Like when you wussed out of that rollercoaster at Alton Towers.'

Alright. He always eats greens, vitamin pills, and icky tonic his mum says is good for him.

So he jumps. Heather yells, and the true triumph in that wind-rushing moment is not the audacity of the leap but that Heather actually sounds a bit alarmed.

*

After landing and rolling, he plays a trick. He lies face down in the mud, pretending that the fall has seriously injured him. A mean thing to do, he know, but it gets Heather back for teasing him. Heather scrabbles over to him, yelling his name, along with numerous oaths. He makes sure that he stays perfectly still, even as she shakes him; she speaks the name of God, turns him over, and he laughs in her face.

'Oh bloody hell Nick you bastard. That was well scary.'

'Hahahahahahaha...'

'Arsehole.'

'Hahahahaha...'

'You really scared me.'

This is the first and worst time he is ever punched—by a very angry Heather, in the nose, age twelve. Years later, he will still, when he wants to, push his nose so that it locks in a funny position. He will call it his Heather Nose.

Nick gives Heather a Pepsi later that day, after stuffing two tissues up his nostrils to stop his nose bleeding. The Pepsi secures peace between them, or at least a ceasefire. They high-tail it to one of the fields adjoining the spinney and lie there watching the day slide toward an ending. Heather cracks the can open and drinks. The light of the day fades, and the heat. She moves closer, so that her arm rests against his side.

V. Adulthood

Oh Heather. Why am I thinking about you now of all times?

*

A bottle of purple methadone solution is delivered to Nick's house by a grinning Dev just before seven: the best fix they can get him.

'Twenty quid, Dev? Are you kidding me?'

'No I am not, and that's mate's rates. In fairness, most users are a lot more desperate than you.'

Nick pays.

'This stuff is dangerous, boss. Go easy.'

The door closes, leaving fading footsteps and silence. He holds, in the grubby, scratched bottle with a yellowed label, two hundred virtually unadulterated millilitres of liquid strong enough to stun an elephant, or at least an elephant of a man. It'd kill a mouse of a man.

What about just a man?

Plain bottle. Child-proof cap. Was this really the best they could do? At least it'll last, he supposes, which is the point. And once it kicks in he won't care what it is.

VI. Neither childhood nor adulthood

Nick is sick in an alleyway. Heather laughs nearby, leaning against a dumpster, before slowing, paling, and vomiting herself; she does not hold his thick mane of hair back, nor does he hold hers, elegant and nuanced of shade and full though it has become; he chooses, nobly as he can, instead to laugh back.

But then something strange happens. One lock of hair has slid into her mouth and he plucks it away, against her protestations, wiping her lips with a shred of Kleenex, and she does the same for him. Then they kiss. The incident is never spoken of again.

Afterwards, shrugging it off, she leads him through the night, teaching him things about clubs, taking him into loud, smoky rooms; blokes buy her drinks; they dance; she tells him off for things, nags, laughs, sings, grows angry,

then sad, then happy again, then admonishes, then gushes secrets. They wander home, tired, hungry, grumpy; they eat kebabs. They hug before parting ways with more than a few backward looks. Then for both it is a short walk down ever-familiar streets to ever-familiar familial seats, semi-detached and safe, each to sleep and wake alone.

They are to go to university in a matter of days, her to Caius (—a woman at Caius, his dad exclaims), he to a modern, cutting edge place with a reputation so dire he blushes to speak its name, as does his father, grimacing in silent reproof.

*

On the way to work he begins to feel very ill.

He's had too much. Simple as that. Methadone is meant to be a very strong one. A sip's meant to be enough for three days: not ten gulps for the morning commute.

Oh, he's messed this up badly.

He feels...

Actually, he is starting to feel relief. The streets start to tilt. He thinks: this is rather lovely.

But then Heather's glance flashes from every passer-by, and he hears her voice, and wants to talk back, and he thinks: Nick you fool. You're going to die.

His options: hospital; activated charcoal; questions; counselling; naloxone.

Or: nothing.

He can fix it. He books a taxi to A&E, explains the situation. The taxi'll be five minutes. How long until this dose really starts to affect him, before it puts him under? Will there be time?

He uses a payphone, one of the last in town, his mobile having died. He has change left over after calling the taxi and he knows the number of an honoured faculty-member at Caius off by heart.

He dials.

'Professor Heather Arder speaking. I don't know how you got through but I'm on office hours so this had better be an academic query. Who is this?'

'Heather,' he says.

'Professor Arder, please. Can I help you?'

'Heather it's me. It's Nick.'

About the Author:

Samuel R. Buckley is a writer based in London. He has been publishing stories since 2012, appearing in the Eunoia Review, Crack the Spine, Yellow Mama Magazine, Bewildering Stories, Brilliant Flash Fiction and the Scarlet Leaf Review, among others.

WHALE BONE

by David Massey

The young man accompanied me outside to enjoy the air and sun. So balmy out here always in July. We walked slowly toward this swing, my favorite place to watch the birds, butterflies, squirrels, rabbits, and other charming creatures that ofttimes appear to this view; I was wearing a hooped skirt and, of coarse, this eternal corset, this whalebone and wire torture skirt that made each step I took such a mincing, laborious affair that I could see my companion growing ever more impatient at my pace. By the time we reached this swing, I saw he had lost all interest in me. What a pity that was, too! I felt immediately that I might have liked him very much. Chester was his name. I remember he smoked some kind of aromatic tobacco in a Meerschaum pipe. I would have liked him so. I never liked my husband half so much!

That marriage was arranged for me. My father was determined I should not be an old maid; it was a mark of shame in his eyes to have such a daughter. By that time he already had declared his firm intention of never willing me more than this house: he wished that I should have a husband, that all my needs of clothing and sustenance might be supplied, and he did not mind a farthing paying for my wedding to get me off his hands, albeit he refused to make it a lavish affair.

Oh, I wish for one moment in my life I could have thrown off this diabolical corset and opposed the will of my father in more ways

than only the one I could not help! I had such a slow, painful time getting from the house to this swing, dear Lord my God, that I never thought I should make it this time! I fear I cannot live much longer--perhaps not even to another Sabbath—but come what may, I know I never can attain my favorite outdoor spot again, unless for one hour I can go without this iron let.

This is my last time in this lovely lookout. Let me enjoy it. Here is a praying mantis, high priest of nature, alighted on the arm of my swing. How he deliberates. Don't disturb him, Janette. He is deep in thought.

#

Whenever I consider how my father dropped me forever from his affections, I am so bitter I almost despair in hopes of heaven. He and Mother were not the only ones who mourned the loss of Juliette, they should have known that!. Oh! It grieved me so that she allowed that uncouth, evil Eli McAllister to take her off to God knows where in the frontier state of Georgia. I know she broke their hearts when she did that, but oh, Jesus Lord, she almost destroyed me, her sister. I loved her, too! O God in heaven, I loved her, too! How could they behave as if a sister should be any less heartbroken over the loss of her belovèd other half than they were over the loss of their youngest child and pet? Oh, my belovèd sister! Bereft! Bereft! I became so furious on one winter night in the second week after she left that I leapt up from the dinner table and screamed, "I loved her as much as anybody! Are you blind, Father?" When Father demanded that I sit down and act like a lady, I stormed upstairs to my room. I almost tripped and fell, clambering with all my might to overcome this everlasting corset. Father could easily have manhandled me back to the table, so hampered was I; but he was constrained by his sense of propriety before the slaves. They were his property. He could not show weakness in front of them lest they grow emboldened, and think themselves people, and people might revolt.

I grieve, too, over Daniel, my nephew. Daniel it was who told me at long last how his mother, my sister, died, brutally beaten to death by Eli McAllister with a shovel. How I admire that young man, and wish my conformity to the mores of this paternalistic society had not caused me to break with him when I learned he had involved himself in an affair with his Julia while she was still married to Adam Brooks. I have little to leave for him— there is virtually nothing left of the two bequests that have kept me in food and raiment adown the years—but in my will made out last year at this season I gave him whatever is left after this house and grounds discharge the debts of my estate. I wish I could do more—and how I wish I had contacted that brave young man before I became so weak, poor, and isolated that I no longer can. I have not even Hattie to help me around the house now, and I live in filthy, dusty quarters. I know the neighborhood he lives in, but do not know his address. Shame on me. My lawyer will have to locate him to give what I have left behind.

It's such a pity that I can no longer spend money keeping up the grounds. Weeds have overtaken even this wholesome vantage, where the roses, oleanders, and willow trees struggle. But I do not so much as have the means to buy provisions for another month's larder, were I able to contact my attorney to release the funds. A mercy it is that I am near death. Let it come swiftly and peacefully. The last time I needed food, over six months ago, I was lucky enough to fall and hurt myself trying to get back to the house from this swing, before a witness; Ezekiel Wheaton; that blessèd fellow, who was cutting through my property carrying small game he had killed with his long gun, rushed over to help me up and back into the house. I was able through his goodness to send him to see Horace. I have enough flour, lard, sugar, tea, dried nuts, and salted pork to last me another ten days if I live that long. Then, I suppose, I shall starve.

I should have had the gumption to *make* them give me control over my own finances. I believe Horace has cheated me, cheated me ten times over. But no woman can keep her finances out of the hands of some man in this country unless she has the courage to insist, to fight our courts relentlessly.

I ought not have come out today. I know not how I ever shall reach the back door this time. Oh, I may have to take off my dress and remove this abominable corset in the very yard! However else shall I make it? Will the shadow of my father continue to dog my every feeble baby step right to my last hour on God's earth?

Look! A fox! Had I a chicken coop, I should be worried now! But I have only the delightful sight of his antics. He must have been drawn to this neighborhood by the rabbits that teem in the thick woods yonder. Thou art a sly creature. So wily, even as you see me watching you. Do you think of attacking me? Ah, you are leaving. Well, go thy way in peace, fox.

I remember so well the salon at which I first heard my nephew's name and suspected who he was, recall it as if it were this very morning. It was such a showy and ostentatious affair that my hostess has been driven from memory, a bovine, vain nature, her very name escapes me, I do believe I resented her very much. Everyone, I quickly saw, was there only to see and be seen—mostly the latter! But during my hour there I met Rufus Wilmot Griswold, who had only that year made a name for himself, with his *Poetry and Poets of America*; and Griswold it was who had the contacts I needed with publishers of Christian poetry to have a slender volume of verse by one of my friends printed out.

Poor Tildy! She met her end nine years ago when the horse pulling her gig, frightened, as horses have the sense to be, by a hissing rattlesnake, threw her from the gig onto her head, against some rocks. She perished of the concussion. In retrospect, I regret even the one good office I was able to do her, for Rufus Griswold proved to be a reprobate who divorced his second wife in a public scandal, then hounded poor Edgar Poe, one of the most unfortunate men ever to walk the earth, into his grave and beyond; for he would not let even Poe's ghost reside in peace, but to the best of his ability befouled Poe's memory. Thank God Poe had the last laugh, for his collected works have proved the most popular volumes going now.

I can only thank my lucky stars that the gaudy affair at which I met Mr. Griswold did not seal my heart against all accounts of this or that salon that I might have heard. In the last year that I was healthy enough to make such a journey to New York City, I gained admittance to one of Anne Charlotte Lynch's soirées, and oh, how heavenly it was to meet our hostess. She was lovely, and her character shined through with a more beautiful light still. I believe that splendid lady would have given her life for any cause she deemed the holy and, most of all, the kindly and compassionate one. Would that I might ever have been so brave, or so effectual in bolstering others in their higher ambitions. At Miss Lynch's house I was introduced to Bronson Alcott, Julia Ward Howe, Bayard Taylor, Fitz-Greene Halleck, Nathaniel Parker Willis, and several more whom I cannot recall, inasmuch as I was in such a heavenly fog, and there were so many luminaries to remember..

It hurts my heart so. Thinking of Anne Lynch's character reminds me of that of my dear nephew. When I heard of him at the 1842 gathering, I tracked him down to his one small rented room. I remember I was wearing purple, from bonnet to shoes, and so complete was the concealment of anything carnal in me that the only parts of my body that showed were my face, neck, and hands. Oh, how can I ever forget the compassion, the utter pity that flooded his face as he witnessed my halting gait into his small room? He rued my corset. He let me sit in his chair, taking my hand to help me ease myself into it, then sat down on his bed so we could talk. He told me so much—how that evil Eli McAllister sank my poor, helpless sister in the deepest of hells, one day beating her to within an inch of her life as she was gathering scuppernongs to make a jam for her family, and on a final occasion of satanic drunken cruelty just sixteen hours before beating her to death with a shovel, held the palm of her right hand down on the red hot top of their kitchen stove, then threatened her with immediate death if she did not stop screaming, and dealt her such a blow when she could not stop that he knocked her unconscious. When his mother next morning saw Eli coming back to the house to kill her before she could flee for her life, she screamed at Daniel, "Run, Daniel! Run! Run!" and the little boy, only seven, ran for his very soul into the road and climbed into the back of a passing farm wagon, hiding himself from his father's rage underneath a tarpaulin covering fertilizer. He had not slept in two nights for fear of Eli, and soon fell asleep. When the wagon stopped, he was taken into slavery by the man at the reins of the mules. That man was Julia's father! His little daughter, a five-year-old, dirt-poor farm waif, loved Daniel from the very moment she set eyes on him, and followed him about like a puppy watching his every move except when her father's actions forbade it. And this was Daniel's Julia; hard was it when the world turned so coldly against them for violating the marriage bonds.

I, at least, should have been more understanding. I had my own cross of beaten brass to bear. When I stormed upstairs in such despair because Father would not so much as allow me to feel my grief without cruel rebuke, he yelled, "You will pay for this, young lady. Remember, you shall pay for this." And indeed, I have. He told me he would, at least, bequeath me the house and grounds—he would not have the world know he left a daughter of his without a roof over her head; but the only provision he would make for my daily sustenance was to find me a husband if I proved unable to find one for myself. And this he did, in the last year of his life. Jeffrey Williams, my husband, was a strait-laced 'cold fish,' the kind of man I, at least, had expected my father, a dictatorial Methodist minister, to find for me. In the three years we were married, before Jeffrey died of a mysterious fever that swept through the country that winter, we did not even once know one another in the sense conveyed by the word "know" in The Bible. I had no marriage; I had three years of prison; and my husband did not even have the means to provide for me upon his death. Had my maternal grandfather and my father's brother, in every way a kinder and better man than Father, not opportunely learned of my fate and made each of them a bequest in my name, I should have had no way at all of supporting myself.

And this is what our paternalistic world does to a woman who cannot throw off this iron corset! Oh, I hate it so!

#

The most shameful thing I have ever done is that letter I wrote to my nephew. It is engrained in memory like the badge of my infamy. *Sir. I shall not call you 'dear nephew.' You are beyond the pale of any intimate address. I delayed writing you because I was hearing persistent disturbing rumors about you and Mrs. Julia Paley Brooks; and today I received information from an impeccable source that the two of you are involved in a relationship that looks like adultery. Therefore, I tell you this, DO NOT WRITE TO ME AGAIN. Any correspondence from you shall be burned. This is your last word from me. --Mrs. Janette Williams.*

How could I write such a letter to a young man who had behaved with such chivalry toward me, and laid his heart bare for me? A youth who had loved me from the very hour he met me? He had told me how dreadfully it hurt him to lose Julia when, he knew not why, she had fled his ken and left him no trail to follow. He was so confused. He really did know why. He and Julia had met after thirteen years of being apart at one of Margaret Fuller's socratic dialogues, and fallen in love; but he had vacillated so between her and a woman to whom he had committed to such a degree that, in his eyes, no honorable disengagement was possible, that she had felt snubbed and cruelly rejected, and she left him in search of a man who could value her. She married Adam Brooks on the rebound, and regretted it before even the vows were taken. I do not know that whole story—was only able to pick up fragments of it—but she seems to have regarded her husband, an alleged poet, as the greatest plagiarist and fool residing in Europe. She left him, came back to Boston, and there began the affair that sank herself and Daniel under a relentless dark sky of infamy. It has been a long time now since I was able to hear any of the gossip of gentility, but when last I did hear, in '48, that cloud had not lifted.

It is too bad I was not able to see beyond the blinders our society had placed on me. In this, too, the heavy hand of my father made my perceptions as narrow as those of my compatriots. I feel that this shirt of Nessus I have worn all my life is the very symbol of all that is wrong with my thinking. I'm not sure it will even allow me to raise myself from this swing, much less stumble across the yard to the house.

Well, let me stop thinking so hard and enjoy the beauty a little longer. The butterflies swarm around that pepperbush, how lovely, and what a soothing scene. Even the gnats do not bother me.

#

She broke her parents' heart, and saddened her sister. THAT is how I described the effect of Juliette's leaving home with that brute, when I spoke of it to my nephew. Saddened? SADDENED? Oh, God! it almost destroyed me!! After my father drove me from the table, overwrought and in tears, I went to my room and would not, could not come out for weeks, for I know not how long, while I wasted away and Annabel could barely get me to drink enough water and juice to keep me alive. I wept and wept. And all the while my father stormed about, threatening the gravest consequences if I did not stop my histrionics and begin acting like a young lady. Both he and Mother felt that a sister should feel much less over a sibling's loss than a child's parents might do. And when I told Daniel of Juliette's leaving home with that willful and bullying Eli, the most that could escape my lips was that I was saddened? Oh, may God have mercy on my soul, the long shadow of my father still put limits to my tongue. It rules, to this very moment, even my thoughts. Oh, let me end it, end it, end it now!

Thank God that after I said that to Daniel, tears streamed down my face, and I said, "No! It all but destroyed me!" At least he knew.

After I finally was able to begin eating again and come out of hiding in my bedroom, I felt differently toward my parents than before, and was ever after frosty toward them. I never again told Mother or Father about my feelings for my sister, or, actually, about anything. To their queries I gave such replies as, "You need not enquire about my feelings. You don't care, anyway." And the like. I remember on one occasion I told Father, "Please don't ask me a perfunctory question." I cured them of asking after my feelings—or even about a preference. They would not honor my wishes above either of theirs anyway.

Perhaps such petulance, offered to their solicitude rather than a real declaration of my rights, is why I face penury and starvation now. My father might not, after all, have left me so ruined a winter bough had my only crime been deep grief over Juliette's departure. But I was in his eyes a thoroughly ungrateful daughter.

Well. I have to get up from this swing and into the house, somehow. It is threatening a rain in forty minutes or an hour. Should I get soaked, I might not last out the morrow.

Oh. Oohhhh! --There. I am up. Let me rest. --Now. The fumble-step must begin.

Oh! So hard! Let's see. One, two, three, four. One, two. One, two, three. --Rest, Janette. This is so hard. How did the most elementary thing in life get so hard?

Oohhh!! Oh, hard! Father, I could murder your very ghost! I hate you, hate you, hate you as I never have!! Uh! Uh! Oh! One, two. One, two, three, four. One— !Ah O God in heaven, will I ever get there? Oh!--

--I blacked out. I blacked out! *THIS IS WHAT YOU HAVE DONE TO ME, FATHER*!! I am your daughter, and this is what you have done! But at least I am here, at the door, my trembling hands have a purchase on the handle. And look at that, the dark, wet clouds have blown right over my bonnet, let me—

There. I am inside. But I am so frantic for breath I feel I may have a seizure and die before I can reach a place to rest my limbs. I tremble throughout. Oh, let me—one, two, three, four, one, two, if I count I can get to the sofa. Oh, at last. Now, sit you down, Janette.

How is it that I am so spineless? Is this corset the only spine that I have? It keeps me rigidly upright enough.

Why could I not tell the nearest relative I have left, and one who evidently loved me from the moment I introduced myself as his mother's sister, how I felt about her elopement? And then to turn against him so shamelessly when he found himself in trouble with genteel America!

In the brief time that I was out in the world at large, I met a number of ladies who had freed themselves far more than I ever could from the lets our society places on every step of its women, and on every the tiniest thought I have had. Of them, among the very doughtiest was Lydia Maria Child, a fearless lady who flew in the face of every prejudice held by our populace, from commonest laborer and housewife to most privileged of our élite. She made me ashamed of myself. She not only broke in her personal life from the constraints of society, but waged one-woman warfare on the cruelties of our natures. Mrs. Child felt white women and the slaves are alike in that they both are subjugated by white males, and treated as property. And she deplored the national persecution of the Indians wrought by the hatred of President Jackson. She not only fought for the rights of women and slaves, but for our Native Indians as well; and for every defenseless and beleagured person or thing in the land, and she drew so much ire that the public have turned against her except with respect to some of her more charming verses. Never you mind—like my nephew, she continues her campaigns undaunted. And I know my sweet Daniel continues on because only last year, Dorothea Sweeney, who disapproves of my abolitionist views but cares enough for me to bring me occasional tidings of the outside world, brought me his latest book of tales, and I am so proud of him, I feel it is his best book, it places him in the forefront of our authors of shorter fiction; but I am proudest of him for not giving up his guns. He mans his turret bravely, even in the face of oncoming war between the North and South, which one can feel gathering in all its violence here in this year 185s at my home outside Richmond.

The rain comes down hard now; it drums on the roof and lashes the east-side windows. I reached safety in the nick of time.

If I could divest myself of this Procrustian girdle, I should little fear such lowering skies as I saw a while ago. And I should, I truly trust, be capable of standing my ground as well as Daniel, or his first lover, Margaret Fuller Ossoli, who oversaw patient care for the wounded of the Italian war for independence while French bombs exploded on the hospital grounds, and went daily in peril of her life; and who also was among the earliest and most eloquent of warriors for women's rights; or as well as Mrs. Child, or her friend, Angelina Grimké, a Southern lady who stood in the forefront of Abolitionists, and dared the utmost wrath of slavery sympathizers in the North, who pelted her, men and women alike, with eggs, tomatoes, and rocks, not only because she spoke out against the 'peculiar institution,' but also because, being a mere *woman*, she dared to take the stump. Or even, dare I think, even so brave as Sojourner Truth, who went in peril of hanging by a mob of slaveholders and poor dirt farmers as she operated her Underground Railroad to secrete runaway slaves on their way to Canada and freedom? Perhaps. Who knows what I might have done, Father, if I could once have flung off this accursèd corset? And rid myself of your dreadful shadow. I am so angry. My thoughts grow almost amorphous in my wrath. You were a slobbering fool, Father, you slobbered when you preached. How did I let myself be intimidate—so—so—

I *will* not. I *will* not let you rule my life another day. This whale bone devourer of innocent lives must come off now, and never again be strapped on! It has stifled my every impulse toward freedom, made me hide my sympathies for the slaves from all but closest friends, cut me off from a nephew I love, my only living relative, the only person from whom I could have received reliable sympathy. Now! Now! Oh! Why is this dress—such a—maze of shackles—I'll never even—oh!—oh—let me just----let me just—now—now—all right, now—all right, yes, that was the most difficult—I'll soon have this dress—off, yes, there, now, now this iron let—yes, oh, oh, oh, oh, aah!!! There!! It's off, it's off!! Perhaps now I can live, forage in the woods for food, enjoy the out-of-doors, end my life with blessèd nature, find peace and freedom in these my last few hours on earth. Feel the bark on trees, look at wild toadstools, hear the calls of birds that only live deep in thw woods.

So there, Father, go away from me forever.. Your gripe is broken and shall never crush me again. I will live as I should always have done. Go back in your grave. Reason has taken a stand in my soul, and *I'm not afraid of you anymore*!

About the Author:

David Massey has a Master's Degree in English Literature After 1660 from The University of South Carolina and while there took creative writing classes under George Garrett and James Dickey. He turned belatedly to an earnest engagement with the art of fiction but has made progress of late. He has had three short stories and ten essays on the craft of fiction published in the past two years.

THE LITTLE DOG

by Eric Massey

There once was a little dog. His name was Rex. He lived in a small house in a small town. He didn't know what the town was called because, well, he was a dog. He lived with a man. Rex did not know the man's real name. The man referred to himself only as "the master" so that was the name Rex thought to call him. The man was middle-aged, bald, and grotesquely fat. He was a mean, nasty, unkempt man with a violent temper. He would often beat Rex for no reason at all, at least none that Rex could comprehend. Rex was so terrified of the "master" he would often have nightmares in which the fat man would chase him endlessly down a dark never-ending corridor. He would wake up in the middle of the night frightened and shivering in his cage. Oh, the cage—yes, that was the place Rex called home.

Rex lived for all practical purposes in the small metal crate. It was indeed very small for him now. When he was a little puppy, it was not so bad, but now he could barely move. He was ten now. He was a very old dog indeed and much bigger than before. He had to lie on his side and curl into a tiny ball to sleep. He couldn't stand or even stretch in the little cage. The only time he had any relief was when the man would let him go out to go to the bathroom. The man would take the leash from the wall. He was never nice or gentle when he did it. He would grab Rex by the hair on his head, yank him out, and quickly hook the leash to his collar. Oh yes, Rex had a collar. A beautiful collar, at least when it was new. A bright blue collar with eight diamonds inlaid on it, a collar fit for a king. When Rex was a puppy

he was so proud of his collar, but time had worn out the collar. The bright blue had faded, the stitching had come loose, and the diamonds had fallen out. The worst part, however, was how small the collar had become, or more correctly, how big Rex had become. He was surely a puppy no longer. He was as tall as the master when he stood on his hind legs. Of course, the man did not like it when he stood like that; the man had a weapon for such a time. He called it the whip. "Do you want the whip, beast? Do ya?" he would scream at Rex and crack the whip down on his head. Rex would yelp and fling himself back into the cage. It was too small, but it was safe. When he was in the cage the man rarely spoke to him, only when Rex needed food or to go outside to the bathroom. The bathroom, that's what the man called it; for Rex it was the only time out of the cage, the only time in the yard, the only time he experienced freedom. It was during this time of freedom that his life changed forever.

The master came home promptly at 5:15 p.m. Rex knew he was home because he could hear the car and its unmistakable low rumble as it pulled up the hill into the garage. Rex was excited as usual. He couldn't help it, even though the master was cruel; at least Rex knew he could get out of the cage. He had to go outside badly. He had a bowl full of water in the morning but by now it was empty. It was just enough to quench his thirst, but also enough to fill his bladder. He could hear the man shut the car door. Rex was shaking he was so excited. He couldn't stop writhing around in the cage. He constantly banged against the sides of the cage, but, confined as he was, he couldn't help but make a lot of noise. He tried to calm himself but found himself more frantic than before. He had to go outside. NOW. He could hear the key in the door. Oh, he could not stand it any longer. He started to bark "Ruff, ruff," quiet at first. He tried to stop but to no avail. "Ruff, ruff, ruff!" Rex barked louder. The key rattled in the door. "Ruff, ruff!" He barked louder still. He lost all control. He flung himself against the cage. "Ruff, ruff, ruff, ruff, ruff." Rex barked louder than ever before. The door flew open and in clambered the man. "Shut up, you beast! Shut up, you mongrel!" he bellowed, foam flying from his mouth. His huge girth pushed through the door as he burst into the room. "Shut up!" he yelled as he kicked at the cage. He had a bag in his hand. "Hold on, you puke!" The man glowered as he passed Rex in his cage. He continued on into the kitchen.

Rex squirmed in his cage. He had to go outside. NOW, please, NOW. He could only whimper as he waited for the man. He could hear the man in the kitchen. He was opening the food box. Rex was trying to be patient, trying to wait, but it was too late. Rex did not need to go outside any longer. He wet the cage. His urine ran along the bottom across the papers and into the corner. "Oh, no," Rex thought. He knew what was coming next. The master would be more than angry, he would be . . . terrifying. He would be the man in his nightmares. Rex could only stare at the kitchen door. He was not excited anymore. Now he was frightened. He hunched back against the back wall of the cage. As far from the door as he could get, he whimpered quietly, waiting for the master.

The door finally opened. Rex closed his eyes. "What? What have you done, you stupid dog?" the master screamed at him. He stood over the cage and glowered down at Rex. "You couldn't wait five minutes, you lousy mutt?" The man turned and grabbed the leash . . . and the whip. Rex shivered. The hulking master threw open the door to the cage. Down came the whip. "Smack-crack!" The whip made a sickening noise as it hit poor Rex. He cried out in pain. "Crack" came the whip again. "Stupid dog, I'll show you!" The man slobbered the words. "Crack!" Down came the whip again. Rex screamed out in pain. "Shut your yap!" The man let Rex loose. Rex fell prone to the floor. He dared not move. He just whimpered. "That's better," fumed the man. He attached the leash to Rex's too-small collar and jerked him roughly up. "Now, we will go outside and you can do your business right, mutt!"

The man led Rex by the leash to the back door. Rex was hurt and in pain, but he still had hope because the yard was just beyond the back door and the yard was temporary freedom and the possibility of more. Rex began to formulate a plan in his head, a plan for escape from his cage, from his master, from this place, a plan for freedom.

The man opened the door to the back yard. The sun was suspended in the sky high above Rex as he walked out into the back yard. The light beamed down on his back.

He felt warm and alive. The cage was too small, too confining and too dead, he needed the outside. He needed his freedom. His freedom was limited, however, to the fifty by fifty-foot back yard. His freedom and interaction with other dogs was limited by the eight-foot-tall privacy fence around the entire perimeter. This was the problem with his escape plan. He had a plan, but everything would have to work perfectly.

The grass felt dry and parched under his feet. The ground was hard but it felt wonderful, much better than the cold metal. The master was stern and heavy-handed with Rex as usual, but Rex knew the routine. He knew what the master would do in a situation like this. He would not leave the cage a mess. He would bring it outside to clean it with the water hose. Rex hated and loved the water hose. He liked the water but hated getting a bath. It was often awkward and usually painful, as he would get hit by the master many times.

His mind was wandering. The master would clean the cage. Yes, but what would he do with Rex? If Rex would behave, he might tie Rex up to the clothes line. This was his best hope. Tie me to the clothes line. The shed by the back corner was the only way over the fence. If the master were distracted for long enough, just maybe he might be able to climb over the fence. "But what would I do if I got out?" he thought. He had never met another dog or another person other than the master. He had never been anywhere. The thought made Rex pause for a moment.

"What are you doing, dog?" the man growled. The master pulled the leash taut. Rex immediately pressed up against the master's leg. He rubbed and fawned on the man.

He was trying his best to appease him.

"Dog, you done pissed me off!" The man rudely punched him in the head and shoved him abruptly away, but he did not use the whip. Rex continued to show the man affection. "Damn you, stop it!" the man cursed under his breath, but he didn't hit Rex this time. "Dog, I'm gonna tie you up to this pole and you better act right, you hear?" The man leaned in close with the whip in his hand. He took the leash and tied the lead end around the metal clothes line pole. Rex nodded and smiled inside. This was it, this was his chance. "I'm gonna get the cage out here and clean it . . . then you." The man smirked when he said it. "Behave!" he yelled back as he walked toward the house.

Rex knew his time was short. It was now or never. He bent over to the leash and began to gnaw on it. The leash was old just like his collar. It was tough, though. This was taking longer than he thought. The master was inside. Rex could hear him cursing as he tried to get the cage up and out the door. Rex was panicking. He kept gnawing. Gnawing. His jaw grew tired. The man was almost to the door. The man backed out the door very slowly, his huge rear end leading the way. He was dragging the cage out the door. Rex stopped

chewing and quickly lay down on the leash. The man stopped and turned and stared at Rex. Rex looked dully back as if disinterested. The man continued his work. Rex waited. The master, sweating and cursing, finally got the cage outside to the water hose. He turned again to stare at Rex. Rex just closed his eyes. "I'm gonna get some soap, dog, then I'm gonna clean this cage, then you." He smirked a wicked grin; he knew Rex did not like baths. He turned back and entered the house. Rex immediately began chewing again.

Almost there. Almost. One last nylon thread. Free. The leash broke from the pole. Rex sprang to his feet and ran across the yard to the shed. It was taller than he thought. He ran up to its side and jumped up on the fence and tried to jump to the back of the shed. He slipped off the shed and fell to the ground. He was up instantly and jumped again. This time he made it up on the roof top.

"Dog! What the hell!" the master bellowed from across the yard. "Stop!" The master started running as quickly as his great girth would allow.Rex froze for an instant; he couldn't move.He saw the master and something compelled him to stop, a deep desire to please the master; somewhere in his heart he wanted to stay. The master trundled closer. Rex snapped out of his trance. He shook his head and turned to jump the fence. "Ya-a-h!" The scream was higher and louder than any scream Rex had ever heard. He stood paralyzed face to face with another human. A female human. A woman, he thought they were called. She was several feet away on the other side of the fence, a place Rex had only dreamed about. Her high, shrill scream only started again. Seeing a big, shaggy dog on the roof of the shed must have been too much for the woman. She, too, was paralyzed, seemingly unable to move, just like Rex.

"Dog, damn you, dog!" It was the master's booming voice. Rex turned just in time to see the master hit his leg with the whip. He fell forward against the fence. The woman screamed again and ran towards her house. The master, cursing, yanked his leg and pulled Rex down from the roof of the shed. Smack onto the ground Rex landed on his head. It almost knocked him out. It might have been better for him had it been so. It would have spared him the beating to follow.

The master whipped him mercilessly. Over and over again the whip came down. Time and time again the master beat him. There would be no end to the beating until the master finally grew weary, until his own muscles became too exhausted from the incessant beating. Rex cried out until no sound came from his throat. The master grabbed Rex by the leg and dragged the broken body back into the house. The cage had been returned to its place just as it was before being cleaned. The master shoved Rex back into the cage. Rex offered no protest. He lay there in his own urine. No sound or complaint. He slipped into unconsciousness or sleep or somewhere in between.

A deafening noise woke him from his deep sleep. It was the sound of thunder only it sounded like it came from inside the house. There was another loud bang and a flashing, whirling light. Smoke filled the room, it was coming from all around. Rex heard shouting. Faintly he heard the sound of the master yelling, but not at him, at someone else. Rex heard cursing from the master, then loud, banging sounds. It was a sound that frightened Rex so much that he shivered and urinated on his papers. Pow, pow, pow went the sound. The master let out a blood-curdling yell. Rex could hear other men in the house shouting. Rex shivered in his cage, darkness and smoke all around him, with strange men in the house. The door to his room burst open. Several men dressed in black clothes and helmets and carrying guns poured into the room. Rex knew about guns: The master had some and they were loud. That must have been the loud banging noise he heard.

"There, there he is, we have him!" one of the men called out. Another repeated the same words into a black box on his shoulder. Rex was deeply frightened. What was happening? Who were these men? Rex was overwhelmed. "We have you. Hold on," said one of the men dressed in black. He opened the cage. Rex froze, too frightened to move. "It's okay, we have you now. It's all right." The man bent down on one knee and reached out his hand toward Rex. Rex growled softly. The man moved his hand closer. "It's okay." He was very calm.

Rex could hear a lot of confusing noises coming from other rooms in the house. The man touched Rex. Rex stiffened. "It's okey. You're safe now." The man's voice was low, calm, and very soothing. "Come on, it's okay." He smiled gently. Rex moved slightly. The man waited. Rex moved closer and fell over a little. He was heavy and sore from his beating. He fell into the man's arms. The man picked him up and carried him outside the house. He moved past the men in the kitchen, where the smoke was still thick in the air. Rex was carried past the front door and out of the house into the front yard. He was immediately blinded by the blue and red lights emanating from several cars and trucks in the road in front of his house. They seemed to be everywhere, and people seemed to be everywhere. He never knew there were so many people. He did not see the master anywhere. The man carried Rex to a strange-looking bed with wheels and laid him gently down on the bed. Rex smiled because the bed was soft. He was so tired that even with all the commotion he knew he could fall asleep. The man placed his hand on Rex's head and held him gently but firmly down. Rex closed his eyes.

Carol Parker was the first one on the scene. She had gotten the call first and in a matter of two hours had managed to get the proper paperwork and manpower to accomplish her task. She dreaded the entry into the house because you never knew what you might find. She had seen many cases of abuse, but she feared the worst. The police entered the house quickly and overpowered the man inside. Shots were fired, but fortunately no one was seriously injured. She paced restlessly outside beyond the roped-off area. She remained in the safe area until everything was clear, when an officer approached her walking briskly. "We have him. He's over here. Follow me," he said. The officer wove his way through the crowd and led her over to the gurney. She approached the medic. "Is he okay?" she said, concern evident in her face.

"Um, he's okay, he has several broken bones and a lot of bruises and cuts, but he'll be okay," the medic said. Carol stepped to the bed, reached out her hand, and placed it on the little boy's arm. There was almost nowhere she could touch him without finding a bruise. She very gently caressed him. The little boy opened his eyes.

"Hey," Carol said quietly. The boy smiled faintly.

"Son, what's your name?" Carol's voice was soothing and calm. The little boy tried to answer but nothing came out.

"It's okay," she said. Carol gently straightened out the faded blue collar with the missing diamonds that the medic had handed her. She wiped the faded dog tag until she could make out the engraved name. "Is your name Rex?" she whispered. The little boy smiled and nodded. Carol wept.

THE END

About the Author:

Eric Massey has been married to his high school sweetheart Heather for over 29 years. He has five children ages 28 to 15 years and one grandchild. Eric graduated from Winthrop University with degrees in Psychology and Music. He also received a B.A. in Biblical Studies from Covington Theological Seminary and an M.A. in Pastoral Counseling from Victory Bible College. He has served for over 20 years as Youth and Worship leader at several Augusta area churches. He recently finished a screen play entitled "Riverbed" a story of failure, loss, and redemption tentatively scheduled for release in late 2019. "The Little Dog" is Eric's first published short story.

AMBIVALENCE: A LOVE STORY

by Claudia Piepenburg

October 20, 2016
6:00PM

"Mrs. Williams? Alice Williams?" The doctor resists the urge to click his fingers an inch in front of the half-shut eyes of the woman sitting by the door. He's seen this reaction before, too many times; and even though he knows that she needs to be shocked into the reality of this moment, he can't. Doing so would be too callous, too cruel, too much like a cringe-worthy scene from a mediocre movie where the villain slaps the hero in the face and screams: "Snap out of it!"

"Mrs. Williams?" Sometimes, he's learned, raising your voice by even half an octave makes all the difference.

"Yes? That's me." She's small, probably not much taller than five feet and less than one hundred pounds, so frail that despite the fact she's sitting he fears she might topple over. Black eyeglasses perch just at the top of her forehead, looking like they'll slide down her face at any moment. Her hair is cropped close; it looks blonde, sun-bleached white but he knows it must be gray. When her lids pop open, as if he *had* struck her in the face, he sees that the eyes hiding beneath them are the color of still blue water.

What a beauty she once was—still is. I wonder what he thought, the first time he saw her.

"Mrs. Williams, I'm doctor Robertson. Mel's primary care doctor has filled me in on your husband's case. He couldn't be here today; he has an emergency surgery. I'm sorry."

Sorry because I have to tell you what you already know but don't want to be told and sorry because what could be more heartless, cold and final than your doctor not being available to deliver the news because he's moved on to care for someone who'll be alive tomorrow.

She closes her eyes, all the way this time, so it looks like she's shielding them from blinding sunlight or a probing laser or perhaps a white-hot explosion. They remain shut while her mouth opens.

"Mel, short for Melvin of course. I always hated the name Melvin. But it was his father's name so..."

"Oh, I understand Alice. I so understand. You know what my first name is? Reginald. Can you imagine? A name like that for a guy born and raised in Brooklyn? But my mom loved an English actor named Reginald Denny who made some movies with Katharine Hepburn and Greta Garbo, so she and my dad named me after him, although I'm pretty sure that dad wasn't all that hot on the idea. I use my middle name, John, as my first name. Only my wife—and well, now you—know that my real name is Reginald."

Please open your eyes, please. Please. I'm rambling and I'm trying to connect with you and I want you to open your eyes and look at me and you need to listen to me and not make me stand here anymore because I really want this to be over because even after all these years, I'm not good at this.

"Reginald is a rather old-fashioned name, isn't it?" He realizes he was wrong—her pupils are icy blue. "Our children won't be here when you…when you turn everything off. You need to know that so you don't have to worry about the time, about waiting I mean. We aren't waiting for anyone."

Am I sorry?

"How many children do you have?"

"Two. Our daughter is off traveling around out west somewhere. Maybe Colorado now, I'm not sure. Last time we heard from her she was in Oregon. She's looking for herself, that's what she says, anyway. Mel told her that saying she was looking for herself was just an excuse to keep her from having to look for a real job—something other than working in bakeries and making artisanal chocolates."

Her voice is hard and chilly, as cold and penetrating as the eyes that bore through him.

So I'm not sorry, I guess.

"Your other child…"

"A son. A son, daughter-in-law and one grandson. They live in Berlin. He's in banking, finance—that sort of thing. They've been there for six years. Our grandson is four, we saw him once when they came for a visit not long after he was born. He wouldn't know us from Adam."

Knowing all this makes it easier and so much harder.

"Well, then since they can't make it to say goodbye," (*God, I sound so sloppily sentimental. I wish I hadn't said that*) "we can proceed, but first I need to explain a few things to you. Your husband…"

"Is essentially brain-dead because he suffered a massive stroke, his second by the way but I'm sure you know that, you've read his chart. We used to talk about this Mel and I, about something like this happening."

That's a good sign, she's prepared. She knows what to expect.

"So you understand then that…"

"There were times when we talked about it and we'd both decided that he'd be the one who'd end up like this unless I got in a car accident or something—we'd talk about it and I'd think, depending on how angry I was with him, what year it was…you know…early in our marriage we never talked about death, about being brain-dead and feeding tubes and all, but we did later, after the kids were born—and there were times in those days when I felt like I was the only one doing all the work, the only one working at bringing up our children, the only one working on our marriage, the only one working on our lives—there were times in those days that I would think that it would be such an easy thing to do, something I'd almost look forward to…the doctor coming to me and saying 'Mrs. Williams, he's gone and we have to pull the plug.'"

Her eyes look as if they might shatter at any second.

"I…I…wish…"

"That you weren't standing here right now? That you aren't hearing me saying these things? That you didn't have to be here? That you knew what to say? I understand, doctor, I wouldn't know what to say to me, either."

She stares at his hands. They're touching,

just below his belt, making a pyramid shape, his elbows jutting out on either side of his torso; the pose makes him look awkward and uncomfortable.

"Are you married doctor Robertson? I don't see a wedding ring."

"I am, been married for almost fifteen years now. I don't wear my ring when I'm working. I was in surgery this morning, for four hours. I don't wear any jewelry including my wedding ring when I'm in the OR. There aren't restrictions against wedding rings per se but I'd rather be safe than sorry. Germs you know. We scrub up well but one never knows."

When she stands and walks toward the bed she seems not quite as old on her feet, not quite as fragile. Her back's to him now but he hears her clearly.

"Mel didn't have to worry about germs, about infecting anyone. He was a comptroller. A guy who worked with numbers, just a glorified accountant, that's all. But he quit wearing his ring about ten years after we were married. Told me that he lost it, said he must have taken it off to mow the lawn or when he painted the shutters and couldn't find it after that. I didn't bother him about getting another one; didn't nag him. Afterwards I figured it had been easier for him to meet women when he was wearing his ring anyway. Precious metals are an attraction, never a distraction."

She strokes her husband's head, knobby fingers moving through his hair, parting it, then patting the thin gray strands into place.

"Of course I didn't know that he already had a girlfriend by that time. Seven-year itch, that's what it was. What happens after seven years? And why seven? Why not five or ten? You know, they made a movie about that...the seven-year itch. You're too young to remember. It starred Marilyn Monroe. There's that famous scene of her in the movie, standing over a subway grate and the train comes by and blows her dress up around her and you can see her white panties. Mel loved that movie. He loved Marilyn Monroe. Mel loved women. Women loved Mel."

If I leave the room now she won't even know that I'm gone. Maybe I should leave her for a while, I don't need to be here anymore. She knows what's going to happen.

"Alice, would you like me to leave you alone with Mel for a bit? Is that something that you need?"

Turning to face him, he sees that the ice has melted; remnants pool in the creases that form a halo around her mouth.

"It's too late now. Too late for me to say some things I should have said long ago. I waited too long. All of us do, don't we? We all wait too long because we don't know how long we have."

"Yes, Alice that's true. It's human nature."

She turns back, resumes the stroking, parting, lifting, patting. He's watching a ritual.

Her face is softening, the lines and creases dissolving, disappearing as if they were ripples on water. And when she speaks he knows the words aren't meant for him. This is a private one-sided conversation.

"I could have had an affair, I could have. That's what I'd tell him. He was a nice man. Not a handsome man, not handsome like Mel but a nice man. He was a widower, his name was Paul. Paul Jackson...or maybe it was Johnson... was it Johansen? I don't remember after all those years. I met him at PTA conference. Mel was away on a business trip and Paul was there because his wife had died two months before. He talked to me Paul did, for a while after we'd met with the teacher. Stopped me in the hallway and started talking about silly things, things he thought a woman would want to hear I guess. He mentioned a movie that I knew he never would go see by himself and then he brought up gardening, talked about tulips for quite a long time. He was very nervous. I looked at his shirt once and thought I could see movement, up and down just a little, right where his heart was. Funny…I remember the conversation so clearly but I can't recall his last name."

She's bent over at the waist, her right cheek touching the side of her husband's face, just below his left eye.

"I didn't though…have an affair. That was the first and last time I talked to Paul. I never saw him again. I used to think about him now and again but I haven't in years…not until just now."

During the two or three seconds that he glances at his watch he's become visible to her again, and the guilt jabs his stomach, hard. As if her ear has become an eye, she speaks, this time to him.

"I guess you'd like to get this over with, right doctor?"

"Well, Alice…whenever…"

"Now, I'm ready now, doctor."

And Alice leans in, closer than before, and whispers in Mel's ear.

October 20, 1955
6:00

"Alice, look who's standing over there. It's Mel Williams. He's standing by the wall all alone and he's looking over here."

The girl in the blue poodle skirt and white bobby socks discreetly pokes Alice in the ribs and not so discreetly tilts her head to the right.

"Mel Williams? Hah! That louse, that cheater, that heart breaker. He can look all he wants. Let him look. He's probably looking at you anyway, Hannah."

"One, two, three o'clock, four o'clock rock, five, six, seven o'clock, eight o'clock rock…" Bill Haley's vocals drown out Hannah's reply. Alice shakes her head, grabs Hannah's hand and

pulls her outside the gymnasium door where the 1949 state football championship team stares down at them from inside their glass-fronted box.

"What did you say? The music's so loud, I couldn't hear you." Usually soft-spoken, Alice brings her right index finger to her lips, laughs and her sunflower blonde ponytail whips from one ear to another as she shakes her head from side-to-side. "Gosh. It's so loud in there that I'm still screaming."

"I said that Mel's looking at you, right at you Alice. Isn't he dreamy? Those eyes, that smile, the dimples and his big broad shoulders. And he's looking at you. You gotta go back in there."

Alice presses the palms of her hands flat into the wall, right shoe-less foot against it, left leg jiggling, just from the knee down.

"Are you kidding me? Mel Williams? Didn't Betty Mitchell just break up with him last month? I heard that she caught him making-out under the bleachers during halftime with that slutty redheaded cheerleader from Wilson High. Right there under the bleachers. *Our* bleachers, at *our* school while poor Betty was buying a soda pop. Heard that Mel gave Betty the money to buy the soda, told her that he wasn't thirsty, he'd just hang around and listen to the band until she got back. Listen to the band…right. Mel Williams? Nuh-uh!"

Arms folded in front of her now, pushed tightly against her blue angora sweater, her hands buried under her armpits, Alice shakes her head "no, no, no" and stares at the clock on the wall behind Hannah's head.

"Let's go get a milkshake." The words don't come out nearly as sure as they'd sounded inside her head.

"A milkshake? You just told me last week that you want to lose two pounds and besides we just got here. Come on, Alice. Let's go back in. What *I* heard is that Betty wasn't very nice to Mel. Thought she was too good for him. You know, Mel's mom died last year, he's still gotta be feeling so sad. Come on. Let's go back in."

"No!"

"Ain't that a shame? My tears fell like rain. Ain't that a shame? You're the one to blame..."

Neither one's surprised to see Mel walk through the open gymnasium door.

"Hey, girls. Whatcha doin' out here? All the fun's inside."

Alice raises her hands and hugs her shoulders, pulling them in like she's folding wings around her body.

"We're...we're thinking about leaving. I'm not feeling..."

"Well, *I'm* going back inside. You two stay out here." Hannah's skirt swirls around her calves when she leaves, as if she's already dancing.

"That true? You not feeling well? 'Cause if you're getting sick, I can drive you home. Your name's Alice, right? Alice Ryzner? We were in the same English Comp class last semester. I remember you Alice. Maybe...maybe you remember me? Nah. Probably not."

His brown eyes remind her of a fawn she saw once in the backyard. She was ten. Her mom called her to come and look at the creature nuzzling around the roots of the maple tree. When Alice stepped to the window, the deer had lifted its head and before it scampered away, it looked right at her, its eyes big and sad and scared.

"I remember you. You told funny jokes, you made me laugh."

"I did? Wow! My jokes made you laugh. I didn't think girls like you thought guys like me are funny."

She lets her fingers brush against his forearm, only the slightest touch, barely perceptible.

"I thought your jokes were very funny Mel."

And this time saying his name out loud feels personal and real and intimate.

"Well then maybe I'll tell you some more. And if you're not feeling too sick, could we have a dance. Just one? And then I'll drive you home if you want."

Alice's fingers tighten around his arm, the way you'd hold onto a crystal goblet—tight enough to keep it in your grasp, to keep it from falling but not tight enough to break it.

"I'm feeling so much better. My headache's gone. I'd love to dance with you."

Mel takes her elbow, leads her to the door, opens it and as they walk into the gym he leans in, very close to her ear and whispers, so she can hear what he's saying over Presley's boisterous vocals:

"You're the most beautiful woman I've ever seen Alice Ryzner. And I'm going to fall in love with you."

About the Author:

Claudia Piepenburg spent the majority of her career as a copywriter, editor and journalist. Her articles have been published in Runner's World and Running Times. Since 1992 she's been a contributing writer to Road Race Management, a monthly running industry publication. From late 2015 through early 2017 she wrote for Carlsbad Lifestyle, a monthly digital and print magazine and the website yournorthcounty.com. She was a freelance reporter for The Coast News Group from April to September 2018.While employed as senior copywriter and managing editor at Road Runner Sports from 1999-2004, she wrote seven books, one titled Running for the Soul is still available on Amazon. In early 2017 she completed her first novel and is currently looking for representation. Also in 2017 she began writing her second novel and wrote twelve short stories and several poems. Her short story Where Do We Go From Here was awarded an Honorable Mention in the Glimmer Train May/June 2018 Short Story Award for New Writers. Although her short story Breathing Lessons was not published in the New Yorker, the editors sent her an email thanking her for her submission, told her that they regretted that they weren't able to publish it and thanked her for giving them the opportunity to read her work. She's a member of Publishers and Writers San Diego; the National Writer's Union; a co-founder of North County Writer's Community, a group of both published and un-published writers who meet weekly to write, critique their work and discuss their craft; and a member of the Oceanside Mission Writers' Critique group.

JULIE IN CHICAGO
by Eric Lutz

Julie sat on her balcony. It was midday on a Wednesday. She wore khaki shorts, a lime green bikini top, and sunglasses. She drank Tecate and listened to Otis Redding on her phone. She had called in sick to work. She wasn't sure what it was, but she had for weeks been out of it, feeling a familiar but implacable ache, almost like hunger, as though she had recently lost something she didn't know she had. She'd hoped maybe some sunshine might help.

Every so often, the Brown Line thundered past her apartment.

Every so often, she went inside to grab another beer.

...

Mike came over that night. They hardly greeted one another when she opened the door. They went straight to her room.

"How was your day?" he said, taking his messenger bag off his shoulder and setting it down in front of her closet.

"Fine," she said, moving her clean laundry from her bed to the floor.

She turned to face him. He walked toward her. They kissed. They undressed. He lay flat on his back on the bed. She mounted him and moved on him until his face twisted the way it always did and she slunk down on top of him and climbed off.

"Did you finish?" he asked her after a little while.

"No," she said. "I never do, though."

"I'm sorry," he said.

"No, I mean like I can't," she said. "Some girls aren't able to. It's not you."

She turned her head to look at him. He nodded like he understood, but she could see in his face that he was still thinking it was him. Maybe it was, she thought. Him and all the others – perhaps none of them had been able to give her what she wanted. But what was it that she wanted?

She touched his face. There was a couple days' stubble on it. She ran her fingers up the sandpaper of his cheeks until she reached his hair. He wore it like an adolescent, with no style to it. He put his arm underneath her and pulled her close to him and dozed off. She lay awake, her head on his chest, hearing his heartbeat and feeling hers, feeling at once close to him and very far away.

...

She arrived twenty minutes late to work the next morning. Her project manager, Bernice, tapped an imaginary watch on her wrist and raised an eyebrow at her.

"Sorry," Julie said.

Bernice sighed.

Julie walked to her cubicle, sat down, and started up her computer. Hers was the slowest in the office because she had been the most recent person hired, and the only computer left was the old one nobody wanted. She waited more than ten minutes for it to groan awake, opened her spreadsheet, and began to transfer data from the paper in the manila envelope on her desk to the spreadsheet on her computer. After a few minutes, she opened her browser and began to search for jobs.

...

Lauren was making stir-fry. Julie sat with her ankles under her at their kitchen table, drinking a glass of red wine.

"You should see someone," Lauren said.

"I'm fine," Julie said.

Lauren stopped stirring the vegetables in the frying pan.

"You're not fine," she said.

"OK, I'm not fine." Julie stood up, got an ice cube from the freezer, and plopped it into her wine. "But I just don't know --"

"Will you stop with the ice cubes?" Lauren asked. She laughed.

"What?"

"You always do that and it's so weird," Lauren said. "It's a hick thing to do."

Julie nearly spit out her wine.

"How is it a hick thing?"

Lauren turned back to the vegetables.

"It just is," she said. "It's so weird."

They laughed a little more. Then the laughing was over and Lauren turned to Julie again.

"I worry about you sometimes," Lauren said.

Julie frowned, smiled.

"Because I put ice in my wine?"

Julie laughed.

Lauren didn't.

"You know what I mean," Lauren said.

...

That Friday night, Julie went to a bar with Lauren and her boyfriend, Tyler. The bar was called the Furnace. It was dimly lit and everything in the place was made of dark wood. The bar was around the corner from Tyler's apartment. Julie and Lauren took two trains to get there. Julie sat on a stool and leaned against the wall and Lauren sat beside her near the aisle.

"I'll get the first round," Tyler said, and went to the bar to order some Scottish beer Julie had never heard of. Julie tried to find it on the menu, but couldn't. She looked up and caught Lauren's eye.

"Are you going to get food?" Lauren asked.

"No," Julie said. "Are you?"

Lauren shook her head. A minute later, Tyler returned with the beer and sat down across from them on the other side of the table.

"Cheers," Tyler said.

They all clinked glasses and drank. The beer was dark and tasted like coffee.

"I like this bar," Lauren said after a little while.

Julie nodded, even though she didn't like this bar.

"I come here to read sometimes," Tyler said. He worked from home as a copy editor for a trade journal, but had, ever since Lauren met him a little more than a year ago, been three-quarters of the way through writing a play that he hadn't let anyone see a page of.

Lauren once told Julie she wished he loved her as much as she loved him.

Julie wanted to say that she felt love only in retrospect, only as a memory.

They talked about a shooting that had occurred in Tyler's neighborhood the previous night. It had been all the way over by the other

Blue Line stop, but Tyler said he could actually hear the gunshots. He said it like he was proud of it, like he'd won something.

After a few minutes, his phone vibrated on the table. He looked at the screen.

"It's Lou," he said to Lauren. "They're at the Patio."

"Do you want to go?" Lauren asked.

"I'm cool hanging here with you guys," he said.

Lauren looked at Julie.

"What do you think?" she said.

"I don't know," Julie said. "Whatever."

"Yeah?" Tyler said.

Julie finished her beer with one huge, final sip.

"It's up to you guys," she said.

Tyler looked at Lauren.

...

It was a cool, breezy summer night.

"This is a perfect night," Tyler said.

The patio was three blocks away. Julie had never been there before, but Lauren said she would like it. Lauren was her best friend and cared about her more than anyone ever had, but sometimes – particularly around Tyler – she could confuse what Julie liked with what she liked.

When they arrived, a bouncer checked their IDs. Tyler and Lauren were admitted, but Julie was stopped.

"This really you?" the bouncer asked. He had the skyline tattooed on his huge arm. It made her want a tattoo of her own.

"Yeah," she said.

He lifted his eyes from her card to her, then looked back at the card.

"What's your birthday?"

"Julie?" Lauren said from the doorway. "What's going on?"

"May 23rd," Julie said to the bouncer.

"She's older than I am," Lauren said.

He turned to Lauren, then to Julie again, and handed the ID back to her.

"You look different," he said.

"Thanks," Julie said, and walked inside.

"Prick," Lauren said.

"I liked his tattoo," Julie replied as they made their way through the crowded bar toward a booth in the back. The place was dark and loud with music and voices. They spotted Tyler and followed him to the booth where his friends were sitting and stood around it.

"I didn't see it," Lauren said.

"It was cool," Julie said.

"Hey," said a guy with long, greasy hair. He wore tan shorts, a blue button-down, and brown boat shoes.

"Lou," Tyler said. "This is Lauren's friend Julie."

Lou stood up halfway and shook her hand.

"Hey," he said. "I'm Lou."

"Julie," she said.

"What took you so long?" Tyler asked.

"The guy almost didn't let her in," Lauren said.

"Who?" Lou asked.

"The bouncer guy at the door," Lauren said. "He thought she had a fake."

"He said I look different," Julie said.

Lou smiled.

"Can I see?" he asked.

"Sure," Julie said. She took out her wallet and handed him the ID. He looked at it and back at her and back at the card again, just as the bouncer had.

"You do look different," he said, smiling.

"I do?"

"Yeah," he said. "Maybe it's the hair? I don't know. I can't place it." He handed the ID back to her. "You look great either way," he said.

Tyler and Lauren went to the bar to get a round. Julie stood silently by the booth and watched people move on the dance floor.

"So," Lou said. "How do you two know each other?"

"Lauren?" Julie said. "We're roommates. We went to college together."

"Cool," Lou said.

Then they went quiet again. Julie watched people dance. Lou looked at her and past her.

"I'm sorry," he said after a minute. "What was your name again?"

"Julie," Julie said.

"Julie," he said. "I'm Lou."

...

Julie left Lou's the next morning. She went to the park. A series of copper, human-like statues stood across a lane of grass from one another, mirroring each other's varied poses. She walked around them, then between them, and then sat on a bench in the shade.

Then she left the park and walked to the beach. Gulls squawked and flew and dove at the shore. Julie took off her shoes and walked in the sand. The cold clean water lapped at her ankles. Kids ran screaming into the lake, their skin purpling like frozen chicken breasts. The sky was blue and cloudless and nearly indistinguishable from the water where they met at the horizon. She took off her overshirt and lay on the sand in her tank top. She fell asleep and dreamed of ice. She woke up shivering in an early afternoon breeze.

She started home. A couple blocks away from her train stop, she saw a woman reading the palm of a middle-aged man. The woman wore a thick gray shawl, a dark bandana, and a patch over her right eye. Though she was thin, she stood with the kind of hunched posture Julie typically associated with stout women.

"Rich, what are you doing?" the man's wife asked.

"Can't you see?" he said. "She's going to predict my future."

"No no," the old woman said, her voice scratchy and accented. "No predict. I *see* your future. I see it and tell."

"She's seeing my future," the man said, nudging his son with his elbow. The small boy laughed. The mother grabbed his hand.

The old woman held the man's hand in hers, running her fingers over the creases in his palm, staring hard at it as though it were a map. When Julie got closer, the woman looked up. Their gazes met. The woman's eye was milky blue. Her face wrinkled into a kind smile. Julie smiled, too, but just with her lips, and then looked down at her feet.

...

Julie and Mike finished having sex and lay on top of her sheets, cooling off.

"You got some sun," Mike said to Julie. "Looks great."

"It's sunburn," she said.

"Yeah," Mike said. "But it's *your* sunburn."

Julie groaned and rolled over so that she was turned away from him. She faced her bookshelf, which was filled with books she hadn't read in years and all manner of tiny knick-knacks she no longer had use for. Clothes that she no longer liked spilled out of her closet and drawers, as did shoes that were breaking at the soles and stained with street-salt from the previous winter.

"I want to have a yard sale," Julie said.

"OK," Mike said, like it was his yard, too. Like either of them had a yard.

"I'm tired," she said.

Neither Mike nor Julie said anything for a little while. Then, Mike rolled onto his side, too, and pulled her body to his so that they were spooning.

"I like you," he said.

She relaxed her body into his and rested her hand on his hand, but did not respond.

"Do you like me?" he asked.

"No," she replied.

"You don't?"

"No," she said. She turned to face him, they kissed, and she pet his perfect eyebrows with her thumbs. "I hate you."

...

"I'm cold to him," Julie said.

She drank Jack and Coke. Lauren sat on the other end of the couch and flipped through channels on the TV.

"I like him," Julie said. "I don't know what it is."

"Is it just him?" Lauren asked. "Or is it with other people, too?"

"I'm not sure," Julie said.

Lauren turned on tennis and muted the TV. She turned to Julie and put the remote down on the cushion between them.

"I guess what I'm asking is, is the problem with him or with you?"

Julie thought about it. On TV, the tennis players volleyed back and forth. They looked more like teammates than competitors.

"I don't know," Julie said.

Lauren looked at Julie for a long time. Julie didn't return Lauren's look, but watched her out of her periphery, trying to discern the expression on her friend's face. It was confusion or worry. Soon, Lauren turned back to the TV and turned the sound back up. The players made amative groans when they struck the ball.

"I've always liked you with Mike," Lauren said.

"Yeah?" Julie said.

"Yeah," Lauren said. "So for whatever that's worth."

...

It was Saturday. Julie lay her clothes on boxes she'd set out in front of her building and stacked books and movies in the grass. She and Mike sat on her front steps all day. Cars slowed down but didn't stop. People casually went through her stuff, smiled, and kept going down the sidewalk. Occasionally, someone would buy a tee-shirt or a scarf. She sold her old purse and a copy of *One Hundred Years of Solitude* that she'd started numerous times but never finished. Huge stretches of time passed without anyone coming by at all.

"We should have advertised," Julie said.

"Maybe," Mike said. He put his hand on her knee and she put her hand over his.

In the evening, she gave up and she and Mike went upstairs. He opened two beers and they sat on the floor of her living room, peeling price stickers off the things she'd failed to sell.

"Hey," she said, her hands interrupting the work his were doing on one of her old umbrellas. He looked up at her. "I'm sorry," she said.

He smiled and grabbed her hands.

"For what?" he asked.

"I'm just sorry. For a lot of things." She pulled her hands away from his and picked up a bunch of the crumpled orange stickers they'd strewn on the hardwood. "I mean, it was a long day," she said.

"No problem," Mike said. "It was great."

He kissed her on the neck. She smiled and watched as he took a big sip of his beer and returned to the umbrella. With his short nails he picked away at the sticker. She wondered what he saw in her. She wondered why his sweetness never relented against the weight of her coldness.

He looked up and smiled.

"What?" he said.

"Nothing," she replied. She drank from her beer and returned to the pile of clothes.

...

Julie was on the Red Line, on her way to work. She wore a gray skirt, white blouse, and dark sunglasses. She stood gripping a rubber handle and swayed with the veering of the crowded train as it rumbled from stop to stop toward the Loop, all faces turned down into books or phones or newspapers, or watching the shell game being operated by a man in an orange Hawaiian shirt.

"Follow the ball, follow the ball," he said, shuffling a bean under bottle caps on the piece of cardboard on his lap. "Who sees it, who sees it."

Julie followed the ball as it appeared and disappeared beneath caps and rotated positions on the board.

"Fools," an old woman said, shaking her head at the crowd.

Suddenly, the train came to a halt.

A man in a gray suit standing near Julie let out his breath.

"Shit," he said. He looked over at Julie.

"You said it," she said.

There was a beeping sound and a voice over the monitor announced that the train was stopped for an emergency on the tracks.

Julie angled herself to look out the narrow windows of the train car. The next stop was maybe a hundred-fifty yards down the way.

"He jumped!" someone a few seats down yelled.

"God," an old woman said. "Glory be."

Julie tried to see what was going on, but could only see police standing between the people waiting on the platform and the electric tracks. It was a sunny morning. A flock of birds broke over the top of the low-slung buildings and power lines. She moved from the window.

"Follow the ball, follow the ball," the man still said. "Follow the ball, follow the ball."

"Fools," the old woman repeated.

The man in the gray suit looked at Julie.

She looked at him.

...

Bernice called Julie into her office. She said she liked her a lot, but this was becoming a problem. She said she'd given Julie enough chances, but that she had proven herself unreliable.

"That's horrible," Mike said over dinner that night. "I'm so sorry."

"Yeah," Julie said. "Well."

She broke a piece of bread off the loaf and sponged the olive oil with it. Mike poured more of the house red into their glasses and cleared space for the waiter to put their plates in front of them.

He ate riso tonnato.

She ate stuffed eggplant.

On the walk home from the restaurant, Mike took Julie's hand.

"I've got my own little work situation going on," Mike said.

"Yeah?" Julie said.

They passed by a row of bars. People smoked in the doorways.

"Yeah," Mike said. "You remember Monica?"

Julie did. She had met her at a barbeque in May. It had been unseasonably cold and Monica had come unprepared for the weather. She'd had to borrow a sweater from Mike's boss, who was hosting the barbeque.

"She asked me what my situation was," Mike said. "She asked me if I was seeing anybody."

He squeezed Julie's hand and looked at her, smiling expectantly. He seemed to be waiting for her to say something. When she didn't, he said: "What should I have said?"

Julie shrugged.

"Say whatever you want," she said.

Mike kept on smiling, but now it was a little dimmer, a little more desperate; it was as if his face had become stuck that way.

"What do you say?" Mike asked. "I mean, what would you have said?"

"I don't know," Julie said, frustrated.

They kept on walking. When they got to her building, they stopped. She turned to face him and he turned away, staring up at an almost full moon.

"I'm not sure if I can keep this up," Mike said.

"What do you mean?" Julie said.

"I mean, I just don't know," he replied.

"Mike," she said.

He looked at her and past her.

...

Julie waited for a train.

It was a warm night. A breeze blew by on the platform. A full moon hung in the sky above the top of the brick buildings. A guy took a picture of it on his phone. Julie leaned in behind him and looked at the screen.

"Strawberry Moon," he said.

Julie nodded. A train came.

...

She arrived at Lou's. Julie sat cross-legged around his coffee table. A group of them played a drinking game. Julie pulled a nine from the deck of cards that had been spread around a can of Miller in the middle.

"Bust a rhyme," Lou said.

"Duck," Julie said. They went around the circle, each person making a rhyme – puck, suck, fuck – until it got back to Julie. She thought – there were a million words that rhymed – but could not think of one.

"Drink," they said to Julie.

She laughed and drank. Then she said, "Stuck. God damn it, I should've said stuck."

"Too late," Lou said.

...

Lou's roommate, Chris, came into the living room.

"They're about to start the fireworks," he said.

Chris had the build of a runner and a head shaved clean and bald. His jeans and tee-shirt fit him well and he had nice, welcoming eyes.

Lou shut off the lights and everyone headed out onto the balcony. The sky was dark, except for the light of the moon. Julie leaned against the railing next to Chris.

"It's a Strawberry Moon," she said.

He smiled at her. His teeth were white and nice.

"Right," he said.

She smiled back at him.

They waited quietly for what seemed like a while. Then, a thin shadow shot up into the sky and burst into a bright umbrella of blue, dissolving into little ghosts of light raining down over the lake. Everyone clapped and cheered.

"So how's it going with you?" Chris asked. "Need another drink?"

...

Julie and Chris lay head to foot on his bedroom floor.

"I'm sorry to hear that," he said.

They were quiet a long time.

"I'm a hard person to be with," she replied.

They kept laying there, staring up at the ceiling. Julie wondered if her feet smelled.

"I'm not so easy myself," Chris said. He sat up. "It's just – it's just so hard, you know?"

Julie sat up, too. She nodded.

"Yeah," she said. She scooched over to him and lay her head on his shoulder. They sat like that. They kissed. He leaned up against the end of his bed and Julie sat on top of him. They kept kissing.

Chris pulled away.

"I can't," he said. "I mean I shouldn't."

Julie nodded.

"I'm seeing someone," Chris said.

He lay flat on his back. Julie moved down and lay her head on his shoulder.

"Is that OK?" he asked.

"Sure," Julie replied.

Chris fell asleep. For a long time, Julie watched his chest rise and fall with breaths and exhalations. Then, she slid out from underneath his arm and went to the window beside his bed and peered through the blinds.

She looked out at the city, but saw only her own reflection in the dark window. She heard the sound of voices in the living room, everyone still talking and drinking. She pulled her phone from her pocket and texted Mike.

"I miss you," she wrote.

She sat on the bed and looked at Chris sleeping on the floor. He looked like a kid, like a little kid who'd fallen asleep on the carpet during story time. She reclined on his bed and checked her phone for a text from Mike. She fell asleep.

...

Light poured in through the window. Julie was alone in the bedroom. Her phone was dead. She wondered if Mike had texted her back.

She sat up and found her shoes on the floor and slipped them onto her feet. Her head felt heavy and she sat there for a minute steadying herself before standing up to leave the room. The apartment was a mess of empties and open chip bags and discarded paper plates. Chris was asleep on the couch. She crept to the door and quietly left for her apartment.

The world was awash in yellow sunlight and the city filled with people. They took pictures in the shadows of giant buildings and asked strangers for directions, jogging and pushing strollers and walking dogs and holding hands and begging for change. Julie simultaneously felt at home and homesick.

She was a few blocks from her train stop when she saw the old woman again. The palm reader. She stood with her back to a building and scratched at something on her thick wool shawl. When Julie got closer to her, the woman turned to her and her face lit with recognition, as if at an old acquaintance, as if at a granddaughter.

Julie stopped in front of her.

"Child," the woman said, opening her arms in a gesture of embrace.

Julie felt heavy. She wanted to fall into the old woman and sleep nestled against her soft body. Instead, she held out her hand. She held out her hand and the old woman smiled and took it in hers.

Julie looked at the woman.

The woman smiled and traced the creases in her palm.

THE MESSAGE FROM THE CROCHETED DRESS
by Maggie Gleason

I had been in San Cristobal de las Casas before. It's a town with rectangular channels of short, rainbow colored buildings and cobble stone streets located in the shallow valley of a mountain range in southern Mexico. Almost six years to the current date, I was there. I had visited this place with a close friend, who had lived and traveled extensively throughout Mexico after college, picking her way across the country's vast natural diversities and rich history. I had felt so lucky to have had the opportunity to journey with her to this land. I thought of her as the ultimate travel expert, as she was fluent in Spanish and knowledgeable of locals only transportation options, like riding a small, rickety bus to a near by town, filled with chickens, children and amused locals, that thoroughly enjoyed placing the live chickens on the white girls' laps. She traveled with trust and an energetic connection to her surroundings. She led me to small, delicious food vendors, life enhancing live music and colorful, intricate markets filled with bright, hand stitched textiles, beaded jewelry and kind, talented artisans. Always present, encouraging and directing your attention to the next sensory experience. And knowing the additional touches that were needed to propel you into a more well rounded experience was a speciality. Knowing that a guided boat tour along the Sumidero Canyon could be slightly enhanced with a cold beer bought off a floating snack bar, knowing that climbing to the very top of a hidden waterfall in the jungle, even though you were scared of slipping, falling,

breaking an ankle or your head, could change your perspective of the surrounding nature, of where you were. And knowing that the purchasing of a pair of earrings from a local artist would be remembered more vividly paired with a conversation you have with them about the procedure of their work. These were some examples. Small nuances of life magnified and integrated to increase your pleasure. It seemed that rich life experiences were always right at her finger tips, magically appearing with a quick notice, turn of the corner and a smile. I longed to travel with this same type of peace and oneness with a place. That energy. I had even given up a job opportunity to go on that trip to Mexico with my friend, as my soul ever so subtly told me that someday, this trip would have more significant meaning in my life than my brand new career, as the ink on my Master's degree was still wet with newness. And now, I was back there with my partner, who I loved, trying to fulfill my dream of being the new age Indiana Jones, the ultimate world explorer, with my hat and whip positioned just so. Calm, steady, observant, inquisitive, present. Ready to conquer and to prove myself to myself. Can I be the unique, travel shifting person that I envisioned in my mind's eye?

Even though I strived in my unconscious dreams to be a world explorer, to see it all, there was a mystic about Mexico that made me want to explore this country first. As a young child, I had an innate fascination with the country, that encompassed the food, music, textiles and the language. Something in my soul was drawn to it, felt immediately connected to it. And so my interest began with a restaurant. My parents used to take me to a place called "Marita's Cantina", a small, Mexican themed restaurant in the suburb of Philadelphia. The exterior of the building was white, plain, with dark, stormy windows that inhibited your ability to see inside. I think my parents avoided trying it for many years, for fear it was some basement like dive bar filled with clouds of smoke. But upon entering, I felt transported. The swirled, plaster walls were painted colors of warm rose and saffron, which fell upon the large squares of terra-cotta tiles on the floors. I used to pretend the tiles were a hopscotch board, drawn out of chalk. And as I jumped and skipped across the cold floor, I made sure to not touch any part of the cracks as we waited for our table. My eyes were always drawn to the colorful paper flags that criss crossed along the ceiling, with detailed cut outs representing all the colors of the rainbow. I wished for my room to be covered in those flags, giving me to keep a small piece of this atmosphere. Salsa and chips were exciting. My heavily chili spiced french fries an amazement of culinary expertise. Sometimes a Mariachi band would play in the restaurant. Five men with large guitars and trumpets, studded suits and booming voices would wander around to the different tables, and serenade the patrons, as they sipped their frozen margaritas with salt. Due to my fear of being noticed that had already taken hold of me at the young age of 4, I never wanted them to come over to our table. I would hide my face, and immediately start to feel overwhelmed, like, "Ugh, people are looking at me". However, I found the sound of the music so intriguing, the high pitched, quick, yet soothing notes. I enjoyed it, but felt strange in front of my parents doing so, never really knowing if it was ok to enjoy something so much that was so foreign.

Another childhood fascination with Mexico came in the form of a dress. My favorite dress. I had been gifted a short, white, hand crocheted dress from a family friend, a hippie hand me down from the 70s. I was told it was a Mexican wedding dress, and it was my most prized possession. I wore it every chance I could, begging my mom to let me wear it everyday, sometimes to bed. And even in situations where wearing white could be problematic, I would strongly insist. "I have to wear it!" This stubborn stance would always then result in a freak out about any tiny drop of dirt that settled into the fabric, which then needed to be hand scrubbed just right. My ultimate goal was to keep it pristine forever. One time at the creek, I was wearing my Mexican wedding dress, and as I was climbing up the slippery rocks back onto the gravel path, I fell and skinned my knee, a large, wide scrape that was dripping bright red blood down my leg. I remember crying not because I was dramatic, or because of the pain. I cried because if I got one drop of blood on my white, crocheted dress, it would be a tragedy. I hiked my dress up to my neck, and ran to the car, demanding that we immediately go home and for my dad to drive fast, so I could save my irreplaceable garment. I remember the day when I discovered I had out grown it. I was no longer a 4 year old girl, but a 9 year old, and my mom tried to explain to me that it was inappropriate to wear a dress where the hem line was at the same level as your underwear. And, as I was not yet as fashion savvy as I am now, knowing that all that dress needed to morph into a top was a perfectly good pair of legging, I had to let it go. Giving up that dress, knowing that it could no longer be mine, was a sad day. There was something in my soul that wanted to cling to that dress forever. I wanted to wear it until the crochet split and frayed off of my body. In fact, it had already started to by the time I painfully placed it in the good will pile. This tiny imprint of a desire from a piece of clothing. Instead of wanting to wear jeans and a Minnie Mouse t-shirt, I wanted more.

More crochet, more texture, more evidence that I was more than a sheltered suburbanite.

And the different language, something that was both loved and feared simultaneously, was my next exploration many adult years later. I had started taking Spanish lessons 3 months prior to leaving for my self guided tour to Mexico, and I was finding that communication was a struggle. The vocabulary, the grammar, the word order, that I understood. As long as I was completing a structured lesson, where everything was predictable, I felt OK, semi-confident. I mean, in reality, I felt like a 4 year old learning to read their first book by themselves, but still, I was trying. I was doing it. However, toss a spontaneous question into the barrage of wordplay, and I became frozen with the lose of all words and functioning. It also did not help watching my teacher's facial expressions, staring at me with concern and disbelief that I person's brain could melt out their ear so fast. Surely, this would all go away when I actually entered the country, right? It had to.

Especially because it had been a life long dream of mine to speak another language, to be bilingual, even trilingual. As a child, I became so perplexed when I heard other languages spoken. Like, how could people know what each other were saying? I used to try and make up my own languages, creating nonsense words, and assigning them different meanings in my head. I would then try to use these words in conversation, but obviously the adults around me wouldn't know what I was talking about, and would quickly try to divert my attention to something else, as they surely worried that I was insane and hearing voices. Oh how I wish my parents would have put me in a child based language class, since it was not offered at my elementary school. And when I got to high school, the first opportunity where a foreign language was offered, I was encouraged to take Italian. I planned to continue learning it through college, fulfilling my soul dream of becoming a rich, cultured person, who could speak another language. However, that dream swiftly died during college, when I attended my first higher level Italian class, only to realize that I could not understand a single word. My teacher spoke, and my heart stopped. I was unable to form one single sentence or understand one short, simple question. I quickly dropped that class, as the whole hour was filled with body numbing panic. And so, 12 years later, I began my slow pilgrimage towards a skill that had been an intense obstacle for me.

Now, Paul and I had been in Mexico for almost two weeks. To prepare for the language barrier and my inability to think, I had tried to anticipate every situation, sentence or question that I would need to utter. I brought with me my Spanish dictionary, all of my notes and worksheets. I studied on the plane. I studied in the cab. On the bus. On the beach. But I was finding the hope of my super natural ability to easily communicate with the local people quickly disintegrating. During all verbal interactions thus far on the trip, instead of genuinely listening to the person I was talking to, I would immediately panic, struggling to pick up a word or two. All learned information would leave me, my brain paralyzed, unable to locate a single Spanish word to respond. And also, everyone seemed to talk so fast! I could not separate one word from another. Each Spanish response formed one long, compounded word. I was not prepared for that. Good thing that Paul is a lot calmer than me. He, of course, easily adapted and could decipher meaning through the context clues of the situation, and translate the general message to me, even though he was not the one who devoted loads of time and effort to learning this language. "The man said they are cleaning the room, and we should come back in two hours." Oh….OK. Why didn't I assume that? During social interactions, my head was usually in my hands, leaning on whatever table or counter was in front of me in total overwhelm. My eyes always wide and glazed over. Plus, it didn't help that even in English, in my everyday reality, when someone spoke very fast or mumbled, and I couldn't understand them, I would panic as well. Or my mind would immediately go to self-consciousness, as in they must be talking about me, or trying to deceive me in some way. This was never the reality, but being able to communicate and having knowledge of exactly what was going on in a situation gave me control and steadiness, in a world that I always considered out to get me. Unpredictability was never appreciated.

We arrived at the bus station in San Cristobal in the morning, after spending the night in transit. After we retrieved our backpacks, we walked toward the line of waiting cabs. It was still early, but the edges of the city were already bustling with activity. Cars, trucks and bicycles filled the streets. Vendors were selling hot coffee and tamales for breakfast, surrounded by a cloud of gasoline fumes and spices. We got into a cab, and I told the driver the name of our hotel. As we began driving, he started to point out various city monuments and relay the history about each one; a church here, a statue there, the mountains in the near distance. And as much as I longed to ingest all of the information about where we were, to learn facts about the culture, to really help my spirit to absorb into this place, my mind could not process the Spanish language. Nor was there room in my brain for anything but the constant grasp towards a second of comprehension. I could not relax. I kept cycling through a series of negative statements, based in the depths of my total overwhelm. "What did he say? That sounded like one giant word. This is hopeless. What am I doing here?" I slumped back in my seat, needing to zone out. I'm not a traveler. I'm not one with the world. I am a wanna-be. A wanna-be adventurer, who has no business being anywhere but the same small dot on the map where she has always existed... Then, the cab driver spoke again. He told me that the

hotel was not located on a street that he could drive on. And without any extended processing time, panic or grasping for words that were quickly evaporating, I responded, "Está bien. Podemos caminar." "It's ok. We can walk", I said. Such a simple sentence. Such a simple message, yet it meant everything. A warm wave of pride flooded within me. Wow, I just did it. I just communicated with someone in Spanish, in real time, in a real way, and it felt normal. Had my brain just played a trick on me, or had a portal in my brain just pushed itself into finally opening? In that moment, I felt powerful, like I had muscles that moved a large boulder out of my path. I had experienced many other moments of joy on that trip, but this one, surrounding my brief integration into a foreign language was incredibly satisfying. A step on the confidence ladder was climbed during that 30 second encounter.

Now, this does not mean that I was suddenly tapped by a magical being, and became a fluent Spanish speaker in that moment. During the rest of the trip, I continued to struggle to communicate quite frequently. In fact, during our last day in Mexico City, we were approached by two people, who asked us for directions in Spanish. My first thought was, "Why are they asking me?' My second thought was that I couldn't believe I looked like I knew where things were in one of the largest cities in the world. Did I look like I belonged? However, my internal emotion was total panic, and I uttered, "I didn't understand", using only English. The couple looked at me blankly, then caught each other's eye and snickered. "You should try to learn Spanish", one of them remarked as they quickly walked away. I was stunned at the insult, and as the words quickly pierced through my body, I started bawling. Walking and crying, like I had been split in two, because I was trying! The whole trip, I had not once allowed my frustrated internal dialogue out into the open. I had kept all of my feelings of mild embarrassment to myself, and tried to only celebrate the small communication victories out loud. I had realized that this was a totally normal learning curve, but I still needed an emotional release, as I was exhausted.

Even English, my native language, can overwhelm me, as there are many instances, while speaking english, where I have no idea what a person means. Maybe they mumbled or used a word that I didn't know. Maybe I didn't hear them correctly or misunderstood them. These kinds of communication breakdowns fill me with such anxiety, for the ability to communicate is such a necessary comfort for me. In order to feel safe, you must always be able to read a situation accurately, right? Otherwise, you might never know what someone could be plotting in your moments of confusion, right? To say I have unwarranted trust issues would be an understatement. However, this is really how much language means to me. This is about the magic of understanding words that, as a young child, seemed to be the dialogue in a make-believe story. This is how much exploring new countries and cultures means to me, as my fascinations as a child most definitely have been giving me hints as an adult. It is important to me to no longer let the weight of my adult life stand in my way, like a boulder that is sinking into the mud on my path. Because in reality, currently, I am still that little girl in the white crocheted dress, exploring the creek while eating tacos on a terra cotta floor, dreaming of how to explore new lands to finally become understood.

About the Author:

Maggie Gleason is a Speech-Language Pathologist with over 10 years of experience, and I live and work in Philadelphia, PA.

LOST TIME: A ROAD TRIP JOURNAL
by Jordan King

May 19, 2016

We had planned for ninety days. Thirty to sell and sixty to close. If it went to plan we'd be ready right when our new house was. But our house sold the first day to the first person who saw it. Above asking price no less. We asked to postpone the closing, but the buyers couldn't wait. They had their own schedule to maintain.

My office was a laptop, and my wife, Jody, homeschooled our nine year old son, Logan. So we put everything that wouldn't fit in our car into storage and took a six thousand mile road trip to kill the time.

I had to make a last minute doctor's appointment and made a desperate appeal to my doctor to give me more pain killers for my chronic back pain so I could actually function during our trip. He gave me way more than I really needed and I should have known better than to take them all with me without mentioning it to Jody.

Logan was the best traveler. He didn't complain or ask if we were almost there. He looked out the window at the landscape passing by and asked questions about mountains and buffalo, about my childhood and why I ever wanted to leave.

I hadn't been to Colorado in five years.

Before that there was another five year gap. The six years before that, I was scattered all over the country and across the Atlantic. Fixing airplanes, shining boots, and saying *yes, sir* and *yes, ma'am.*

As we drove through my old home town, I barely recognized the place. Everything was different. The Colorado I grew up in was open, empty and quiet. By then the town was nothing but traffic and noise. The hills and fields I wandered as a kid were gone. In their place was an endless expanse of subdivisions and shopping districts, each one a copy of the last. The only hint of wilderness was the occasional coyote or bear that wandered into a neighborhood following the smell of wasted food in lines of blue trash bins. Every road was brake lights. Every lake and river crowded by fishermen. Every trail was torn up with overlapped footprints.

May 24, 2016

The whole morning in the car on the way to Grand Teton National Park, the base of my skull throbbed and my vision blurred. In the spot I knew too well between my shoulder blades, something was wrong. The discs were over-inflated balloons, impinging on nerves.

My right hand was numb and in bursts would come back to life just long enough to burn.

We pulled into the parking lot. The distinct mountain tops, like the tilted tip of Gandalf's hat, were covered in low clouds, but the beauty of the surrounding area and the lake at the base of the mountains was enough to make the stop memorable.

When I stepped out of the car, the back spasm I hoped wasn't coming took my breath away. Jody asked if I was okay. *Just stiff*, I lied.

I took a double dose of Percocet and muscle relaxers when Jody wasn't looking. I hid the pain to avoid ruining our day, but I also hid the excessive amount of medication from Jody in particular, who knew from years of experience that I lacked self-control.

I'm grateful for the pictures we took that day; otherwise I wouldn't remember a thing.

My back problems started in 2002 with a herniated disc; one too many times contorting my body inside an aircraft wheel well or carrying a hundred pound toolbox all over the flight line.

In the years that followed the diagnoses piled up and my symptoms intensified exponentially. At first the myriad of doctors I saw all agreed I was too young to be having such problems and that it was too early for them to perform any kind of surgery. A few years of failed treatments later they all told me it was too late for surgery and I'd be dealing with the symptoms for the rest of my life, barring some new medical discovery.

We hiked trails for about two hours before I had to stop for a break. I took off the backpack I was carrying and set it in the rocks along the shore of the lake. I remember the quiet and how fresh the air was, but at that point I was so consumed by the pain that very little of the beauty and tranquility seeped through my scattered frantic thoughts.

I took another dose of Percocet hours before I should have, and then turned around to grab the backpack so we could keep hiking, but Logan beat me to it.

What are you doing? I asked him.

Dad, I know you're hurting. I can see it on your face. Mom already has a bag. I can carry yours for a while. Really, it's not too heavy.

I couldn't make eye contact with Jody when Logan said that to me because I knew I'd start crying if I did, so I just thanked him, touched his freckle dusted cheek and continued down the trail. He carried the bag for me the rest of the day; he was adamant that I let him.

May 29, 2016

Our next destination was Missoula, Montana. The movie *A River Runs Through It* had been one of my favorites for a long time and for nearly twenty years I looked for an excuse to visit the town the movie was based in.

At the beginning of 2005 I was single, a few months from leaving the Air Force, and had plans to move to Missoula. I would attend grad school and get back to the natural world I had been missing since first leaving Colorado. My back hadn't yet developed into the nightmare it would become. By the end of that year I was married, had two adolescent daughters, and a baby boy on the way. No Missoula, no grad school. We moved to Moore, Oklahoma and I got an administrative job at the law school. It was a strange twist of fate, but a beautiful one.

The next ten years, though not even a whisper of what I had planned, were the best of my life, despite the constant pain. The girls had grown into wonderful women and moved out to pursue their own lives, and Logan was already a better person than I'd ever been.

As we crossed the state line into Montana, I looked at Jody then into the back seat where

Logan slept, not quite believing so much time had passed.

I could tell why Montana was called "Big Sky Country." It really did seem bigger than everywhere else, or that you were closer to it. There is probably a scientific explanation, but I never want to find out because it would take away the mystery and magic of its beauty.

Driving through Montana was like traveling back in time to the Colorado I grew up in. It was open, vast, and quiet. Every town was small, and slow, and polite nods from strangers on uncrowded sidewalks.

Glacier National Park was our last stop in Montana. The lake at the entrance of the park was the loveliest place I'd ever been.

A barely visible path off the main road led us to the shore of the lake. The beach wasn't sand, but pebbles the size of corn kernels, smooth as glass. Where the pebbles ended the mirror began. Two rows of evergreens, two stacks of mountains, two rows of clouds rolling across two skies. The three of us huddled together on the beach and mirrored the scene in our own way, with silence. There was a hint of breeze that put soft ripples in the water and gave the occasional tree cause to creak.

I took a small handful of those pebbles with me. Any time I'm overwhelmed by the noise and pace of the world I run my fingers over the smooth pebbles, close my eyes, and listen for the sound of that breeze.

June 2, 2016

On our way out of Montana we stopped for a break from the car. Even the rest stops were beautiful and empty. My back hurt. It was a dull, ever present realization. I hadn't experienced a symptom free day in over five years. By then I was grateful for symptom free hours in the day, and even those were rare.

Jody said that would make her go crazy and my response was to ask *what makes you think I haven't? Do I even resemble the man you first met?*

When I first met Jody I was confident, healthy and very active. I had dreams, goals, and the optimism to believe I could accomplish anything I set my mind to. By the time we had that conversation about symptom free hours I was completely broken down by years of constant pain. I still looked like the man she fell in love with, but felt like every other part of that person had vanished.

The pain wasn't bad when we got to the rest stop, just there, and after a failed attempt to convince myself I didn't need it, I took an extra dose of Percocet. My supply was getting too low, too soon, but I took them anyway.

Behind the small brick building with bathrooms, water fountains, and highway maps was a river. Jody made a phone call and plotted the rest of our trip to Buffalo, Wyoming while I walked with Logan to the river. We sat on the river bank and put our feet in the cool water. I held him in my lap, and rested my chin on the top of his head. His soft hair tickled my beard. Neither of us said a word, just looked at the water as it rolled across rocks until Jody said it was time to go.

We walked through the long green grass holding hands. Jody watched us; one hand shielded her eyes from the sun. We looked at each other and she smiled, the little one where the left side of her mouth curved up. *We made him* I thought and her smile widened.

There was no reason for choosing Buffalo, we just didn't want to drive further. The town had seen some desperate times. There were abandoned houses and decaying businesses down every street, but there were also signs of resurgence. A park near the cabin we stayed in was one of them. There were several tall slides, obstacle courses, baseball fields, and a new imagining of a tire swing. It was a massive steel octopus with chains for dangling tentacles and large multicolored plastic mold tires attached to the bottom of each chain. The whole contraption spun. I got it going fast enough to make Jody nervous and Logan squeal. A group of local kids wanted in on the fun, so I stopped it so they could each get on. They kept screaming *faster* and *more*. Their laughter was my fuel, and I kept going until I was exhausted, pouring sweat and grateful my back was quiet.

I was surprised I hadn't hurt myself, but it was always so unpredictable. One day I could play with Logan and feel fine, the next day I'd have a back spasm and be bed ridden for a week because I dried my hair too vigorously. Even though I was fine in the moment I knew there would be a price to pay later. At the time I didn't care because Logan had so much fun. I would care later.

The parents of the local kids on the octopus swing came over and talked to us. Everyone kind and welcoming and full of stories. They said the town had been revived when a fracking company came. That's why everyone was driving new cars, and new houses and chain restaurants were built in between the crumbling remnants of the old town.

The only thing missing is the girls, I said to Jody when we got back in the car. *I know* she said and instantly welled up. I felt bad for bringing them up, but their absence was weighing so heavily on my mind that day, and I'm sure she'd thought of them already anyway. It's still so hard to believe that they're grown and out in the world.

June 6, 2016

We made a pit stop in our old stomping grounds of Moore, Oklahoma. We didn't live there long, less than two years before moving to Ohio, but that's where Logan was born though he had no memory of it. The only real plans were to visit our old house and the hospital he was born in.

The first stop was to the hospital. Although a hospital was there, it was brand new and looked nothing like the hospital Logan was born in. A quick internet search showed us that the original hospital had been destroyed by a tornado the previous year. No one was killed, the warning systems there are top notch, but the room Logan was born in was gone forever.

Our old house was so small, smaller than I remembered, but there was so much laughter and happiness there.

A vivid memory hit me as we sat in our car outside that house. When it was time for Logan to start sleeping through the night, no more midnight feedings, we let him cry it out. Jody had already been through that twice, but for me it was a first, and it was harder than I imagined. He cried and we sat there listening, but only for a few minutes before he went back to sleep. He didn't cry in the night the next day or the next, or ever again.

As I sat in the car, remembering, Jody and Logan got out to take pictures. An unexpected wave of sadness hit me when I realized that Logan's sleep training was one of the few vivid memories I had from that house. I was on Oxycontin at the time. The crippling desperation of the pain, coupled with the memory erasing ability of that particular drug, especially when abused, left me with patches and shadows where the first eighteen months of Logan's life should have been.

When they got back in the car, I was bitter about the pain and how it invaded every aspect of my life. Soon the bitterness faded and turned into disgust with myself. I couldn't help the pain, couldn't stop the injury from happening, or the healing from going all sideways, but the missing years of Logan's life were entirely my fault. I had abused my prescriptions over the previous ten years to the point that I should have been dead, many times over.

My disgust turned to unmasked self-loathing when I thought of how many times I'd openly wished for death. But even in that moment of self-realization I still had drugs coursing through my blood stream. I had more drugs in my pocket, in the glove compartment, in my duffle bag in the trunk, and in my toiletry bag inside that. I wondered, and not for the last time, just what exactly I was going to do about that.

June 10, 2016

We'd travelled through fourteen states and over five thousand miles. We'd been in wilderness, small towns, and big cities, and spent time with three generations of family members.

Our last destination was Fort Walton Beach, Florida. We rented a condo on the oceanfront and didn't even consider getting into the car again for a whole week.

We bought boogie boards and rode the waves, built sand castles, and laid on the beach for hours on end. Every night we'd huddle together on the sand, watch the sun go down and listen to the waves. Rows of pink and orange light shot out of the western horizon and mixed with the darkening blue sky that revealed distant stars. Tight formations of birds flew overhead. The waves crashed on an endless loop, the milky foam slipped to our feet buried in the sand, and then retreated to start all over again.

My back had gotten progressively worse throughout the week and it got harder to ignore and pretend like everything was okay. Our last night there, as we enjoyed the quiet peace of each other's company during one final sunset, another back spasm came. It was even worse than the one that happened at Grand Teton, worse, in fact, than any spasm I'd had in years.

It started slow. The back of my neck got hot and my face started to tingle in waves that mimicked the ocean. The muscles in between my shoulder blades suddenly cramped and I heard a pop. A jolt of electricity went from my spine to my fingertips and my vision doubled. My spine felt like it was wrapped with barbed wire and every movement, every breath, was a mistake I could never take back.

We went back to our room and against Jody's wishes I slowly hobbled across the street to the liquor store and bought the strongest rum I could find.

I laid down with Logan on his bed and listened to him talk about his favorite parts of the trip and how grateful he was to have experienced it, but that he was also eager to get settled into our new home and play his guitar through the amp again. We made sure there was space on the road trip for his guitar, but it just wasn't the same without it being plugged in and turned up high. I kissed him goodnight, told him how much I loved him, closed his door and went into the kitchen to make a drink.

I took a triple dose of Percocet, a double muscle relaxer, and half a dozen Ibuprofen. They numbed me a bit, but on the inside I was still raging. I didn't really want to die, that's what I tried to convince myself of anyway, but if I happened to catch a break and never wake up, then I would've been fine with that.

When I woke up in the morning, Jody was shaking me and crying. Logan sat against the wall of our bedroom hugging his knees, looking at me, crying the same desperate frightened tears his mother was. I guess they'd been trying to wake me for a while.

It had taken over a decade of abuse, several involuntary detox sessions, countless lies and arguments with Jody, but the looks on their faces that morning changed me for good, though I knew it would be a long road ahead.

I can still see their expressions. The mixture

of confusion, anger and fear in their eyes. It's a visual that will always follow me.

but you're only making it worse. Wake the fuck up.

June 12, 2016

First sober twenty four hour period in five, maybe six years. It was a strange, long, maddeningly uncomfortable day but it wasn't as bad as I expected and, unlike many days before it, I could remember everything. I didn't tell Jody I was trying to get through the day unmedicated, mostly because I thought I'd fail.

I was using a mixed bag of Percocet, muscle relaxers, marijuana and alcohol which meant that I hadn't taken any one thing long enough to have to detox. Having gone through that before I was grateful for the reprieve.

One of the many things that convinced me Jody was the woman I wanted to spend the rest of my life with was her complete disinterest in playing games. We had always been equals and I could count on her to not bullshit or manipulate me.

She hadn't said much to me since we left Florida. What needed saying couldn't be said around Logan. When he got into the shower at the last hotel we stayed in before returning to Ohio, she finally spoke up.

She said she knew that I'd lost time and that I'd suffered. She said that all the years of watching me go through the pain and treatments and doctors and finding nothing more than a perpetuation of the misery had all but broken her. Then she told me that even though I'd lost so much already, I was lining up to lose everything. She took a deep breath and looked into my eyes for a long time without saying a word. Then she gave me the best, most honest, most Jody advice I could have asked for.

Now with that said, stop being such a pussy. We need you. You're in a bad situation,

June 20, 2016

Closed on the new house. Logan was so excited. The first thing he wanted to do, after picking out his bedroom, was plug in his amp to test out the new acoustics. Jody and I sat against the wall in the empty living room and listened to him play *Thunderstruck*.

I had heard of people who seemed born fit for something, whether it was music, or math or sports, but I had never known anyone like that personally until Logan started playing guitar. It won't surprise me if he's playing in stadiums one day.

As I listened to him play, I realized that I wanted to be around to find out. The pain was a daily struggle. It never stopped, but I could do a much better job of managing it. I could manage it without substance abuse, without putting myself in a position to wonder if I'd wake up. I wanted to wake up the next day. Wanted it more than anything. I just didn't fully realize it until that moment.

I could rarely hide anything from Jody, and right then she seemed to be reading my mind. She said that I'd get through it, that it would get easier, that she believed in me. I nodded and kissed her, uncertain of why she believed in me, and for the first time in years I started to see some of that old brightness return to her eyes when she looked at me.

Entire chunks of Logan's childhood and the girls' adolescence are missing. They float somewhere in the shadows of memory and I can never find my way through them. The pain I can deal with. It's been with me long enough that I expect it to be there when I wake up in the morning the same way I expect the sun to rise, but that lost time will always haunt me.

About the Author:

Jordan King is a creative writing MFA student at Miami of Ohio. Lost Time: A Road Trip Journal is a formal experiment; he wrote it as a series of journal entries. It's about a month long six thousand mile road trip the author took with his wife and son in 2016.

JOY

by Allen Long

In December 2016 in the San Francisco Bay area, I drove to my orthopedic surgeon's office in considerable pain. Despite near-agony in my right leg, I experienced a sudden overpowering joy. It began as a warm glow in the cradle of my stomach, then quickly rose like a helium balloon to fill my chest, throat, and mind with golden light and one of the most ecstatic bursts of happiness I've ever experienced.

I was sixty and on my way to my one-month check-up following full knee replacement surgery. I'd spent three days in the hospital and then eleven days in a rehabilitation hospital, where I received three hours of physical and occupational therapy each day and ate the worst food imaginable. I was only supposed to spend five days there, but my doctor extended my stay when he discovered a blood clot in my right calf.

I'd finally been discharged, but I found myself in great discomfort at home, despite prescription analgesics.

In my experience, euphoria comes upon us when we least expect it. In most cases, we have no idea why we're flooded with this wonderful feeling. And maybe, most of the time, the wisest course is to simply embrace rather than analyze it. However, I have a strong sense of why I was struck with elation that day, and here's my reasoning.

For starters, that was the first day I'd driven since my return home, and it felt good to drive again and reclaim my independence. Also, I

love my car, a silver 2005 Honda Civic coupe that has plenty of power, handles well, and provides a smooth ride. Second, the interior of my car was warm and snug on that wintry day. Third, the day was bright and sunny, and I'm a swimmer and sun-worshipper who revels in the bright light and heat. Fourth, I'd been happily married to my wife Elizabeth for twenty-one years, and marital bliss put me in a generally happy state that made it easy for me to experience occasional bouts of joy. Finally, *Led Zeppelin II* boomed from the stereo, a perfect album in my opinion with its mix of heavy metal, blues, and acoustic cuts, along with Robert Plant's and Jimmy Page's superb singing and guitar playing, respectively.

Led Zeppelin II holds a special place in my heart. The first time I heard it, I'd wandered up to my junior high's gym in Arlington, Virginia, on a bored winter Saturday in early 1970 to maybe shoot some baskets or play in a game, even though basketball's not my sport. When I stepped into the gymnasium, *Led Zeppelin II* blasted forth from a record player just inside the door. I was transfixed. This was some of the most exciting music I'd ever heard--I felt an exhilaration similar to my first exposure to the Beatles. I listened to the entire album.

The person in charge of the stereo was a pretty girl with black bangs named Myra who was in my seventh grade English class and treated me like scum--I was a pimple-faced straight-A student with an out-of-fashion crew cut my parents made me sport so I wouldn't be mistaken for a hippie. I disliked our teacher, who constantly held me up to the class as a shining example of the ultimate student, and, naturally, many of my peers despised me.

"God, I love this!" I said to Myra.

She smiled and made my day.

Within twenty-four hours, I'd walked several miles with my buddy Will to Giant Music in Falls Church, where I bought *Led Zeppelin II*. I was a budding electric guitar player, and I quickly taught myself a number of Jimmy Page's easier licks. The hottest guitar solo on the album occurs on "Heartbreaker," and it was way beyond my ability. However, I had a friend named Craig V. who was an exceptionally talented player.

One day when he was at my house, I jokingly asked him if he could play the "Heartbreaker" solo. I assumed no peer of mine could even begin to deliver the goods, but Craig played the solo note-perfect without any visible effort. He didn't crack a smile, but I know he thoroughly enjoyed putting me in my place, oh me of little faith. This is one of my favorite memories of Craig, who ended up playing with such headliners as Steve Winwood but died of a heart attack in 2010 at age fifty-three—heart trouble ran in his family. I miss him deeply.

So, as I drove, *Led Zeppelin II* reminded me of how much I love to play guitar. Even though I owned two exquisite Fender and Hamer electric guitars and a gorgeous mahogany Martin acoustic, I hardly ever played them, since I'd made a decision a few years earlier to dedicate my free "artistic" time exclusively to writing. I immediately vowed to start playing again and to maybe resume my lessons with a local master player when I retired in the not-too-distant future.

Another reason for my happiness was that I didn't have to return to work until March. I'm an assistant nurse at an inner-city hospital, and

I greatly enjoy taking care of appreciative and cooperative patients and helping compassionate nurses, but my peers and I often encounter verbally abusive nurses and violent, mentally ill patients. Also, I had high hopes my doctor would give me permission to swim soon, so I could swim five days a week for the next two months before returning to work.

In addition, I was proud when my physical therapist—nicknamed "the bulldog" because of her ability to inflict pain--complimented me on my willingness to suffer agony so I could heal quickly. This made me feel connected to my brother Danny and my son Josh, who had also recently demonstrated a strong ability to handle post-surgery discomfort. This also reminded me that I'd toughed out some really grueling practices when I played football and wrestled in junior high and high school. I remember thinking then, *if I can endure this, I can endure anything.*

I also thought about how I've successfully overcome child abuse, a nightmarish first marriage, a nervous breakdown, and other difficult periods in my life. Now I rejoiced in feeling physically and mentally tough.

Finally, as I sped through the rolling green hills, I thought about all the books I wanted to read during my medical leave—I could consume one or two a week for the next two months!

It suddenly stuck me that I was still the same person I was in high school—I remained passionate about reading, writing, guitar playing, and swimming—only I was even tougher now and with forty-two more years of experience, knowledge, and wisdom than I had at eighteen. This is when the joy struck. I suddenly had a deep, clear reminder of who I was.

I'm still marveling about how I could experience such bliss while in near-agony. This reminds me of a conversation I had with my doctor many years ago. At the time, I was afflicted with undiagnosed anxious depression and felt constant near-panic about my bad job, my failing first marriage, and money. I told my doctor, "I just need things to settle down for a while so I can relax and be happy."

My doctor smiled and said, "The trick is to be open to happiness, even while you're suffering."

About the Author:

Allen Long is the author of Less than Human: A Memoir (Black Rose Writing, 2016). He is a regular contributor to Adelaide. Allen's memoirs have also recently appeared or are forthcoming in Broad Street, Eunoia Review, and Hawaii Pacific Review. He has been an assistant editor at Narrative Magazine since 2007, and he lives with his wife near San Francisco.

TWO SUMMERS
by Rachel Cavell

It wasn't fully explainable, the fog of sadness clouding the morning last summer when Integral Tree and Landscaping came to chop down the tree that had lived alongside our house for over one hundred years. Rising twenty feet from alongside our driveway this tree, almost overnight, lowered a tired branch into an unwitting dagger. The tree is "declining", wrote Angelo from Integral, having "numerous smaller dead branches and a history of multiple branch failures" and this, less ominous than a second opinion offered by a laconic local arborist, declaring "four seconds" from detachment to death should one of its larger branches unmoor unannounced. Our daughter moved away from the Hudson Valley to New York City several years ago and it appeared that the tree, too, had also outgrown our home; the imagining of its slow decay resulting in the midnight loss of one of its extravagant gnarled branches through the window and into her room, onto her bed perhaps, on a night when she returned home was one thought too many. The day of its dismemberment we took photo after photo of our tree as it lost height and limb, becoming unrecognizable to us in its slow undoing.

These trees we live with come in and out of focus, the maple behind our kitchen over time the single most important architectural feature of our house, standing at the back of our small blue-stone yard with a grey trunk that dwarfs the delicate wrought iron patio furniture I inherited from my grandmother, as uncomfortable to sit in as the dresses worn by its original settlers. Rudimentary science tells me that this maple was less significant when we bought our house twenty years ago, but it was nearly invisible to us then. We couldn't have known that it would come to protect us, spreading its branches and rocking at summer storms that pass down our block.

When I was five years old my mother and I lived in Berkeley in a cottage on Dwight Way tucked behind a bigger house and accessible from the street by a driveway that turned into a pathway that opened into our front yard. My father had moved to New Jersey when he left, and seasons were punctuated by his arrivals and departures and by greeting cards of the sort that aren't made any more: Cards the length and width of a cereal box, textured with real felt and real sparkles smiling greetings like "Someone in Princeton Luvs You," or crawling with cats whose tails are made from yarn, meowing: "You're the cat's Pajamas." It is before breakfast and I see him striding down our path to the cottage at first hazy and indistinct, rounding the corner where the driveway ends and opens up to our front yard, its fuchsias dripping down from the branches, sprinkling him with the water off their spidery legs as he brushes by them with a tuneful hum and an almost imperceptible skipping step. I know it is May because this day is my birthday, and he must have taken the "red-eye" from Newark to Oakland arriving in Berkeley not long after I would have woken up and maybe before I even had the chance to start wishing he didn't live on the other side of the map thumbtacked over my bed. I ran down that wet path, nightgown flapping around my legs, his laugh low and sweet as he catches me. And I know that if this is not a dream, my running towards him that like might have provided exactly the sight to make that nighttime airplane ride at the end of long academic semester worth it.

There is still a park in Oakland called Children's Fairyland, although then there was a creature who inhabited it named Robin Goodfellow, and she had long brown hair and played the tin pipe and I thought she loved me although it was probably my father that she loved, and she came and she played for me on that birthday and in this particular memory she is following my father down the path that morning, chirping out "happy birthday to you" on her recorder (though this particular detail feels unreal to me now). Checking this memory, I searched on-line for Children's Fairyland and Robin Goodfellow and found to my astonishment many photos of Children's Fairland from 1950 to the present, unchanged, with its entrance still a free-standing large multi-colored pastel F-A-I-R-Y-L-A-N-D behind the oversized shell of an old woman's shoe. Surely she once found me curled up and laughing inside that shoe, and I imagine I might find us hiding in there if only I could see into my computer screen.

My father visited us in August last summer. Walking with my step-mother into our living room in Rhinebeck with his soft beige sweater thrown around his shoulders and his jaunt, he is so much like the man he was and looks for a second like the picture I have of him standing in front of Sather Gate, gazing out from the university onto Telegraph Avenue the world placed then just the way he figured it. But a longer look reveals something else, a man of ninety with a smooth round moon face, wide-whale corduroys and loafers, clothes similar to those he would have worn during the heady days spent teaching and writing. And I notice that as he walks into the house in Rhinebeck

that he has visited many times, he hesitates for a moment as he expects to but does not recognize it, as if he wonders whether it is (as he has been reminded) his daughter's house, but feels now uncertain that it is the house of someone he knows.

The world falters in little ways, and sometimes it fails us in big ways. The dog end of that tree cut down by Integral still sits in our backyard a year later. I am aware that it will be a vestige only to future inhabitants of our house, basically unseen and certainly unremarkable. But this stump, our stump, stands out to us now. It serves as a daily perch for birds and squirrels as it provides a constant reminder of where our tree stood before it outgrew us. That very first evening last summer after Integral had left, I sat and watched as one of those squirrels began to scamper up the stump and when it came suddenly to where the tree wasn't anymore, planted itself at the ledge, looked up, and began to screech, long and continuously. I lived alongside this tree for more than half of my adult life, and had never realized until that night how many squirrels had lived or played in its velvet branches until I heard a squirrel make a noise of mourning and terror.

My father died unexpectedly at the end of this June. Calling their house in Brookline from a trip back to Berkeley, I looked out over the eucalyptus hills behind the house we were visiting as my stepmother answered sadly but calmly and told me that we'd lost him that morning, just like that. Lost him. As if bringing him back may be a matter of finding him. As if his never coming back suggests some failure on our part to look hard enough.

Taking down the tree alongside our driveway took two full days, and cost us over $4,000. The cost was obscene, but felt like a bargain compared to the thing we spent it to avoid at all costs, the dismemberment of a limb when we least expected it, the difference between life and death nothing more than the mindless swell of wind.

Another picture of my father sits in our house. I imagine he's in Amsterdam, Berlin maybe, as a large and low Neoclassical building hugs the cobblestoned plaza where he is standing. He is wearing a Fedora tilted slightly off center and a trench coat and is looking off to the right, away slightly from whoever is taking this photo. My father isn't smiling in this picture but he is relaxed, confident, in mid-sentence or mid-thought and his stance is active -- he is on his way somewhere or he knows where he's going--. For so long the world was a place completely known or knowable to him; and what wasn't known he set out to conquer. That moment when the world would become unfamiliar to him would have been as far away then as the horizon is invisible to us now, as we sat in our back yard last July, that summer night the tree was finally and fully gone, gazing out towards the empty sky where it had been.

About the Author:

Rachel Cavell is a lawyer; and also, a teacher with the Bard Institute for Writing and Thinking up the Hudson River in New York. She had also taught in the Bard College Prison Initiative Program (a course on Walt Whitman and Manifesto); and with the Bard College Language and Thinking Program.

THE LANDLADY

by Robert Steward

Paris, France 2001

"I like your clothes," I said, before taking a sip of my *café au lait*.

"Thank you, Robert." My landlady touched her headscarf. "I make them myself."

Her silk floral caftan hung loosely over her large frame. It was burgundy, with purple spots, gold suns, azure swirls, lilac flowers and hints of mustard and antique rose; it was all held together with a silver brooch, set in the middle of her chest. She had a pale round face, puffy cheeks and a double chin; two large eyebrows hovered over brown eyes and black rimmed glasses, and her burgundy lipstick matched her nail varnish and flowery earrings. She looked bohemian, like an artist.

Behind her, stood café Zebra, with its French windows, black and white striped awning and blackboard, displaying the *plat du jour*. It was getting dark now, and the old-fashioned streetlamps lit up one by one, accompanying the neon lights of the boutiques, bistros and bars.

"So Robert, how are things at your school?" she asked.

She had a quiet, refined voice with a slight Spanish accent.

"Fine, thanks," I said.

There was an awkward silence. I didn't know what else to say.

A waiter weaved past with a tray of coffees.

"And the apartment?" she asked. "Is everything okay?"

"Yes, everything's fine, thanks."

"I hope the smell of paint has gone," she added.

"Oh yes, I hardly notice it now."

"Good," she said. "Good."

I took another sip of coffee and remembered something from our first meeting.

"So, you lived in Barcelona, then?" I asked.

"Yes," she replied.

"Whereabouts?"

"Sorry?"

"In what part?"

"Oh, in Gràcia," she replied absently.

"Oh, so did I!" my voice rose, as if now we had something special in common.

Suddenly, it all came back to me; the bars in Plaça del Sol, the smell of the Gràcia food market, the sound of children playing outside my apartment.

"Do you know Plaça de John Lennon?" I asked.

She pursed her lips and frowned.

"Yes, I think so," she replied vaguely and studied the back of her hand.

"So, were you born there?"

"No, actually, I'm from Bolivia."

"Really? So when did you move to Barcelona?"

"About ten years ago. Before that, I lived in Argentina."

"So, you've travelled a lot, then?"

"Well Robert, we had to leave Bolivia for political reasons," she said in a low voice.

Her expression remained fixed at the memory.

"Oh," I said, a little unsure of what to say next. "So, what made you come to Paris?"

"I've always wanted to come here," she said, adjusting her headscarf. "It has everything: art galleries, museums, classical music, theatre--every night of the week."

I nodded approvingly. Paris wasn't just a city, it was an education, in art, cuisine, culture; it was an education in life.

"And I just love art." She sighed, playing with her brooch. "I can spend hours and hours just wandering around an art gallery. Only last week I was looking at a painting in the Louvre and found myself completely absorbed by it. There was a half-naked woman holding the French flag in one hand and a rifle in the other, and the people from the revolution following behind; I must've been standing in front of it for over twenty minutes."

"Really?"

"Yes, it was so vibrant, so fiery that I even started to cry."

"Gosh."

"And then a museum guard approached me and asked if I was okay. I must say, it was all a little embarrassing." She smiled.

"No," I said softly, shaking my head.

"Finally, I just had to sit down--I was so... so overawed by it all."

"Amazing."

The word eccentric didn't come close to describing her; neither did the words odd, peculiar or unusual. But I liked her; she was fragile, sincere; she had a fascinating charm about her.

I sipped my coffee. She sipped hers too, with her finger and thumb pinching the cup handle, her other fingers in the air. When she put her cup down she rubbed her shoulders. It was starting to get a bit chilly.

"By the way, I've got the rent for you here," I said, reaching into my jacket pocket.

She lifted her hand.

"Wait," she said.

Her face became serious, her eyes watchful.

She took an envelope out of her burgundy handbag.

"Here," she said softly but firmly. "I'd like you to put the money in this envelope."

She slid it across the table and looked away.

I took the envelope.

"No, not here," she whispered.

I looked around, slightly confused.

"Go into the toilet." She nodded towards the café.

"The *toilet?*"

"Shhh!" She put a finger to her mouth.

"Oh, okay then." I found myself whispering.

I got up and went into the café. It was full of people eating, drinking, smoking. The bar was L-shaped with two red dome lights hanging from the ceiling. One corner of the bar was filled with wine bottles and spirits, and in the middle sat a silver coffee machine with La Marzocco written on the front. Behind it stood a barista, making some coffee. He was bald with a hooked nose and handlebar moustache. He wore a white shirt and jacket with a black bow tie. He seemed like a caricature of himself.

"*Où sont les toilettes?*" I asked.

"*Là-bas,*" he indicated with a wave of his hand.

Past the bar, the café looked cosier, with wallpapered walls, brown leather armchairs and felt covered chairs. On the wall hung a picture of a black cat, called *Tournée du Chat Noir*. It was one of my favourites.

The toilet was down a winding staircase, the cubicle small and dimly lit. I took out the French bank notes from my pocket, counted them out and put them in the envelope. It felt like I was doing something sinister, like doing a drugs deal or selling stolen goods.

If anyone could see me now, I thought, looking into the mirror.

I couldn't help but laugh.

I put the envelope into my jacket pocket and unlatched the door.

The café looked smaller now, the atmosphere more intense. I started to feel self-conscious; maybe my landlady's paranoia was becoming contagious. Eyes looked up at me from everywhere, the barista from behind the coffee machine, the waiter from behind his tray of drinks, the customers from behind their tables. It was as if they all knew. I tried to avoid their glances as I went outside and sat down.

"Ah, there you are," my landlady whispered. "Have you done it?"

"Yes," I replied.

"Okay." She looked over her shoulder. "Give it to me under the table."

I took the envelope out of my pocket and passed it to her under the table. She looked around again and put the envelope into her handbag.

"Wait here," she said out of the corner of her mouth and walked into the café.

I sat at the table and waited.

I wonder if I'll have to do this every time, I thought.

A waiter walked past.

"*Er, l'addition s'il vous plaît,*" I said, catching his eye.

I waved my hand as if writing a cheque.

"*Tout de suite,*" he replied, and walked into the café.

I looked at the other people sitting outside. Two women sat crossed legged at a table; they seemed to be gossiping about something. At another table a man sat alone, reading a book, and at another, a woman also sat alone, smoking.

Paris was a good place to be alone.

I stared into the distance in a pensive mood. I felt relieved to have my own apartment; no more living out of a suitcase, no more flea-ridden pensions in Gare du Nord, no more embarrassing phone calls enquiring about flats to rent. Now, I had my own place, my own bed, my own kitchen, my own bathroom, my own--

"Robert?" my landlady said, breaking me out of my spell.

"Everything okay?" I asked, scratching my head.

"Yes," she replied, and sat down.

She adjusted her headscarf. She touched her ear, wrinkled her nose and finally settled down to playing with her brooch.

She seemed more serene now, happy to sit in silence.

"It's a nice evening, isn't it?" I said finally, looking out onto the cobblestone street.

"Yes, it is," she said.

She moved her head as if she was looking at a picture.

"Oh Robert, what a wonderful tree!" she exclaimed.

I looked over my shoulder. The leaves were starting to turn yellow; in the lamp light they looked almost golden.

"Oh yes," I said, turning back to her. "It's beautiful, isn't it?"

"I never noticed it before." Her eyes glistened and her lips turned upwards into a gentle smile. "It's so small, so fragile, so... so *joli.*"

#

About the Author:

Robert Steward teaches English as a foreign language and lives in London. He is currently writing a collection of short stories, some of which have appeared in Scrittura, The Creative Truth, The Ink Pantry, Winamop, The Foliate Oak Literary and Communicators League magazine. You can find them at: twitter.com/ theroadtonaples

THE SMALL GIRL

by Patrick Hahn

I'm lying on the sofa in my bungalow, reading the same issue of *Discover* magazine for the twenty-ninth time. They don't have much in the way of printed matter in this country, I'm thinking to myself, when I hear a knock at the door. I already know who it is, even before I get off the couch and fling open the door to find the Small Girl standing my my doorstep.

The Small Girl is sixteen years old. Polio has left her with a paralyzed arm and a limp. One eye wanders, and she slurs her words, as if talking with a mouthful of mush. Her name is Ayeshetu, her nickname is Ama, but I usually just call her the Small Girl.

"Oh Joy," I exclaim. "It's the Small Girl. Now we can have Christmas after all."

The Small Girl gives me a lopsided smile. This is all part of our riff, our daily ritual.

I turn around and walk back inside. The Small Girl follows me, without being invited. This, too, is part of our daily ritual.

I clap my hands together. "Hey Small Girl," I exclaim. "Make yourself useful. Fill up my water barrel." The Small Girl grabs a bucket and does as she is told. Meanwhile I get down on the floor and begin doing my exercises. Some people might find it fatuous for me to be doing pushups while this little girl – excuse me, this one-armed little girl – fetches water for me, but I believe you are not doing anyone a favor by treating them as if they were helpless.

When she finishes, I hand her a note worth about twenty-five cents in the local currency. A pittance, to be sure, but this is a country where the average salary for a working man is about seventy-five cents a day.

After she pockets the note, I ask her "Did you pray for me today?"

"Yeth," she lisps.

"What did you pray for?"

"Dat you will give me money," she replies.

My jaws drops. Never in my life have I encountered such an utter lack of guile. The Small Girl watches bemusedly as I double up with laughter.

"I am hungry," the Small Girl intones.

I hand her an orange. The Small Girl smiles condescendingly and shakes her head. "An orange," she patiently explains, "Doeth not thatithfy me."

"Okay," I say. "You can have bread and margarine."

Again she smiles condescendingly and shakes her head. "Bread and margarine doeth not thatithfy me."

"Okay," I reply." You can have rice and margarine."

Another condescending little smile, another shake of the head. "Rithe and margarine doeth not thatithfy me."

"Awright," I respond. "Whaddya want?"

"I like thtew."

So I go to the refrigerator, fill a bowl with fried rice, ladle some eggplant stew on top, and hand the bowl to her. I ask her if she would like to sit down, but she says No. I ask her if she would like a spoon or a fork, but again she says No. As always, she eats her food cold, standing up, in the kitchen, with her fingers.

After she finishes, she washes out the bowl, and as usual she does a half-assed job. I have to stand over her as she washes the bowl again and make sure she does it right this time. "You know Babe," I tell her, "If you want to make your living as a professional free-loader, you're gonna have to learn to tread a lot more lightly in other people's homes."

"Pashick," she says, slurring my name, "Give me money to do my transport."

"WHAT DO I LOOK LIKE?" I roar. "A FREAKIN' BANK?" The Small Girl remains expressionless.

Impulsively, I ask her "Who cuts your hair?"

"No Body," she murmurs.

"Whaddya mean 'Nobody?'" I demand. "Somebody must cut your hair."

Without missing a beat, she replies, "Pashick – give me money to get my hair cut." Again she looks on bemusedly as I double up with laughter.

We repair to the living room, and she picks up a copy of Gideon's Bible lying on a side table. "Should I take?" she inquires.

"Why do you want my Bible?" I ask.

"I want to read the word of God," she replies.

"Yeah, sure you can have it," I tell her.

The Small Girl asks me if I believe in God. When I say No, she starts getting agitated. "Look," I tell her. "You've met one person in your life who doesn't believe in God, and he's paying for your education. There's twenty million people in this country who do believe in God, and not one of them will pay for your education. Why do you think that is?"

"You let God worry about dem" she replies.

We sit down on a couch, and the Small Girl reaches into her shopping bag and pulls out a tattered notebook to show me. Every page is filled with original poetry she has written. It's all in her native language, so I can pick out only a word here and there.

She has told me that her ambition is to go to university and get a job in broadcasting. I wonder if she has any idea how badly the odds are stacked against her.

The Small Girl announces that it is time for her to go. I see her to the door, and then she turns around and says "Pashick – give me book."

"Huh?"

"Book," she says, oddly emphatic." Give me book." I have no idea what the Hell she is talking about, but presently she makes me understand that she wants some writing paper. So I pick up a yellow pad, tear off five, sheets, and hand them to her. She carefully folds the sheets in half and places them in her shopping bag, along with the Bible, the loaf of bread, and orange I have already given her.

The Small Girl promises to come by tomorrow. "Oh Joy," I exclaim. "I can hardly wait."

I watch her hobble off. She has no idea how much I admire her.

\#

PAU HANA TIME

by Kirby Michael Wright

IT WAS SATURDAY MORNING at the Moloka'i Ranch. The rooster light broke in through the bedroom window at the bungalow. Chipper Gilman was snoring under the quilt. Julia Wright had already perked fresh-ground Kualapu'u coffee and was sipping the dark brew from a tin cup. She liked it black. Today was Lazy Day. Chipper would get up late the way he always did on Saturdays. They'd planned to head to town in the Ford to buy staples. The kerosene refrigerator was working fine and Julia wanted to stock up on perishables such as cheese, bacon, butter, and eggs. She got all the cream and milk they needed for free from the Cooke Dairy. After shopping, they would motor to the west where they could enjoy a day at the beach. Lazy Days invigorated Chipper for the workweek. Julia cherished every minute with him because he was relaxed and good company.

Julia put on a pair of khaki knickers and pulled a green top over her head. She looked at her reflection in the kitchen window. The clothes seemed slightly big and her face looked thin. She promised herself to eat more while laying out Chipper's denims and white cotton shirt. She kept his hat on the wall since wearing it made him think he was driving cattle or handling sheep.

*   *   *

The Model T puttered down a narrow road past the Kaunakakai Courthouse, a shed-sized structure with a shingled roof that Sophie had told her doubled as a jail. Julia guessed that was where they'd sign their marriage license when the time came. The ring on her finger felt loose, as though it might slip off. The road curved right, taking them to box-shaped buildings on either side the dirt road. The buildings were painted forest green and had been built so close together they seemed connected. Most were two stories. Second floors were facades without windows. Chipper parked outside Kanemitsu's Bakery. Julia went in while her man leaned against the doorway. Bert Kanemitsu, a chubby man with salt-and-pepper hair, stood behind a glass display case of donuts, cookies, and custard pies. The case buzzed with flies.

"'Morning, Bert," Julia said.

"Almost noon," he replied. "Da regulah?"
"Please."

Chipper pulled out rolling papers and a tobacco pouch.

Bert grabbed a pair of steel tongs and snatched a long john. The donut had a twist. Bert stuffed a half-dozen in a paper bag.

Chip sealed his rolled cigarette by sliding the outer paper over his tongue. He spit out a flake of loose tobacco and tucked the cigarette in his shirt pocket. He followed Julia out. The strolled the walkway devouring donuts. The Chang Tung General Store displayed hand-crank eggbeaters, machetes, alarm clocks, and orange cast-iron pots and pans that fit neatly into one another.

"I love cast-iron," Julia said.

"Only the two of us," Chipper said. "That set's for a big family." "You're right, Chip."

They strolled Ala Malama Avenue and finished their long johns. Chipper stuck the cigarette in his mouth. He scratched a cowboy match against a kiawe post and it flared to life. He lit the tip and took a long pull. Julia stopped to admire the lady mannequins inside Imamura's Clothing.

One lady wore a yellow chiffon dress with an empire waist. Her friend looked sexy in a salmon-colored tea dress with a turquoise cloche hat pulled down over her ears. What caught Julia's attention was a pair of ivory-and-black lace up boots the tea dress mannequin had on. Sue had worn a similar pair the night they met the handsome brothers. Julia thought it strange how the lives of two sisters could turn out so differently. She doubted Sue could have weathered the storm had Harold been the stable one and Fergus the playboy. Julia wondered how strong her sister's marriage was in Oregon, seeing how her Englishman had been spoiled by his father's money.

Chipper puffed and blew smoke. "You want those boots?" "No. Can you see me in one of those dresses?"

"Maybe if we lived in Honolulu."

Chipper paused outside Kikugawa Liquors and peered through the plate glass window. He exhaled a stream of smoke that bounced off the glass and stung Julia's eyes.

She rubbed an eye. "Jesus," she said. "Sorry."

Bottles of rye, Scotch, and bourbon were on display. A black-and-red toy train on a track looped around the booze. Chip sucked hard on his cigarette. "Could stand some Wild Turkey," he said.

Julia winced. "Too expensive."

Chip exhaled. "Wild Turkey helps me get some shut-eye." "You're asleep the second your head hits the pillow."

Chipper flicked his cigarette. It bounced off the walkway and sprayed embers.

Julia killed the smoldering butt by grinding it out with the heel of her boot. She kicked the butt into the street.

"Wouldn't mind some shots now," Chip continued. "Come with me to the Midnight Inn. Whadya say?"

"No." Julia crossed Ala Malama. Chipper followed. She grabbed a shopping cart and pushed it through a bustling store owned by Uta Misaki. Uta was a seamstress who'd opened her doors back in mid-January to help the Misakis survive. Uta and three generations lived on Mango Lane in a two-bedroom cottage behind the store. Uta's cashiers were Filipinas in their teens. Uta believed these girls were trustworthy and the most affordable labor on the island.

Misaki's was a canned goods paradise. A shopper could find almost anything in a can, including lamb tongues, silkworm pupae, and fish assholes in cheese sauce. There were lots of bottled goods too. The store had a butcher shop stink that mixed with the odors of insecticide, sour milk, and Mochi Crunch. Along the store's eastern wall, shoppers could find dairy, produce, and packaged meats. Most of the meat came from Moloka'i Ranch and the milk products carried the Cooke Dairy label. Julia envied Sophie and George for having a monopoly on so many goods. She filled her cart with eggs, bacon, cheese, and cans of deviled ham. Chipper was hunting for something in the rear of the store, where they kept ammunition and fishing gear. She tossed in carrots bound by string and found bottles of powdered curry, Worcester sauce, Kikkoman soy sauce, and ketchup. Next came a ten-pound burlap bag of rice. Last but not least was a quart jar of Halawa Valley poi. She knew the poi was fresh because it was purple and smelled freshly beaten after she spun open the lid. Julia steered her cart to the front of the store. Chipper flirted with Crystal at the register. He tossed a pack of rolling papers and a pouch of Bull Durham tobacco onto the counter.

"Said you were givin' up smokin'," Julia told him.

He wrinkled his brow. "When?" "New Year's Eve."

He lifted the bag of rice out of her cart and rested it on his shoulder. "Quit nagging," he said.

Crystal tallied the total. "Eight dollah pifty," she said.

Julia pried open the clasp on her black coin purse. She pulled out a wad of folded bills and tossed Crystal the wad.

Crystal counted the bills. "Twenny cent mo', missus."

"Fo' the luva Pete," Julia said. She dug around in her purse and clanged loose change over the counter.

Chipper winked at the girl. "Nearly broke da bank."

The girl giggled. She placed their groceries in small wooden crates.

*   *   *

Chipper killed the Ford's engine at Papohaku Beach. The shore was deserted. Julia slipped into her two-piece while Chip pulled on his canvas trunks. She'd prepared a picnic basket at the crack of dawn. They'd have kalua pork, rice, and kim chee on tin pie plates. Sophie had given her bottles of beer.

Julia looked across the Channel of Bones. She made out Oahu's south shore and the pali rising above it. The cliffs looked black from a distance. She wondered how her boys were in Kaimuki. Julia told herself she'd visit on Thanksgiving.

Chipper took Julia's hand and they waded out. The water was cold for October. Limu drifted by. Owama schooled in the shallows and some jumped out of the water as they approached. Chipper dove in. She followed. They dog-paddled out past the breakers. There wasn't a person in sight. To Julia, it seemed as though the ranch didn't exist and they were the only ones on a deserted island. This was the paradise she'd imagined as a girl, one that belonged to her and the love of her life. The deeper water felt warm to Julia and it was calm.

Chip practiced his crawl stroke, something Duke had taught him before he left to fight. He showed Julia how to turn her head for air while rotating her arms and using a flutter kick. The crawl seemed unnatural and awkward to Julia. She had trouble keeping her head underwater during her strokes. She quit swimming, stuck out her head like a turtle, and gasped.

"I nearly drowned!"

"Lesson's over," Chipper said, floating on his back. He sucked in seawater and spurted a blast over his head. "There she blows!"

Julia quit her dramatics. She knew she was complaining for attention and that he wasn't buying any of it. She enjoyed it when Chip acted goofy. It reminded her of the Makai Boys, when Waikiki was his oyster and the responsibilities that came with being an adult were a million miles away. Remembering him as a young surfer and waterman helped her revisit her younger days, the time of playing with her brothers and sisters in Palolo Valley. They'd laid claim to the fern and guava grottos of empty lots, challenging kids from neighboring families for the rights to build forts from busted pallets, sheets of cardboard, and termite-infested planks.

Tommy had been the head of the Wright clan, a fearless leader who kept his younger brothers in line. They'd lost their father and Tommy became the authority figure they all secretly craved. He'd taught Sharkie and Jackie the basics of football and baseball. He'd gone down to Waikiki to show his sisters how to dive and tread water. He'd protected them from bullies and was always ready to fight at the drop of a hat. Locals always showed respect for the Wrights whenever Tommy was around. He was short in stature but stocky. If someone tried to beef Sharkey or Jackie, he held up his fists and swung for the moon. Tommy's short fuse made him dangerous. Most challengers backed off when he clenched his fists.

Catarina appreciated the protective nature of her oldest son. The fight had gone out of her after her husband was arrested, tried, and sent to jail. Benjamin's journey to Honolulu Prison cast a pall over her and the children. Relatives such as the Colburns and Carlos Long looked down on the Wrights for Benjamin's crime, and she couldn't free herself from the quicksand of shame.

Julia floated on her back beside Chipper. The sky was filled with fat white clouds. A plover flew over her. Chip whistled to the tune of "The Army Goes Rolling Along."

"Hungry, Corporal Gilman?" Julia asked.

"And how. Thirsty too. Did you bring provisions, Private Wright?" "I'm always prepared, corporal."

Chipper swam over to Julia. She lowered her legs and treaded water. He wrapped his arms around her. She liked the way he pulled her close, as if protecting her from something dangerous lurking in the sea. The trades toyed with her hair. She brushed the bangs out of her eyes. He pressed his lips to hers. They kissed. It's these little things in life, Julia thought, that's what counts.

She was sure her love for this man would last until the day she died.

About the Author:

Kirby Michael Wright won the 2018 Redwood Empire Mensa Award for Creative Nonfiction

ON FREEDOM - MAN'S EVERLASTING ILLUSION

by Dr. Raymond Fenech

You can't say that you're advancing freedom when you use free thought to destroy free will. The determinists come to bind, not to lose. (G. K. Chesterton)

Truth be told if you examine the definition of freedom by the Oxford Dictionary every one of these statements are arguably subject to debate.

Take the first (a): *Do we have the right to act, speak or think as we want?*

A foreigner was filmed by a mobile phone from a passing car on one of the most popular promenades walking stark naked. He didn't walk very far before a police car came up with him, sirens and all and arrested him for indecent exposure.

b) *Can you actually speak your mind?* A lot of Europeans in Italy, Malta, Sicily, England, France, and Hungary are all worried about the influx of refugees that are crossing their borders, or arriving clandestinely by boats to their shores. When politicians try to make a stand against this, human rights societies, several churches from different religious denominations, and activists immediately claim these people are racists, Fascists, Nazis, heartless, uncharitable even anti-democratic.

Maybe you can think whatever you like, but thinking and actually putting your thoughts into action can be dangerous. An investigative journalist has proof the government of her country is hand in glove with organized crime. He is in league with the Italian and Russian Mafia, has a secret account in Panama and that her country has become a tax haven for money gaming companies, money launderers, and drug and human trafficking. There is all sorts of evidence to put this Prime Minister and his cronies behind bars. So she writes her thoughts on her personal blog.

At first, she is riddled with libel actions, but as more proof becomes more intense and further investigations continue to portray the government for what he really is, the investigative journalist, one fine day leaves her home on an errand, climbs into her car which explodes into a ball of fire. She was killed on the spot. This is a true incident that took place over a year ago in my country, Malta. Perhaps now you are wondering how this can happen in a country that is member of the EU? More food for thought – how is it that over a year has passed since this gruesome assassination and the persons who hired the killers are still at large? Perhaps you might be asking yourselves what has the EU done about this since its investigative delegation that visited Malta soon after the incident came to the conclusion that the Rule of Law and freedom of expression in Malta are under serious threat? Well apart from all the drivel I heard in the EU parliament, no concrete action has been taken against the Maltese government so far.

b) *What is fate?* If we consider personal experiences, does anyone of you actually know what is round the corner? My late father used to tell me when I was still a little boy: *Life is full of twists and turns. No one can ever know what lies behind each corner we turn.* Forget that fate is often thought of something supernatural, that it is something we have no control over. But is it really a supernatural power that keeps us guessing to the end what will become of us? Or is it really the fact this is part of the natural process of things?

The will or principle or determining cause by which things in general are believed to come to be as they are, or events to happen as they do: destiny … fate sometimes deals a straight flush … he had no idea that he would become the right man in the right place at the right time … - June Goodfield.

c) *The state of not being imprisoned or enslaved.* Aren't we enslaved by our own conventionalism, the laws of our own countries, even the laws imposed on us by society itself? Can you for example refuse to pay your taxes without harsh consequences? Can you decide not to pay your fines for over-speeding, parking your car where there is a no parking sign? Aren't we imprisoned by our own stereo-typed lives?

Freedom comes from our perceptions. We may have grown up in what others consider to be an oppressive regime, but if we have never experienced or heard of any other way, then we may think we are experiencing freedom.

Freedom as we experience it is dictated within a range of permitted choices within whatever society we live in. Being social animals, we will relinquish certain rights to some freedoms to remain part of that society, sometimes this means that we relinquish freedoms that we know we should be allowed to practice. We compromise.

The controllers of our societies attempt to control our freedoms. This can range from the implementation of law in more liberal societies, to severely brutal enforcement of restrictions in oppressive societies.

The problem with the freedom we experience is that it is not a naturally evolving thing. It is an artificial freedom based on the will and actions of those in power. Even in a society that is considered democratic, those in power will impose their own views and wishes on the population under the guise of it being for the greater good. (Freedom – Is Freedom an illusion? - By the Order of Truth 2013).

D) *The state of being unrestricted and able to move easily.* Is this possible at all? How many times do we feel compelled to break away from routine and come up with a camping idea for the weekend? Ask yourselves how many times these sudden impulsive cravings have actually been put into action and you managed to get a good group of friends prepared to remove the chains, which bind them to the everyday boring routine to join you on this impulsive adventure enabling you to move easily into the direction of that momentary dream? But most will all find some sort of excuse, perhaps these excuses for not being able to do what they want will be described as *'other commitments'*.

E) *Unrestricted use of something (force and violence in this case).* Perhaps some of you have watched the film, *Purge*. Well this is a futuristic story when the US government tries to decimate the population by declaring a night whereby all and everyone had the legal right to perform anything they wished, from rape, murder, burglaries, armed robberies, muggings anything that would be considered criminal and severally punished in any law abiding country. Has this ever happened in any law-abiding country? How horrified were you if you watched the film? Doesn't this somehow transmit the subtle message that clearly states: *God forbid something like this ever happened.* So, in other words you want freedom, but not too such an extent, right?

F) *Freedom from the state of not being subject to or affected by (something undesirable).* Can this actually be put into practice? How can a decent, law-abiding citizen of any country live within a system and actually be free to choose what is always best for him only.

I am a writer and recently had the opportunity of a job I have always dreamt about, an associate editorship with a leading literary magazine. But I needed to move from Malta to be able to be closer to work and couldn't because my brother in-law being handicapped is totally dependent on my wife and myself. The law here states that since his sister is the closest and only blood relative, she is legally duty-bound to see to his financial maintenance. Despite the fact I am not legally bound to fork out money for his upkeep, especially when I know he brought this situation upon himself, I love my wife too dearly to abandon her. So am I really free to think about myself? Had I been single, maybe, but then perhaps some other relative within

my own family would have needed my help. Is it an easy choice to abandon someone in need when he needs you most?

There is no such thing as a condition of complete freedom, unless we can speak of a condition of nonentity. What we call freedom is always and of necessity simply the free choice of the soul between one set of limitations and another. (G.K Chesterton)

At the present moment, my country has been taken over by building developers. They are all close friends of the government because he has given them the green light to build anything, anywhere, at any cost. So, if you happen to have been unfortunate enough to have invested your life-savings in a bungalow, or a terraced house in an area where no high-rise buildings could be built, you suddenly find yourself surrounded by such high-rise apartments blocking your views, the sunlight and creating the most horrible claustrophobic environment one can imagine. Not only, your privacy has been robbed from you because these minute apartments all have windows overlooking your garden, where in summer you used to enjoy sunbathing.

Before, in your street, you could park your car right outside your door, especially when you come loaded with shopping. Now that is no longer possible because the whole street, which used to have 100 houses, now is a street which has 800 houses as a result of which cars have a problem where to park. This is not to mention, the dust, noise and diesel fumes caused by excessive traffic, building machinery and equipment which creates serious health problems for the residents that suffer from asthma or hay fever. He who governs in a dictatorship has the power to dictate by use of force. In this case, it is actually money dictating to political clowns in exchange for *'little favours'*, such as pledging their financial support during the election campaigns to the government in power. Corruption is everywhere and there isn't a single institution, whether governmental or private that is not controlled by the privileged few.

A man can be free of government in the case that there is no government, but he will not be free from man altogether. The abolition of government still leaves social rules to dictate the actions of man. Let's say a man lives in an anarcho-syndicalist society and they have just freed themselves of the shackles of government. Any rules that the society puts forth, as just as they may be, limit the man. For instance that man would not be free to take things from another's possession without permission. There will always be rules of some sort, even if that society is rid of religion there will be laws of the land to keep peace and prosperity. (Philosophy, The Politics of writing - Is Freedom an Illusion? June 20, 2015).

There can be no freedom until men remain subject to society's conventionalism, slaves to stereo-typed life styles, materialism, without leaving space for spontaneity and for imagination, that mental faculty which can work freely within us, spurn us on to look at life from a different perspective, seek pastures new when the old ones have become like chains, keeping us imprisoned in our own self-created glass houses. Feeling safe here is an illusion, it's the only way we dig our heads deep into this space so we cannot see outside this space, thus finding it much easier in convincing ourselves that within it is actually the limit. In fact, there is nothing more untruthful, more frustrating because outside this space there is true freedom. The whole point is whether we have the courage to emerge from within our limitations and dare go beyond, where no one, or few have ever dared venture.

*Let me ask you a question: Do you live a life of freedom or bondage? Before you disregard my question, let me explain... **It's possible to choose bondage in a culture of freedom.***

I was born and raised in a communist country and I personally experienced not being able to do what I wanted, dress how I wanted or buy what I wanted. When communism fell, I saw many struggle to keep up with the changes and handle their newly gained freedom.

Some jumped on new opportunities, opened new businesses, left the country or changed careers. Others gave in to their anger and confusion. The country was free, but sadly, some people's minds were still held captive.

Even though I live in a free country now, I see a lot of the same stuff around me every day. People THINK they're free, but in reality, they don't even understand freedom. They're trying to cope with it by heading in the opposite direction. (Silvia Pencak)

Men have to break free from the bonds of everyday life, the eight hour or more work mania that has enslaved them for centuries. Humans' quality of life is wasted considering the fact that modern technological advantages have not been used in their favour, so they could work less and enjoy life more, without effecting their standard of living. Instead, the advantages have all gone in favour of the rich entrepreneur who has made himself and his pockets fatter by exploiting science and making men more productive without their realizing. The EU is even trying to extend retirement age to 65. So far it is voluntary whether you choose to continue working so far or not, but does this make sense at all when people's life expectancy has increased dramatically? What about the aftermath of such a law? Did the bureaucrats even take into consideration that when people retire they make space for the young people to take their place thus creating vacancies for those who want to start shaping up their careers and their lives? Who can predict that 65-year olds will actually remain healthy to the point they can produce the same quality work as when they were younger? Does it make sense that with all the technological advances, people should at all spend three quarters of their lives slaving away and working until basically they are ready to collapse? Was men really born to work until he falls dead only? Doesn't men have a sacrosanct right to have enough of their years on this short journey to be free to enjoy what's left of their lives?

We might fancy some children playing on the flat grassy top of some tall island in the sea. So long as there was a wall round the cliff's edge they could fling themselves into every frantic game and make the place the noisiest of nurseries. But the walls were broken down, leaving the naked peril of the precipice. They did not fall over; but when their friends returned to them they were all huddled in terror in the centre of the island; and their song had ceased. (G.K. Chesterton - Orthodoxy,153).

Where is your freedom if you have to work a certain amount of hours to receive a financial remuneration? Where is your freedom if you have to wear a uniform, your break is at a set time and you cannot take leave in certain months? Where is your freedom if you cannot leave your office during working hours — sometimes not even when this is necessitated by things outside your control – your son fell ill at school, your closest relative is on his death bed in hospital?

It is enough for you to look around and ask yourself a simple question: Where is all that time which modern technology was supposed to have gained for us gone? On the contrary

life seems forever increasing its pace. There is more stress and most common illness, heart attacks, strokes and several psychiatric problems such as a break downs are caused by the speed of life which humans are failing to keep up with. And we travel with cars, trains, airplanes. We have smart phones, computers, tablets — yet the high quality, quantity and accurate work that these help us produce is never enough for our employers. They want more and more and aren't happy with all this progress!

Yet this is not the worse part of men's exploitation by those who dictate, either because they are financially or politically powerful. The worse is that *leaders* have managed to steal our identity, our very soul. Who can deny that we are just a number on an identity card, a passport, or a license?

Italian psychiatrist, Professor Mazzullo, a special guest on an Italian TV show once said to a woman who was arguing that she had chosen to be a career woman, but still wanted to have a family and children as follows: *Life is full of choices, but you have to remember that when you make up your mind and make your choice, as soon as you do, you are immediately renouncing to another, or even more than one choice.*

If I had freedom of choice in mind, it immediately went out of the window. Simply because in the real world, there is no freedom of choice, because humans have the capability of being multi-tasked. But in some cases this would mean that one of those tasks suffers neglect, or not enough attention, simply because there is only so much one can do.

The point this woman wanted to make was that she was sure she could be a professional but at the same time have a husband and children and be able to do both. The truth is that as we have so often experienced ourselves, you cannot, because each human being has his limitations. In other words, as the common saying goes: *Something has got to give*. So freedom, as long as we live within the self-erected walls, the laws, the rules, all the conventional behavior, the stereo-type way of living, the expectations, ours and those of our relatives and friends is in fact an illusion.

Maybe we have restricted our own freedom, because we expect so much out of life that we are not aware that the more one has, or achieves requires certain responsibilities and these same responsibilities limit our freedom. We find ourselves imprisoned in our own self-created harnesses that prohibit anything outside what we get so used to, we end starting to accept as normal life. Is it?

Men must not forget that they were made of body and soul and that in the end only the Soul survives. Perhaps only through death men can actually achieve their real freedom.

There is no such thing as a condition of complete freedom, unless we can speak of a condition of nonentity. What we call freedom is always and of necessity simply the free choice of the soul between one set of limitations and another. (G. K. Chesterton).

The End

About the Author:

Raymond Fenech embarked on his writing career as a freelance journalist at 18 and worked for the leading newspapers, The Times and Sunday Times of Malta. He edited two nation-wide distributed magazines and his poems, articles, essays and short stories have been featured in several publications in 12 countries. His research on ghosts has appeared in The International Directory of the Most Haunted Places, published by Penguin Books, USA.

GERANIUMS

by Noel Williams

A slow approach to Turner in the corner of the gallery

This hull emerges dazzling
in the blue blaze of air, breaks through
a pulse of sun, emptying light
through a lancet of bulwark and bow.

That baulk of sky, concrete grey,
caulked with a knife of white gold
blurs in a trailing haze
which might be a tree but floats

like a creature from Lovecraft over wet scree.
Behind it the cliff unfolds
drops the shawl of water crease by crease
in a tumult of tumbling brushstrokes.

On the back-side of the canvas I try
to find any clue, peer though this,
search out a hint behind the lines.
Scuffed prints of oiled hands. A turpentine kiss.

Skydiving over Machu Picchu

Stripped by the tumble dryer of the wind
tossing everything away, except delight
of fear in a friendless, birdless sky,
flat against gravity, the world doesn't move
and I am not falling.
Below me clouds fumble comfort
until, when I drop absolutely into their embrace
they spread desire-thin, ghost-kisses.

At once I'm through and there -
there is the impossible city of my long imagining
in free fall towards me. Viracocha, sea-foam god.
I fill all horizons so the worship of these walls
stretches up to me, my prodigal home.

Then the silk snatches me
as if I start breathing again
and snap back to the world,
elbows on the desk,
spreadsheet unfolding like the doors of a Cessna
over the sulking city.

Geraniums

I'm peering in the bleak green excess
that sprawls from pot to pot across our yard,
the fallen clematis, the sprawling
infiltration of nextdoor's tendrilled tomatoes,
wondering what we need to do for flowers.

Only geraniums strut this unwatered earth.
Pouting in leafery, lipsticked among snailshells.
They fend off slugs and you, my love,
an equation you're not pleased by,
shy behind kitchen glass,
eyeing the brazen flirts.

Spoil heap

In his album he'd pictured each stage of its
building:
concrete laid, bricks squared,
hills framed in the dormer,
glass snapped for the greenhouse
behind the drills he'd seeded where
shading her eyes, my mother bound her hair.

Now I'm back with my hardhat and hammer -
he'd only changed the gate, planted
a plastic canoe with geraniums
where the greenhouse fell.
As the wrecking ball swings, as the cellar door
buckles,
I smell paraffin, acetone, fixer:
the darkroom where he'd loosened her hair.

My blow cracks reluctant brick,
like the thrash of glass in that 60s storm
when I cowered under my eiderdown,
as she fled through broken beds towards dazzling halls
while he stood in splinters,
lost in the tumble of her hair.

Dust clears.
We can see the hills of Loxley
and the river greening where Ivanhoe rode.
From the spoil I steal a wire of white glass
for my girl to wind in her hair.

Pansies

And it was all a dream.
God wasn't giggling through his fingers.
The remote could, after all, rewind what hap-
pened.
Press the red button to erase guilt.
Are you sure? Are you really sure? And she

she did not squander wanton loveliness
nor starve herself to death for want of love.
She watered pansies on the roof, a brindled cat
sprawled in sun-scraps, her skirt splashed on
tar-paper,
her hair snagging light,
teasing them from their black soil,
dark as bruises, white as hot coals, brief as
butterflies.

About the Author:

Noel Williams is the author of *Out of Breath* (Cinnamon, 2014) and *Point Me at the Stars* (Indigo Dreams, 2017). He's published quite widely. He's co-editor of *Antiphon* (antiphon.org.uk), Associate Editor for *Orbis* (www.orbisjournal.com), reviewer for *The North* and *Envoi* and an occasional writing mentor.
Blog: https://noelwilliams.wordpress.com

WOULD THAT...
by Margo Poirier

WOULD THAT.....

**Would that answers
could come with
the same ease as breathing**

**Would that peace
could come with
the same ease as falling asleep.**

**Would that love
could come with
the same ease as peeing.**

CARLTON DAYS 1

Living in the present moment the
rubber band of memory bounces
back to tall, ancient halls of
Melbournian academia where
literary luminaries aimed their
poetic arrows fair and square,
finding their mark in earnest
hungry minds who

having had their fill
of Chris Wallace-Crabbe,
Vincent Buckley and just a smidgen
of Beatrice Faust leapt with
brimming confidence into the
bubbling cauldron of newt and
fresh white mice to spawn and ooze
their own creative genius all over
the crumbling pillars of higher learning.

Yet it was Dylan who claimed my heart,
Thomas and not Bob whose words would
firmly sink the poetic flag into Virgin territory,

ripe for Settlement.

The present moment reclaims me,
a ghostly mantle of old poets
brushes my shoulders a final time,
falls to the floor and leaves me while
 remnants of whispered sonnets drift with
wisps of pipe smoke from beneath
the door of Vin's study.

CARLTON DAYS 2

Remember, my love,
wine in coffee cups
at that cafe whose name
I don't remember -
and Jimmy Watson on very
special occasions when
coins would tumble willingly
onto wine glass counters and
we would drown our study worries
lying briefly in the arms of Bacchus?
Those were the days my friend.
We sang because we *were* the days.

Floor dwellers in older than old
rented cottages, walls hung with
hippy hessian decor, we
drank, smoked and drowsed to strains
of Cohen and Baez, tripping over chipped,
empty coffee mugs, reciting dreadful
poetry of new genius because we were
spawned with flowers in our hair and honey
on our lips, inventors of free love, creators
of new possibilities.
But only in Carlton.

About the Author:

My name is **Margo Poirier**. I am a poet and a writer living in the Adelaide Hills. My first poetry anthology 'Moon Shards' was published in 2000. Over a span of twenty-five years my poetry has appeared in numerous literary anthologies and radio broadcasts. More recently, Ginninderra Press has published two chap books of my work which also features in two of their anthologies. I have had two books published: 'Unzipped' 2013– a short story anthology and 'A Previous Life', 2017- a novel. I am a qualified Massage Therapist and Professional Counsellor and have just finished another novel.

LETTER TO A YOUNG POET
by Korkut Onaran

AFFINITIES

A starfish lives in a five-hour day,
an octopus in October.
Words are crawling all over me!
'Cheek' sits on my cheek.

'T' is Christian, 't' is born again.
'K' is my name, 'O' is my last name.
'O' is an instigator (my notebook's blood
oozes in the heart of 'o').

Who says the letters cannot be sexy!
I can have an orgasm
just thinking of 'o.'
Then there is the capital 'B.'

Add to the mix
a few 'i's,
a few 'I's, then you have it:
an orgy on the page!

A silence settles in my memory;
I remember only the poem.
The word foot takes over my foot.
It feels as if I am losing my substance.

A beautiful April morning outside!
Or is it that
I make it so as I scribble?
I flip a coin.

On one side it reads: nowhere.
On the other side: now here.
The coin hangs in the air
and does not land.

The word heart
steals my heart.
That's when I disappear
into the notebook.

DEW

Like a spider crab, I change
my shell once in a while,
very slowly usually,
and sometimes I don't even
notice that it is happening.

But when I try to remember and cannot
certain touches, the names
of certain streets, or colors
of certain gazes,
I realize that
selves that I thought
would always be a part of me
are gone

as will be, one day,
the rest of me.

COEXISTENCES

It takes time to clear up the morning
and leave behind the dreams.
Some of them are really sticky; they
show up in the middle of the day
even weeks after I've seen them. The other day
I am in the bookstore going through what's
new
and there it is: one of my dreams hiding
on the shelf behind some books!

My eighty year old self is sitting
across the bar. Next to him
is my teenage self, drinking. They are
in a deep conversation, as if grandson
and grandfather. What are they
talking about? Are they aware
of my presence? Do they know
that I am writing about them?
Probably not! How could they?
There are years in between us.
Then again, anything is possible.
What an amazing world!

Here comes Bach! He is everywhere:
in this very moment, among people,
in the sky, in the architecture of a flower!
On the face of a woman,
eyes closed, facing up,
receiving the sun light on her face
with such delight!
This, as well, may be a dream!

Coda: As I sit here
at this picnic table facing the lake, I am
thinking of how poetry and music
make love! They give
birth to all. No wonder why
I am so loyal to the poem.
She makes sense of everything.

READING ONE OF ADÉLIA PRADO'S POEMS

The poem tells me that
she feels touchable today;
she wants me to touch her.

I hold her words
in between my lips,
touch my tongue and taste them.

Then I speak them
with the softest of my voice
ever so slowly

hoping to preserve
somewhere deep in me
their aftertaste.

LETTER TO A YOUNG POET

Live life
as if its ups and downs
are large breasts – you climb

and kiss the nipple: then
before you open your notebook
die a little – explore

the words
as if they are flowers
unconditionally receiving

your gaze, your attention,
your intention!
Let them

seduce you; let them
procreate in your mouth –
in your poem

About the Author:

Korkut Onaran's The Book of Colors has received the first prize in Cervena Barva Press 2007 Chapbook Contest. His poem House has received the second prize in 2006 Baltimore Review Poetry Competition. His first book of poetry The Trident Poems has been published by World Enough Writers in February 2018. His poetry has been published in journals such as Penumbra, Rhino, Colere, White Pelican Review, Crucible, City Works Literary Journal, Water –Stone, Review, Atlanta Review, Bayou, Common Ground Review, and Baltimore Review.

EMILY

by Luke Francis Beirne

EMILY

I: Emily, February 14th
The wind started:
blowing and gusting
across the ground,
fresh snow covered
most of the red.

Frayed strands
of a welcome mat
poked through the snow
at her feet.

Blinds hid most of the room.
Bottles and cans were scattered on the floor.

She knocked.
She listened.
She waited.

From the back of the house:
The tilt of a white hill;
A valley densely covered
in lightly powdered evergreens;
The air was crisp;
The sky blue.

She lifted herself
to the window
and peered through.

A reflection of the snow
and the trees behind her,
and the sky – the moon
and it hung out of place
in the blue.

In the kitchen:
A coffee pot sat on the counter;
An ashtray on the table,
littered with cigarette butts
and roached joints.

She'd sat at that table
many times, years before
and lost days to coffee
and evenings to wine.

And as they talked,
and laughed,
they danced

around the big topics
and, sometimes,
when the wine was heavy,
and the time was right,
they addressed them directly.

The dance itself
was enough
most of the time.

There was a mark
on the window above the chair
that Ronnie used to sit in.
Emily touched it gently.

She could feel it,
trace it – catch it
in the ridges
of her fingertips.

She stepped back,
looked from a distance,
but could only see it,
from the angle
she'd been at before.

She moved close
and touched the glass again.

Looking down:
Lying in the snow,
completely unseen until now,
a small brown bird.

Half buried,
its right wing stuck
straight up in the air.

She could have stepped on it,
but hadn't.

Besides the tufts of feather,
the snow around the bird
was smooth and untouched.

She looked for something
to move it with,
but couldn't see
a thing to use.

She pushed
a mound of snow
over the bird
with her foot.

And walked back
around the house
to her car.

II: Emily, February 14th

When mom died,
she'd found her in the closet
in the middle of the night –
something had woken her,
and she didn't know what.

She tried to scream,
but couldn't,
so, she leaned against the wall
and cried for a very long time.

Eventually,
she crawled back
to her room
and got into bed
and hid beneath the blankets.

She was young:
She didn't know
what else to do.

She lay there – awake
and praying and crying and shaking –
until the birds began to sing
and the sun grew up the wall
and ceiling from between the curtains.

After a long, long time
she heard her brother scream –
she didn't know which,
she never found out.

She heard her father cry,
for the only time in her life.
A power like nothing else,
And broken.

The ambulance
came up the road:
The crackle of tires
on the gravel driveway
and doors opening
and closing and boots

on the stairs; the calm
rushed sounds of
paramedics working
and angry yells
from her father.

She hated the birds
outside of the window
and she hid under the blankets
to get away from the light.

No one came to wake her,
and so she lay there
and lay there
until it was all quiet
in the tidy little house.

About the Author:

Luke Francis Beirne was born in Ireland and currently lives in Canada. His short story "Models" was published in the Honest Ulsterman and also won the David Adams Richards Prize for Prose from St. Thomas University.

REDUCTION

by Jonathan Dowdle

Riff

In the rebound, resound,
Where all thoughts go to drown,
And we sleep beneath the sea,
That buries us in echoes bleed;
How are we to sleep or dream
Between the stitch and the seam,
Plucking grief from the bleed,
Where nothing is ever released.
Our sorrows sigh, they sigh for us,
As the fist is wrapped up in the cuff,
While we are still speaking dust,
From the graveyard of each blush,
As mistakes collapse in on our heads,
That we have not overcome,
Spinning the cycle now,
Pounding down like rain on drum,
And how should we dare to fight,
The things that we don't know how
To escape in the night,
Or escape within the day,
Bend our broken knees and pray
To the deaf things in the sky,
Or the things still in the way,
Or the ones that pass us by?
In the rebound, resound,
Where all thoughts go to drown,
Perhaps the surface needs a kick,
Perhaps we need another sound.

Later

What wealth might some shared smile give,
Against the weight, the rising tide,
And where does the fire live,
Outside the chains of pride,
What might we still forgive,
As the soldiers still march on,
Never truly here, my love,
So they cannot be gone.
And who with heart, with pulse in hand,
Speaks their secret beat,
To spell out God's only psalm,
To march, soft, down the street?
What wealth might each kindness give,
A match struck in the dark,
And who, true, learns to live,
Gathered in that spark?

Reduction

In the beat of the heart,
In the beat of the street,
We lose something,
In defeat to defeat,
Weighed in the judgment,
Executioner's psalm,
I supposed we knew it,
All along.

Don't measure the measure,
Return to yourself,
The same old paragraph,
From the same old mouth.
The mirror reflection,
Is all that matters in the mean,
You'll say you know better,
But you haven't seen.

The gaze in your eyes
When you cut through the throat,
The ending of the song,
In the sudden, stark note.
All that matters
Is the self-sanctified view,
There is nothing that matters
On the edge of the truth.

So silence your grace,
And silence the psalm,
And we'll learn to play,
Just play along.
In the beat of the street,
In the beat of the heart,
Though all this is silent,
As we're reduced to a part.

Broken Fibers And Strands

Let the wind whisper through
Your catalog of thought, absently
Lifting a page of heart,
Written in fire or water, yet,
The highest grace, the lowest regret,
Still, on my tongue your name remains
Among the prayer of prayers
A graceful recollection of
Dancing down the stairs,
While you beat the tide of what
Sisyphus did not dare,
Burning through your worry
While casting off your care.
Let the harbinger dare to speak
What runs deep beneath,
Waiting to be born from this
Moment of apocalypse,
And rise yet beyond the time,
The hands that held you in place,
As the secret slips and dances
From underneath your face.

Blood-Stained Elegy

In time, you become a prisoner of yourself,
Thoughts swing which take the neck, pointing,
Like painted fingers, bone white and jabbing
Into the skull. A thousand other worlds
Still wait to unfold, like a heart, like wings,
Like legs, welcoming, into the mystery;
Still, there are few stories to be built
Between bodies, minds, or hearts,
We learn to fill with fractions
All that has passed, or all that will,
We are books written with the blood of the
past,
Passed, from hand to hand,
We are the graveyards read,
Living elegies to the dead.

In dark hours, I believe, there are no true
streets,
Our journeys turn us inward, we live the lives
of cowards,
Building, brick by brick the familiar tick of the
internal clock,
Spelling out the time of our lives, moment by
moment
Eroding between - all revenge and atonement,
And I step out of this,
Into the silent, dark abyss, leave the moment
That shall not exist to kiss
This path of such resistance.

There are hours I believe
I am no more than the sum of my mistakes,
Still trying to do right by all that might awake
If the right word can be stitched, If the right ear
might still hear it,
Fool of reflection drowning in the lighter
dream,
Where we might become
All that we might seem.

But there is no harmony in such doubt,
Between all we might say, or seem,
I merely want to build the moment

I say: "fuck you" to the dream,
Between all that may have a beat,
Between all that might still breathe,
All love is only finding the body
We create between you and me,
And only in that moment
Are we ever free.

About the Author:

Jonathan Douglas Dowdle was born in Nashua, NH and has traveled throughout the US, he currently resides in South Carolina. Previous works have appeared or are appearing in: Hobo Camp Review, 322 Review, The Right Place At The Right Time, Blue Hour Review, Whimperbang, After The Pause, Midnight Lane Boutique, Visitant, and The Big Windows Review.

NE PLUS ULTRA

by John Casey

This

That moment
Your sweet smile
Elevated me
Asked for nothing
Warmed my world-worn heart
Validated my existence

The honest, nova-bright life of your eyes
That purest expression of a want
Only to love
Only me
And I was overcome

A sublime, singular smile
Ethereal, unconditional, real
This
From then to now and ever on
Is the memory by which
I measure joy

Spring

Crystal flowered vases cast sunbeams astray
Diffused about her figure, as if by nature's
design
She smiles, reposed by the window
Elegant, serene, inquisitive

Luminous warmth caroms through the glass
The resplendent bouquets are caught,
indecisive
Lured by an uncommon radiance
A hopeful smile touched by impending joy
That portends at once both question and
answer

But what does she ask?
What does she know?
Should they lean to the Sun, or to her?

All this, captured in a smile
By the light of the window, at the onset of
spring
With wonder at what may rise anew
Knowing that it will be beautiful
And that it starts from within

Carpe Diem

Work it Earn it Live it Learn it
Climb It Run it Yell it Fun it
Like it Date it Joy it Fate it
How it Why it Hold it Cry it
Love it Leave it Miss it Grieve it
Hurt it Need it Shame it Feed it
Lie it Fake it Lose it Break it
Drug it Thrill it Hate it Kill it
Quam minimum credula postero?

Ne Plus Ultra

Cool, clear air
Oxygen thick
Inhale slowly
Measured
Controlled
Sunbeams peek between trees
Cutting the chill, just enough
Sharp report
Adrenaline rush
And we go

Instant warmth
Coursing
Energized
School of fish
Bumping shoulders
Field of view narrows
The goal
Unseen but known
One simple distance ahead

Find a nice little pocket
Settle in
Sounds muddle together
Overcome by rhythm
Droplets of perspiration
Tingling the brow
Proof of purpose

Personal space
Silently agreed upon
Each of us
In our own little world
Counting up
Counting down
Intermediate milestones

Endorphin kick
Riding the wave
Euphoric endurance
Good time
To break from tunnel vision

Glancing left and right
Quick smiles exchanged
Shared empathy acknowledged
Only we know this
Pace, breath, life
Synchronized

Carry the distance
Passing some
Passed by others
No matter
The goal is common
But
The purpose is mine

Banner ahead
Cheering cuts through
A monotonous
Drumroll of footfalls
Break rhythm
To embrace speed
We shared the distance
But suddenly
It's more personal
Each remaining second
More important
Than peaking pain

Finish
Exhilaration
Waves of emotion
Vision goes wide
Colors and sounds
Back in tune
Bright and crisp
Pats on the back
Grateful for these moments
Breathe it all in
This is one way I know
Life is beautiful

About the Author:

John Casey grew up in New Hampshire and graduated from the U.S. Air Force Academy in 1992. He earned an MA in International Affairs from Florida State University in 1994, then began his flying career as a tactical airlift and developmental test pilot. Casey left the cockpit in 2005 to work as an international affairs strategist and diplomat at the Pentagon in Washington, D.C., embassies in Germany and Ethiopia, and at Randolph Air Force Base in San Antonio, Texas, where he retired in 2015. Since then, he has focused on his writing. His work has appeared in numerous literary journals, magazines and online blogs. Raw Thoughts is Casey's first book, and he is currently working on his upcoming novel, Devolution. He is passionate about racquetball and fitness, music, travel and nature, and the human spirit. His writing is inspired by the incredible spectrum of people, places and cultures he has experienced throughout his life.

BIG TIME

by Dave Nielsen

Time's Up

To see how beautiful a single rock is,
to put one in one's yard
by crane, by a team
of workers.
The beginning of time—
set off by a flowerbed!
Look at the children next to it,
little flashes of light.
And the sun and the moon,
the rock's brothers.
How wonderful!
To see how magnificent a pebble is,
a little fleck of gravel.
To hold it on your tongue,
to swallow it—

the beginning of time
deep inside you now,
like a giant stomach ache.

Experiment

I heard a coyote's puppy
whimpering in the snow.
I heard a woman sobbing in the kitchen.
I heard the snow melt in June.
I heard the door close behind me.
At night, I heard a rat perched on the window sill
nibbling on a plastic cup.
I heard its teeth click against each other.
I heard dry leaves blowing.
I stuck my head out the door
and heard the wind over bare
treeless
  nothing.

Lines on a Very Painful Subject

It isn't fair,
my life is so boring.
When I was ready to write about anything—

I was ready to write
about anything.
A little plastic cup at my desk

stuffed with pens.
My penmanship superb, excellent, superior.
Notebook ready.

My parents loved me—
loved me too hard, really.

The sound of a vent blowing air
over my head. In ten minutes
I shall leave all—
for lunch, I shall leave it all for lunch:

a tomato sandwich,
some grapes—

It's not fair,
my life
  is so boring.

Hero

Sometimes there is nothing a man can do
in the face of mortgages
and rising interest rates

in the face of the sexual impulse
the national debt
children

Sometimes a man is overcome
by spelling errors

and he has to make choices
based on instinct
and limited information

and a sentimental longing
for celebrities of his youth

Sometimes there is nothing

If there were you wouldn't be reading this
Nor would I have ever written it

Big Time

Towards the end they stand and cheer

They clap their hands

They throw their hats in the air

They sit down

Now they are calling for hotdogs

They call and call

They begin screaming at the referee

Pointing and screaming

At the field empty as the sea

Someone bring them

A damn hot dog please!

About the Author:

Dave Nielsen is the author of Unfinished Figures, a collection of poems. His writing has recently appeared in Crab Creek Review, Folio, Forge, and other venues. He is the brother of the famed-poet Shannon Castleton, and the son of the highly esteemed Craig and Jerrie Nielsen. He is married to track star Susan Lee Taylor. The couple currently resides in Salt Lake City, on the East Bench.

WHAT SHE NEEDS
by Sophie Chen

SHAMEFUL GOODBYES

She gave you all she had
interminable affection
day to night fondness
a bundle of peace
on nights you can
hardly think straight
the after hours
where even tequila
couldn't calm your angst
yet you
eradicated her soul
disfigured her body
and poisoned her mind
now her absence
eats you away
consumed with guilt
you realize
the toxicity in you
never deserved her

HIS HUNGER FOR HER

men cry too
though they do it soundlessly
in the darker
stage of twilight
under the blinking tree leaves
over a credulous shadow
oftentimes perceived as
the stronger gender
heartache breaks through
and shatters within the soul
regret finally pours in
as the sky begins to weep
thunder bellows
as if representing
its understanding
of the mayhem in yearning

WHAT SHE NEEDS

his lips the color of cherries
breath of lime and vengeance
soul pure as translucent glass
physique craving to be touched
form in maps
of cities and towns and oceans
unexplored
thick filled to the brim hair
styled up like a wave
on top of his head
eyes seductive and filled with light
so glorious
even the sun feels
a twinge of envy
yet all she desired
was his essence
his abiding spirit
and perspicacious mind.

THE DIFFERENCE BETWEEN HIM & HER

you are addicted to the drugs
she's addicted to the ball point pen
to the words that it births
to the ink that bleeds onto paper
you are addicted to the for now's
she is passionate about the forever
you yearn for nothing but lust
she desires the endearment
you crave new skin to touch
new beer to sip
every weekend
she craves the familiar scent
of the masculine body she loves
over everyone else
every night

About the Author:

Sophie Chen is a seventeen-year-old poet who was raised in Queens, NY. At a young age, she loved to write whatever came to mind. It was not until she picked up poetry by R.H.SIN and Rupi Kaur that she realized she, too, relates to the anguish behind the scenes. Her poetry is her self expression and more can be found on her webpage:

https://blissfulremedies-org.webnode.com/

RESSURECTION

by Barry Silesky

RESURRECTION

A phone call tells me I'm breathing and the
world returns. Isn't that what they mean by God? It
must be what we've been waiting for. There's more of
course, but this is the center. Leaves gather in front of
the dirt, the music has a name I recognize, the terrible
gray cold familiar as the rooms, and I'm here again.
Call it resurrection. Not that I was dead, but I might as
well have been. It's from a kind of faith hanging
around the corner everywhere.

But the job doesn't change. The dirt must be
dug, the cells keep going; I'm not done with
anything. The guy's coming to fix the toilet and I have
to be here. Still, an old friend promises to take me
under her wing on a trip I have to take next week. Call
it the good life, whether I find Him or not. Maybe
enough of the cells will work to fool the onlookers,
make the mind believe these are the right clothes and
they actually fit. I'm still listening to the story. I know
the language is wrong, but isn't the idea the
point? This must be a prayer.

HYMN

He's gone now, whoever it is. Only the idea
hangs amid the day's elements, and it's more than I
can explain. The details that make up its heart keep
drifting away like the cat lumped on the corner of the
desk, temporarily anyway, as if to remind me "alive"
is right here.

Isn't that the point I wanted to celebrate? It's
part of the sacred text I've always imagined, that
hundreds wrote through years and years. The body's f
ailure, in tedious repetition, is an excuse blocking my
view of the pages, the letters I have to answer, the
work that organizes the day. Right now the job is
to answer the phone and eat. The food is tasteless, which
is another thing to get used to. We all want it to mean
something, but it's a question of perspective. This
very account is that view, comprising the work I
intended, and the thank-you too, with the petition for
the rest. Call it a hymn

THE NOISE

The usual hum of machines: call it the world
and try again, and harder, the mind says. This is what
they mean by conscious. It's the prayer I can only
know by this language. Eventually it falls into
nothing, but right now this is the very hand that's
shaking me, telling me to look up, to walk to the next
room, to open the window. The rain is coming, though
it hasn't started yet, but the fact is unmistakable as the
job: look out! It's right there! Whatever's "divine" is
the rain; the name doesn't matter. It's ready whenever
I face it.

This must be the time then. Except it's
overcome by the mind's failure to rise, to be aware and
attend, while the storm passes through. All that
remains is the same static— the symphony in the next
room, the book on the table, the blank, crowded with
more than I can list, and
incomprehensible. Someone's coming even now, and
though I'm never ready, I know how to pretend, say
the words, take a breath and wait. I swear I hear you.

NEW SEASON

    Less than a month and it's spring training
again. A frosting of new snow brightens the street;
there **are** reasons to live. This isn't one, but I'll wake
up soon, and the refrigerator's got plenty of food. In
fact, I'll get something to eat as soon as I'm done with
this. And remember the books set out across the
room? Add a short prayer and the whole day begins to
assume a shape I can recognize. Easier said than done,
but hey, saying is the start. Just don't get hopes up for
the rest. Hard to know when the flu grips down,
something smashes a window, and the storm blows in.
But the possibilities are everywhere. The new world
could be right here, about to begin even now.

    By the end of the week, the paper say, the snow
will start to melt and the star the team needs will
sign. Sky clear, no noise, there's plenty to explain, and
the reason we're looking could be anywhere. Smetana
's death in 1884 for instance. And now they think
Chopin was epileptic. He's someone else who didn't
have visions of a different world. That doesn't mean it
isn't right here, waiting, but more is always required:
the guy to fix the broken fan. That sweater, right
there. Whatever you left on the table. The thing is to
keep watching.

PLANET THEORY

"Today things are more complicated." –The Evolution of God, Robert Wright

All the keys hang by the door and the wind howls. When the cold takes over, we hunch against it, warm enough not to move. There's nothing else to ask for, but the phone rings and more is required. More what is the obvious question and the logical place to start. It begins with anything new, which should be enough, and if it doesn't work, there's a boxful of candy, a light, a postcard that must be answered. Now! The storm in the South Seas may begin the whole process, combined with the faint siren outside dying away. The job: look up. Put on the clean clothes. Do something you haven't done. This isn't it, but anything can be the place the mind crouches, poised in the starting blocks, gun about to shoot. Then it does. A little music? Red? Green? Combined with the dog barking and the El train heading downtown, all the elements are here. The machine keeps humming.

But where is He— the one who explains the love and terror, and makes sense of this manic foraging? Wasn't that the point of the dream I felt so powerfully and can't remember? Maybe. Now I can put in the sound of the plane and look for the new planet they've found.

About the Author:

Poet, biographer, and editor **Barry Silesky** was born in 1949 in Minneapolis, Minnesota. He earned a BA from Northwestern and an MA from the University of Illinois-Chicago. His books of poetry include The New Tenants (1992), Greatest Hits, 1980–2000, and The Disease: Poems (2006). He has also published a book of micro-fiction, One Thing That Can Save Us (1994). He is a noted biographer, and his biographies include Ferlinghetti: The Artist in His Time (1990) and John Gardner: Literary Outlaw (2004). Silesky lives in the shadows of Wrigley Field with his wife, fiction writer Sharon Solwitz.

LOVE

by Katharine Studer

Love

Before the word is spoken
A man might walk on hands
Dangling mid-air without a net or wire,
Concentrating to keep the weight
 of his legs extended straight in the center,
Nudging his fingers to gain an inch,
Choosing his words
like a gambler at a roulette table,
Weighing the odds of winning
a straight bet on a single number.
Before the word is spoken
doors are always opened for her, the
Red carpet rolled out and rose petals
arranged like arrows pointing toward him.
Before the word is spoken,
He might lie in bed at night
Imagining the way her face glows
In moonlight, counting the breaths
she expels in the moments between
her last "goodnight" and her dreams.
Before the word is spoken
Dragons are slayed and mountains
would be leveled
and even the slightest brush
of her hand against his leg
allows him to conjour her
as that sex goddess

pinned up on the boy's
teenage wall, red bikinied
and always smiling, eyes
following him from every angle.

First and Last Breath

Rumor has it
we are born alone
and we will die alone
but that too is just a myth and forgets
the way the umbilical cord
holds its grip through the birth canal
and how that snip that cuts through
the knotted skin and breath
becomes the moment one
faces a solo death,
through her warm tears
we arrived in this world
she bore the clamping down of our becoming
and though they lay it
in her arms or gently place it
bare skin upon her chest,
it is expelled from her, forever.

June 24, 2018

Somewhere on a mud floor
on a Sunday afternoon
she stands barefoot, scraping
the last cup of rice
from an empty
bag and boils it into
a tender ball and drops
It into the beans
That have been cooked
to soft brown skins
and feeds it to her
four children by spoonfuls
until they no longer look at her
with open mouths. Outside
her door, a father is missing,
the blood soaked streets
remind her of the brother
who is in hiding,
the blistering heat
creates a danger of a wide
open door, as an uncle
stands guard, hidden in the bushes
 by the wall that surrounds the house,
But even the spikes that line
the windows and porch won't
Keep them out, she keeps one
ear Listening for the sudden yelping of pleasure
of blood rolling down the street like a stream,
for a car engine's reeved-up warning,
for the thumping of footsteps
that appear from nowhere.
The last time they ordered her
to bare her legs,
so she did
without hesitation or complaint,
now her hands never stop shaking,
as she busies herself
with the exhaustion
of keeping her children in doors--
she pulls their fingers off the toy gun
refusing to allow them to pull the trigger,
reciting riddles

to ridden their curiosity
for the sounds of gunfire, for the crying
Of grandmothers whose wailings
becomes an evening ritual, she
holds the children by the waist to keep them
safe,
they pull back in restraint
like a tug of war--
her arms become jelly,
no mid-day rest, no breath
and still this:

In the U.S.
children are being pulled
off their mother's breasts at the borders
whisked away by strangers
without familiar coos or swaying
as they stand in lines in
unfamiliar places without
their favorite blankets or teddy bears
without rag dolls or stick toys
or the rocks they use to build
those cities their mother assured them they
would find
every night in her bedtime lullaby's, places
of swings and marry-go-rounds
of zoos and summer afternoons,
instead abandoned and numbered and pulled
into cages
without the gripped hands of brothers
and uncles, without the lies
they might recognize that were often
whispered
into tiny ears late at night, between
The gunshots and screaming,

> *Be still*
> *Go to sleep now*
> *Be brave dulce niño mio*

And in New York City, Chicago, San Francisco
and LA, signs are being waved to make it stop,
letters are being written by important people,
yet some shout with stern voices "Keep them
Out,"

explaining the process for the thousands
and thousands of children
beyond the drawn lines
who are being photographed
waiting with sheets of aluminum
draped over their bodies for blankets
Is due—All this on a Sunday
afternoon with the church bells ringing
throughout the plains
 and on social media in the small towns, the
suburbs and farmlands
and cities with named streets
the big announcement reads,
"Christmas Eve
is six months from today."

About the Author:

Katharine Studer teaches writing at Ohio University at Chillicothe and The Ohio Dominican University. She holds an MFA from Bowling Green State University in poetry. She divides her time between Ohio and San Francisco. She has had poems published in The Meridian Poetry Anthology, Blue, The Cornfield Review and The Women of Appalachia Project.

BUTTON COLLECTION
by Howard Winn

BUTTON COLLECTION

Bringing order to our mother's house,
as she sat in her rocking chair
watching a daytime television program,
my sister threw out old candy boxes
containing buttons hoarded
from at least sixty years.
They sounded like shaken gourds
as they went into the trash;
although not in Caribbean rhythm.
Snipped from worn clothes
in a mild fever of saving,
these buttons were of all sizes,
shapes and colors, buttoning down
the past even when occasionally
reused in the present.
They might come in handy,
my mother used to say,
and waste not want not.
I think that she just loved
the myriad colors, shapes,
the quantities, the weight ,
the implicit histories,
the textures of enclosure.

INFLUENCE

Neutral studies indicate that success
comes most often if you are tall,
six feet is a minimum,
apparently,
if one is a believer in statistics,
and pretty, or handsome,
when male,
in the most conventional fashion.
Short or ugly? Or both?
Look for happiness in other ways.
Of course, if you have the aforementioned
characteristics of height and beauty,
the sky is the limit.
Even intelligence or stupidity
will not stand in your way.
if you play your cards well.
Political triumph may follow
commercial success,
or vice versa.
Money and fame will flow your way
when you are adept enough
to pose properly,
say little that is not common cliché,
and put your money in off-shore banks,
as yet unknown to the IRS,
if that is still possible.
Finally,
it would be of incalculable benefit,
if you were a born psychopath,
wearing the mask of humane sanity.
One percent of the population
shares that happy condition,
so your odds are poor,
but, hey, you never know what your
genes might provide.
Check your parents.

NEWSPAPER POLL TAKEN RECENTLY

More people
believe
in extraterrestrials
than
believe
in God
in America
at the moment
when polled.
So,
who will
exit
the final
flying saucer
on that day
of
judgment?
The day the mortal life vanishes
for eternal good health?
If there
is one?
And what if
neither faith is
valid?
No one will return
with the news.

CLEARANCE SALE

Buy a governor from our overstock jumble sale.
They can be had at a markdown of a
few million per gov,
but hurry since some are under indictment
and the sell-by date is fast approaching.
There is still time to arrange a tasteful
gerrymandering preparation to suit every
palate
and pocket book although the purchase
may have to include a few state senators
as a side dish or antipasto before the main
meal,
since the bill of fare is not *a la carte* for the
special
but *a table d'hôte* menu.
Hurry in to the governors' bistro.
It is not meant for just anyone with desires or
needs,
but for those special people with champagne
taste
and the investments to match.

THE SUICIDE NEXT DOOR

He has passed on,
she said,
dead being a word forbidden
to her lips
apparently.
Bleed to death right in
the bathtub.
She shuddered
as she vomited those words
Who would have guessed?
Three police cars,
a fire truck
and one ambulance clogged
the private way
as people excluded from the house
paced and hugged.
Dead.
Passed on.
How about passed over?
What would the obituary say?
The woman in the house,
H
his live-lover
staying the night again,
seemed to have slept through it all.
Now she treads the driveway in tight circles
when not held by friends.
The medical examiner must come
for it to be made official,
and then the hearse,
the plastic body bag,
the evacuation of the black vehicles
with the uniformed stunned
young representatives of the law.
A cat is forgotten, left behind for the SPCA.
No reasons are acknowledged
in the death notice of the local newspaper.
Maybe a lovers' quarrel.
As with that illicit word – DEAD--
reasons remain unspoken by those who know,
if they do.
Life gone bad is enough to know.
No one wanted the cat.
Unloved?

About the Author:

Howard Winn's writing has appeared in Xavier Review, Southern Humanities Review, Long Story, Galway Review, Antigonish Review, Blueline, and Evening Street. His novel, "Acropolis" was recently published. His academic study was at Vassar, Stanford, and N. Y. U. He is Professor of English at SUNY.

PEN SAND

by Luke Skoza

Pen Sand

The block of ice she tries to hide
in the backseat
keeps melting on her hands.
An old lake sits around her feet.

Her white rain coat is so clear, it's not transparent.
One of her frightened hands tries to find her legs.

The mound of rock salt sprawled in her tongue
stretches towards the lake.

There's another sea inside
the moldy food in her colleague's drawers.

She wants to put an assignment on your desk,
but she never has a pen
You always have to discover one for her at midnight.

When her hand finally finds her knee,
the salt in her tongue cooks to sand
and is dry enough to reach her eyes.

Bone Olives

The old apartment sits in broken notes
of two letters.

 Her nose crawled on the stove.
Her legs tingled
and burst into pepper
drifting into the noses of thoughtless cows.

Broken windows in abandoned steel
train cars by the vine kingdom of old power
in reptile buildings.

Her dirty
bird cage behind Gambrinus grunts,

it keeps losing its door next

to someone in her closet.

Old dirt wads of grass pile in her room

sliding over fake furniture

next to her friends in sweaters stuck to their skin
holding watered cocktails
tied to their hands.

Olives are bones in their throats

They could fit in a small town of statues

almost growing new teeth every year.

Toes of ages, faces inside balloons
trying to breathe old bubbles.
Old steel become roots again.
Bone olives still stick to sweaters
soaking the water of old cocktails.

BUS TO SANTEE, SOUTH CAROLINA
by John Horváth

REVEREND TERREBONNE PREACHES TO THE DEAF AND DUMB
OF GRUNDY COUNTY

Bought hisself a brand new doublewide painted
white as angel feathers and a red cross atop so's
whomsoever might could descend to make Judgment
would know foursquare whereabout to find him an'
His. With purple sateen sheets--them slick 'uns--
He hung it all inside. And he called it Everyones
Tabernacle of Jesus ain't no Christ, ain't God, but
God's in your own Self by your own Soul its own
Salvation on this Earth. Briefly, they was called
The "Good-n-Earthy" after Terrebonne hisself.
Then late one Saturday whilst he sat watchin'
His favorite televised save-your-soul19.95 Bible-n-
Salvation salesman he got taken with a little lady in
The corner o' the tube with her fingers just a blurrin'
In the name of the Lord.

Terrebonne got inspiration;
Sent off for a booklet on how to sign
Your way thru heaven's pearly gates;
Then commenced t' study the Gospel 'cording
To St. Peter's fingers til he become THE
Deaf-mute preacher of the Deep South
With his stubby little hands just Am-
Slammin away "are ye washed in the blood
Of the lamb?" and "we'll all sing hymn
Number Sixty-nine." Brother Terrebonne
Happy as a sow in summer mud collectin'

donations every Sunday service, every
Wednesday evenin' fellowship, same
each and every Bingo chapter and verse
'cording to the Testament Friday night
with the Good-n-Earthy ladies' auxiliary
(not to mention his special Rosie's Bar
trips to save the lost from drink Tuesday-
Thursday regular at the crossroads town
past the town just down the way
where he took off his collar--Terrebonne
careful not to offend by a man of the cloth
drinkin' sinners under the table for their good).

The Lord works in mysterious ways--
or so Terrebonne would say
in his own peculiar fingered way.

SOWEGA JEWESS

She collects rags which she weaves
into placemats, carpets, dishrags
and carpetbags that she must trade
for newer rags and victuals. Mamas
warn badly behaved babies saying,
"Gonna sell you to the raghag" who,
everyone knew, sucked baby's blood
Friday nights locked in her candle-lit
shack.

South West Georgia's first Jewess
like a rare earth element in clay
came not so very long ago, ignorant
of directions to the promised land;
and, although some hinted turnabout,
she settled into her small tintop shack
along the tracks. Some said she should
move to the other side. The other side
said let her stay put, some folk move
too much.

Childhood fears became swastikas
until one evening when the train
screamed the Jewish Question was
resolved. Old flesh on rusty rails
some swear still bleeds into gravel
and other insist the old hag groans
under the burden of diesels headed
North to the promised land of milk
and honey. Good old boys chuckle,
their red necks bright with knowing
the South will never die--'cause some
truly believe with true belief.

AFTER THE BLUES

He plays at the corner of Meridian and
    Main Saturdays for socialite mobs
Leaving Late Matinee fictional
    characters battling dangerous foes
Their Silverspoon fantasies left on
    the screen Off to appertif dinner
        and drinks
Or suburban sunrise Sundays when
    their bedcrust eyes ope like
        peonies to daylight
then close on remembering once
    having been something but blind
poor excuses for not having souls

And he plays there the sax
whose crisp riffs
stagger into alleyways where black
    cats tom and soft bitches hang
Their heads down into the trashbin
    hostelries of bankers' sons gone bad
rancid with failure

All around 'em his notes banging
    'gainst bottles o' rye
Cheap beer halfpiss and halfvinegarish wines
And they damn well do love
When it wraps warm misery rhythms 'round
    their can't give a damn lives
He plays all night backup to their
    memories and recalls of when they
        had
real ones until it all dies down to a long
    low note drawn out that dries
under the heat of the sun coming up.

Common playmate, corner princess Tanya
Shares the saxophonist's territory;
Helps him count his coins at night end nightly
Before he departs to sleep where ever
He can find a bedroom cheap for sinners.
Tanya says it aint music, not atall --
Can't sing a lick of that stick – but

that hard as metal thing he's got
under the lamplit corner of Meridian
    and Main Street after the social set
        has gone.
She comes again and again.

She's after the blues.

BUS TO SANTEE, SOUTH CAROLINA

(Busing East toward Santee, South Carolina--
Beulah's broad bottom like a baker's bad cake,
Earl's pale frosted cheeks, sitting five seats
apart among the drunks, loud-mouthed pimple
-plus
kids, and mothers who smoke Marlboros and
hold
wet diaper babies over the roaring engine.
Hear 'em all night.)
Earl's waiting for darkness
and inside lights to play mirror on his window
so he can catch sight of her reading that Book
five seats back, across the aisle from him.
It ain't like that he never been in love;
Never been in love for a while is all.
His women plump and grateful, he thinks,
wanting another; wishing he could stand,
walk the bouncing path all the way back
to the bathroom redlight but not wanting
degenerates watching him, wondering why
or what he goes to relieve; not wanting
apologetic smiles of bad breath mothers
greeting him either, only a chance to move
with a ready excuse to speak with HER--
wanting to kiss Beulah.

　　　Beulah's seen his lean face, sunken eyes
like a puppy's, his oversize ears and rough-cut
hair a little longer than his three day beard.
Three days ago he sat down to start his vigil,
a squint-eye peekaboo with his seat down,
next
one up, pretending to sleep. But she noticed--
a man, she decided, who might have been
someone
some time ago. Something about deviants,
drunks
and derelicts attracted her, forced her juices
to seep down into the sweat between her
thighs.
　　　　　　　Bus Station
　　　　　　　Carrolltown
　　　　　　　Georgia--

She rises to leave and he stands, turning to her.
She begins to pass and he places his hand on her
　　　　　　　(Wanting to kiss Beulah).
She pauses to hand him her Book. "Thank you,"
says Earl.
She leaves and turns to look through the window;
On the wet asphalt through the window,
She alone smiles because Earl is reading:

　　"Give, I pray you, loaves of bread
　　　　unto the people that follow me;
　　　　　for they be faint, and I am pursuing.."
　　　　Gideon 8, verse 4.

About the Author:

Mississippian **John Horváth** (now that I'm 70, I'm dropping the 'Jr') publishes poetry internationally since the 1960s (recently in Burningword Literary Journal (Best of 2018), Adelaide Literary Magazine, Brave Voices (Zimbabwe), London Reader, Subterranean Blue, Ink Sweat & Tears). After Vanderbilt and Florida State universities, "Doc" Horváth taught at historically Black colleges. Since 1997, to promote contemporary international poetry, Horváth edited for 20 years, the magazine at www.poetryrepairs.com.

THAT OLD BLACK MAGIC

by Gary Beck

Machine Learning

Before a car can drive
without a human,
one must first get behind the wheel.
As the driver accelerates,
stops and turns on local streets,
sensors in the car
record what he sees
and how he responds.

A team of engineers
build software
that can teach the car
how to behave
from the human data.

Software is installed
in the waiting car
eager to drive on its own
and mimics the choices
made by the human driver,
making it autonomous.
It won't get drunk,
tailgate, smoke pot, text,
explode in road rage.

Sight

The property of light
does not give ownership
to those who see
only material things,
illumination elusive,
for even the blind
need to find their way
through the darkness.

That Old Black Magic

Old king coal
was once the soul
of American heating,
keeping us warm,
those who could afford it,
in bitterest winter.

Then the arrival of oil
created turmoil
when environmental concerns
and new capitalists
proposed a solution
to air pollution,
stop burning coal.

Conflict wasn't overt
like the Civil War
between Southern agriculture
and Northern mercantilism,
but bituminous magnates
had a lot invested
that they didn't want divested
and resisted stealthily.

There's no doubt the coal barons
bought oil stock, wells, companies,
but they wouldn't give up profit,
no matter who it poisoned.
They finally got a champion
in candidate Trump,
who played the miners for a chump,
promising new jobs
if they elected him.

Only desperate men
could ignore the boom
of shale oil, natural gas
that would end the rule
of traditional fuel
because it was easier to get,
cheaper to get, cleaner to use,

at least in comparison
to dirty old coal.

Coal powered plants are closing,
so less coal is needed.
Fewer miners are needed
while the insulated bosses
no longer dig holes in the ground,
just chop off the tops of mountains,
a massive assault on nature,
but still profitable.

The American way
has gone astray
that once allowed many
comfortable lives.
Now fewer and fewer
of the endangered middle class
still don't realize the goal,
to make them as obsolete as coal.

Loss

My love has departed.
I wait beneath her window
in the pouring rain,
hoping to catch a glimpse
of the one I lost
and I have become drenched,
waiting to see my beloved.

Aging II

The elderly slowly shuffle
through hazardous city streets
menaced by careless drivers,
cracked sidewalks,
vicious predators
in increasing numbers
attacking the vulnerable,
old men and women
incapable of self-defense,
helpless to resist
assault, robbery,
victims of the dispossessed
subtracted from human values.

About the Author:

Gary Beck has spent most of his adult life as a theater director. He has 14 published chapbooks. His poetry collections include: Days of Destruction (Skive Press), Expectations (Rogue Scholars Press). Dawn in Cities, Assault on Nature, Songs of a Clerk, Civilized Ways, Displays, Perceptions, Fault Lines, Tremors, Perturbations, Rude Awakenings and The Remission of Order (Winter Goose Publishing). Contusions and Desperate Seeker will be published by Winter Goose Publishing. Conditioned Response (Nazar Look). Resonance (Dreaming Big Publications). Virtual Living (Thurston Howl Publications). Blossoms of Decay, Expectations and Blunt Force (Wordcatcher Publishing). Transitions and Temporal Dreams will be published by Wordcatcher Publishing. His novels include: Extreme Change (Cogwheel Press), Flawed Connections (Black Rose Writing), Call to Valor and Crumbling Ramparts (Gnome on Pigs Productions). As part of the continuing series, 'Stand to Arms Marines', Gnome on Pigs Productions will publish the third book in the series, Raise High the Walls. Sudden Conflicts (Lillicat Publishers). Acts of Defiance, Flare Up and Pirate Spring will be published by Wordcatcher Publishing. Extreme Change will be published by Winter Goose Publishing. His short story collections include, A Glimpse of Youth (Sweatshoppe Publications). Now I Accuse and other stories (Winter Goose Publishing). Dogs Don't Send Flowers and other stories (Wordcatcher Publishing). The Republic of Dreams and other essays will be published by Gnome on Pigs Productions. Feast or Famine & other plays will be published by Wordcatcher Publishing. His original plays and translations of Moliere, Aristophanes and Sophocles have been produced Off Broadway. His poetry, fiction and essays have appeared in hundreds of literary magazines. He lives in New York City.

UNHOLY MEDICINE
by Mark J. Mitchell

UNHOLY MEDICINE

If Buddha had a cold
would the eight-spoked wheel
still start to turn?

Would the diamond vehicle
convey learned saints
above the summit of Mount Meru?

Would chanting monks
set ancient columns
vibrating with wordless songs?

Would meditation cushions
stay empty, even unmade?
Would zendos be storerooms?

Could there be saffron robed,
shaved-headed teachers wandering
Lhasa, Paris or Enid, Oklahoma?

Where would the loose
compassion find a home?
Who would discover Metta?

Perhaps another could find
a holy tree, could creates
a completely other Bodhgaya?

If Buddha had a cold
would we be left with
"Life is sniffling"?

ORIGIN OF UNEASE

You seem misplaced—a key under the sports
section or check-up card from your dentist.
Not lost, not right though. Morning toast
resists
the jam. The newspaper carries all sorts
of plague news. Outside moist heat hides in
mist.
The day calls you in spite of your desire
for warm comfort in bed, for the banked fire
of heat she left behind. Your alarm insists
you rise. It was some dream—where you were
hired
to gather jeweled sins that mourners dropped
at your own wake. There was a girl with
cropped
hair hiding the keys to your task. You stopped
while she taught you wicked ways to disport
with death, leaving the dream floor damp,
unmopped.

THE WANDERING COMMUTER

...be lowlie wise
—John Milton
Paradise Lost, Book VIII line 171

The ghost of a tic haunts her pale left cheek.
She texts premature sorrows and two weak
apologies while the bus rolls to a stop.
She rises at each bell and switches spots
when doors hiss open. Her skirt is too neat
for work, she knows. But knows that's all she
knows.
There's no learning left in her. Traffic flows
through flashing lights. She unfolds her long
hands
and grabs the stop cord, rising to stand—
grade-school stiff—just to please an empty
ghost.

MILLENIUM TOWER

*The gods are back, companions. Right now they
have just entered this life; but the words that
revoke them, whispered underneath the words
that reveal them, have also appeared that we
might suffer together."*

—*René Char*

The gods of this city, at rest atop
their leaning tower, sip smooth designer
coffee. One says, "It's time to put a stop
to worship of numbers. They refine their
calculations and forget about us."
A goddess answers—drowned out by a bus
passing below. "Temples don't get finished,"
says a stern, old god. "They forget to pray."
"That bothers you?" winks a love god, playing
the fool, sliding to the street like a fish.

"Suburbs can be nice—they're very quiet,
 with wispy trees and green lawns of rolled sod.
Their hearths are screens. No talk. You should
try it
for a bit." This was the laziest of the gods.
"I eat prayers," mouthed the stern one. I miss
smoke
from offerings, ceremonies." (when he spoke
clouds formed around the tower's slanted top).
"We are all numbers and have always been,"
said the slyest god. "I desire days when
people are kind and their sad noises stop."

"When we made them," offered the lost love
god
just back from the cool street, "we taught them
fire
and stone. Make things, we said. We thought
the odds
were long, they wouldn't last. Now we're all
tired
just watching them speed around cherished
grids."
That goddess said something but a truck hid
her sounds. They looked at their city and
wished
for better creatures. Still, the stiff exhaust
was a kind of smoke, a new holocaust.
They breathed deep. Cracked the glass. Made a
fresh myth.

MYSTERY RELIGION

*Ayez pitié de votre Dieu qui n'a pas su vous
rendre heureux*
(Pity your God, unable to make you happy.)
    —*Jules Supervielle*
    God's Sorrow

First bow to darkness. When the hawk-faced
girl
appears, formed from pain, accept her cold
book.
A page will find your touch and texts will hook
your hands. Let your fingers create what God
forgot to write. Let each loop and spiral
seep like blood into your skin. Then meaning
unfolds. Avoid sounds, breezes and seeming
breath. Her hawk face is gone leaving an odd
angled light. A language enters through touch
and knocks your hand aside. Know this is all
a pantomime that's been acted before
that hovers because something—not much,
but something real, is asking you to fall
into dark. Hold this world. There's nothing
more.

About the Author:

Mark J. Mitchell's latest chapbook, Music for
the Other Voices is available from Finishing
Line Press. A full-length collection of poems,
Starting from Tu Fu is coming from Encircle
Publications in September. His novel, The
Magic War was published by Loose Leaves
Publishing. He studied at Santa Cruz under
Raymond Carver and George Hitchcock. His
work appeared in several anthologies and
hundreds of periodicals. He lives with his wife,
Joan Juster making his living pointing out pretty
things in San Francisco. A meager online
presence can be found at https://
www.facebook.com/MarkJMitchellwriter/

ETERNAL AND INFINITE
by Scott Thomas Outlar

Loki's Ammunition

Sometimes we must
set the book aside
for a moment,
exhale a deep breath,
and exclaim,
"My God, that's what a poem is!"

No whitewash on the crescendo
where it all went to hell.

No handbasket to carry
your broken mirage of thin clichés.

Wear your wounds well,
ripped, torn, tattered, shred,
and sip my blood
from the stagnant puddle
of pride and regrets.

There is passion in the words
exchanged between lovers
when the arrow is initially shot,
but there comes a second death
when old letters are discovered
on dusty shelves believed forgotten.

What hand penned such thoughts
from the head rush of sweet amore?

It can't be dubbed a lie
if it felt like truth in the moment,
but even the most sincere hearts
can sometimes be fooled
by trickster gods
on the prowl.

Let Others Fool Around with Stones

Techniques, styles, comparisons,
critiques –

I listen to others
discuss the work
of their contemporaries
or that from the canon

I tune in with interest
to such discourse
and perhaps
even nod or shake my head

but rarely will I ever
opine on such a subject

because in the end
it has no bearing
on the words I write

Thoughts about ghosts
are about as good as a mirage

and as far
as running my mouth
about the writing of others
I'd rather stay mum
and tend to my own

Hemorrhage

Dark in the belly of hunger

A way out
of the whale

waiting in slumber

Watery wombs and tombs
between us

Winter masks/summer shades
quiet desperation

Holding our breath
as lungs fill/collapse

The final fall
hits (hurts) hardest

Black in the night of no moon

A new taste
of the silence

promises of smoke

Eyes with specks and beams
that blind us

Autumn tears/springtime gasps
ring hollow

Biting our tongues
as blood flows/fails

The ancient smile
slips (snaps) loudest

Eternal and Infinite

Are those stars
or the headlights of a car?
O my dear,
we are all just deer
staring at God.

About the Author:

Scott Thomas Outlar hosts the site 17Numa.com where links to his published poetry, fiction, essays, interviews, reviews, live events, and books can be found. His work has been nominated for the Pushcart Prize and Best of the Net. Scott was a recipient of the 2017 Setu Magazine Award for Excellence in the field of literature. His words have been translated into French, Italian, Dutch, Persian, Serbian, Albanian, and Afrikaans. His radio show Songs of Selah airs weekly.

THE PEOPLE WHO VANISH
by Ryan Havely

The People Who Vanish

You wear the wind around you
like a favorite shawl. I try
to hold you against me
and you go to ashes. You
leave like a storm,
tie your hair
with ribbons
like rivers
like ribbons. Others have gone this way.
The self-proclaimed matador
who called himself Gazania
fell through a puddle
and vanished. The old women
say he was dreamed
by a sick child
or the widow whose lover
wandered up the blue ridge
toward Phoenix Mountain
one dawn and never wandered
back. His hat came bobbing
down Cranberry Creek
later that summer. The old women
say a widow can build a man
out of dreams. She left too,
the widow. A pack of dogs
watched her float, sleeping,
into the foggy moon
not long after Gazania

slipped through that crack
in his reflection. Most people say dogs lie
but the old women
know a late mist held the widow
like a girdle that night
and before she was gone
she fluttered in the wind
like a cattail. Your eyes
bare a luster of going, and this is not a place
where the people refuse to *go*.
Maybe you jump
into a kiss of smoke
and scatter, or you dream
a copper hill
rich in Spanish Poppy
and wake there. How you go
is your business, just as the wind
that takes you
is the wind's business
and the hard shadows
you leave behind
like oil stains
offer their empty
to the others
who follow you away.

Chicken Little

Can you imagine a world more sad
more penetrated or irate
more whole and unforgotten
Anything you say before sunset is true
rain falls in straight lines and the drops
never touch   if they touched the sky'd fall
 with them   if the sky falls you'll wake up afraid
if you're afraid   you'll hurt yourself   and others
if you hurt yourself   and others the seas   won't churn
if the seas don't churn   math won't work   if math
won't work the numbers   can't match and   if the
numbers can't match the   sky might fall and
if the sky falls we'll all be   afraid again and if
we're afraid we'll send men with no beards
as far as we can send them and we'll tell
them to draw lines on the earth and wait

to rise like suns from holes in the mud
and run like rivers toward guns
We'll tell them they can't be afraid
because we're not afraid
and the sky hasn't fallen
and the numbers check out

Isn't It Was Love?

Imagine it's about you,
this poem, any poem
you like. Ask me to write
you a poem, and I'm finished.
I wrote it when I wrote
this poem, now, then,
back right now when
I'm wrote, when I writing
with you docked like a canoe,
tied to a tree on a sandbar in my
imagination. Ask what is not
about you, what thought could be,
what thinking would even matter
were you not its seed,
and I will tell you
                    nothing.

Seppuku in the Kitchen

First, cut a green pepper, red pepper, and
onion
into long, thin strips, and set aside. Some
snowflakes melt before they find ground,
yet each is no less a snowflake
than the pebble in your sock is less a stone
than the granite slab on the riverbed—
rainbow trout resting an inch above
in the never-ending water that dreams
of stillness. The trout find peace in high
currents,
find stillness in hurried streams. Next, peel
and dice two large cloves of garlic and chop
a nice handful of cilantro. Put your skillet
over medium-high heat. Do not blame
the nightmare for your terror. The nightmare's
job is to frighten, as the song's job is to tempt,
as the autumn-red oak leaf's job
is to castle windsweptly downward and skirt
along the ground, farther from home
with each gust. Coat pan with oil and add
peppers, onions, and the chicken you
marinated overnight while the red moon
lingered in your window like a grifter
so when you wanted to see out you only saw
your face on the moon, your vapid eyes
at the bottoms of bloodshot craters, boot-
prints
stamped into your skin. Stir frequently.
When chicken is cooked through,
add garlic and one-third cilantro to hot pan,
turn
off heat and stir. Next, kneel and insert blade
into abdomen
just left of navel and cut toward right until
overcome with pain. Finally, pull blade
upward,
cut until blade hits moon and recite your death
poem.
If you've nothing to say, the moon
says nothing, so wash your hands

and start again. If each word
of your breath rhymes with the moon,
it will sit like a jester in your window.
Go with him. Listen to his stories,
laugh at his jokes.
Serve with tortillas.

About the Author:

Ryan Havely earned his B.A. in English from Ohio University and his M.F.A. in Creative Writing from Minnesota State. He worked as a college professor for a decade before moving into marketing. His work is found in such magazines as Pebble Lake Review, Ampersand, Midwestern Gothic, and Main Street Rag, among others.

HUMAN BEING

by William Welch

Untitled [poem for Lent, 2018]

"I'm not Rumpelstiltskin," I said, joking,
then realized how apt it was —
that malicious imp coming nightly
to anguished girls, promising to spin
straw to gold, but for a price.

Imagine if he used his power for other ends,
if he set broken bones without casts,
changed old tires to loaves of bread,
or melted bullets down to water —
how full would wells be in Syria,
how much blood spared?

But, I must consider my own actions.
Haven't I made selfish bargains?
And for all my one-sided loved,
how justly do I deserve the name
       — Judas.

Human Being

the fetus seems like
a question mark that nature
puts before itself

men grown stand erect
their posture straight determined
an exclamation

our bodies recurve
with age as if we're asking
to return again

refind the start of
our sentence and rephrase it
make our sense better

Pismires

Four men, after twelve hours of work,
sat down with bottles of beer by the lumber
pile
where ants all day had outdone their labor.
The youngest, while the older carpenters
talked,
saw a gang of ants struggling in the dusk,
carrying off the carcass of a bee.

It was like watching men move an aeroplane
from a hanger, one of those wooden ones
used in the first world war: rickety things,
flying against the laws of nature,
and on their backs, absurd pilots
showed the wind their teeth and dared
birds to race them toward the sun.

The ants, who lost their wings,
were stealing them back again.
They hauled the bee forward, its rigid body,
striped with dazzle camouflage, unwieldy
on the ground. Its eyes, even lifeless,
seemed to realize where it was going.

"Look," the boy said to the men. His foreman
quipped,
"Now they know how to work," and that was
all.

About the Author:

William Welch grew up in Central New York. He's been fortunate to have traveled more than he once expected and has lived in Brooklyn, NY and Houston, TX. He has done a wide variety of work, from assisting the emeritus director of the Film and Video Center at The National Museum of the American Indian, to learning carpentry. Currently, he resides in Utica, NY, where he works for a community arts center called The Other Side, editing the organization's literary journal, Doubly Mad. He is also studying to become a registered nurse. William's poetry has appeared in Pudding Magazine, The Dr. T.J. Eckleburg Review, Denim Skin and, most recently, Belle Ombre.

SO BRIEFLY HERE

by John Grey

THESE VACATION MEMORIES

Tourists trudge through
the makeshift marketplace along the dock,
inspect the obligatory merchandise:
chess sets, shell necklaces,
coconuts carved into faces.
"Very cheap," says one local after another.

But the visitors have little time to stop.
They're on their way
to a flotilla of buses
that will take them around the Caribbean
island.
They'll hear the history, see the sights.
No need to worry that they've missed a
bargain.
The trinkets aren't going anywhere.
They'll be even cheaper on their return.

That's how the ceramic dolphin

makes its way to a mantle in suburbia.

It keeps company with a diving horse,

a china thimble painted with a pineapple.

It's all part of vacation Alzheimer's.

The history fades.

The scenery's a blur.

They forget everything but what

was made in Vietnam.

SO BRIEFLY HERE

Irises bloom then wait
to be hammered by the weather.
They are born into their own savaging

Some sprout around
the statue of the bending maiden
who has lost a limb
and most likely her desire.

The meadows gleam
but then sandpaper wind
scrapes away their softness.

I can't get over
how battered some beauty gets.

There is no justice
just a withering,
a clap of thunder
raising more young
to the west.

THE CATCH

The stream is as thin and shallow as a
ballerina's leg.
Fishermen's creels lower their sights.

Twilight, bugs pick up the pace.
Water stills but hands start swatting.

Men and a few small fish make their way
homeward.
Should have thrown them back.

Not much more than nothing is still nothing.
Need some cream for those welts.

Conversation in the truck mostly about
how plentiful the trout used to be.

Twenty miles of shrinking expectations.
Then house lights, an expanding whole other.

About the Author:

John Grey is an Australian poet, US resident. Recently published in the Homestead Review, Poetry East and Columbia Review with work upcoming in the Roanoke Review, the Hawaii Review and North Dakota Quarterly.

I ALMOST KNEW THIS
by Frederick Pollack

I Almost Knew This

1

Love is a pleasant, working seaside town.
Strangely, its major industries
are neither tourism nor fishing;
it lives on gentrification
per se. There's a small dock.
Most of the residents came
from elsewhere, but are devoted to the place
and view themselves as natives.
The sea in this allegory
is grief. You have a boat,
but eventually you sell it;
it wouldn't get you far should the waves rise.

2

You know that Renaissance etching –
a favorite once of hippies and New Age types,
still employed as an ad
for some transcendence or other: a guy
in scholar's robes and skullcap kneeling
at the edge of the flowery, forested world,
sticking his head
and upper torso through a crystal sphere
and gazing with awe, arms outspread,
at wider spheres, all sun and stars and light?
A good way to get your ass kicked.

3

I really don't care, do u?
– Melania

Absurd and servile to imagine
that any member of the 1%
(before he pressed the button dropping you
from your chair into a disintegrator beam)
would describe, coldly, logically,
happily, his and their
ultimate plans. Dr. Evil *works for* them,
and for him too the point is focus,
lack of emotional investment, the short term.
The BWA-HA-HA-HAA of cartoons
implies the moral consciousness
it mocks, which is a petit-bourgeois handicap.
(The peasantry, as always, senses this
and pennilessly emulates its betters.)
Likelier that a master
will scurry between his bar
and pills, clutching his phone, shrieking batlike
at a lawyer. Think also
of that disintegrating suet
major donor on a wheelchair-scooter
accompanied by arm-candy ...
Tall, stately, lacking somewhat
the requisite cheekbones;
her thoughts beneath the careful tan
as close as we will get to the superman.

4

A Roger Ballen photo, looking back
in part to his photojournalism:
decayed white inbred *dorps*
of South Africa, angry hulking microcephalics …
But this guy,
sitting on the edge of a bed,
is chalking on a wall, a foot away,
faces. His own, long, pale, and flat, turns
jut-jawed towards you;
the whites of his eyes show.
The faces are small, quite simplified,
demonic, crew-cut. He may be
prevented by his medium
and stylistic assumptions from saying
whatever he would about himself and men
in general. Or perhaps
he is saying everything he wants to say.

5

And in another Ballen shot
(or is this a composite?)
the Witnesses, his charcoal cutouts,
line the implied walls;
they are so used to wanting to be elsewhere
they avidly take in whatever happens.
Animals and parts of animals,
some alive, some toys, help
cords and tangled wire define the space
(Nature is holes and will go down holes).
While on the sheets below,
cluttered with other witnesses,
mice and a lizard
crawl, and from the tangles hands emerge,
seeking Yolandi Visser
of the band Die Antwoord,
who welcomes them perhaps but her hands
are full.
(She has the sort of beauty that ages well
because it's so close to the skull.)

6

Others had horses, abuse from their own
and other bodies, the self-righteous smell
of cows, grandparents, parents mourned
and hated from the womb, a "you" who said
nothing
or went on and on, bourgeois plants
whose names I never learned, the joy
of signifiers liberated
from signifieds, compassionate tourism;
I had only my suspicions.
By now I've forgotten what most of them were,
which is their nature and why they remain
important. I forgot, above, to mention
religious poets, to whom I have something to
say.
If God exists, he can do *one* thing
for me: when I (who never
served, and won't)
ask him to let his servant depart in peace.

Near the Ocean

1

Legendary good-time girls,
not sisters (each has one, good,
scolding, not in contact) but might have been,
shared eye-drops, and make-up
for veins in cheek and nose; see themselves
both as outriders and moral center
of dusty rental complex, an iterated
shack, near the World-Famous Pollo
Piquante, students, druggies,
student/druggies, a teacher, Pier-workers
whom
they don't date, holding out
for sugar, meanwhile entertaining (themselves
with)
too-rich-for-but-sequacious-of-
the-gangs young Latins, scared, good weed
and pills; white wine from morning on,
annoyed by a couple staying in illegal
bnb downstairs, whose door they adorn
that afternoon with tp, markers, then some
eggs lying around in the fridge, that'll show
'em.

2

The sliding-glass door always open, no fear
of bugs (sometimes flies). On the walkway
between the low fence and the beach, tourists
look,
maybe wave, raise phones, must envy
the liquor whose shelves take up most of the
facing
wall; see also (as sun heads towards China) a
jersey, a flag, a medal, some funny-
obscene and/or hopeful incitements
on posters. And friends, always friends,
deployed
on a vintage though frayed and taped beanbag
indoors, or
the balcony. But there's no question who's
the center, the shoulders still wide

as a tank, the belly still vaguely muscled over
the trunks (the friends also always about
to run towards the sea): the loudest, chin
drawn down, neck swelling and red when
he laughs and laughs again, I was I AM NOT
responsible for everything
I saw, so now I see nothing.

Ataraxia

1

The masters of the world are Pyrrhonists
of a sort. It's indifferent to them
whether they appear
before crowds (on the rare occasions
they must) in T-shirt or their native suit.
Someday with equal grace
they will readopt togas or thick perfumes.
They play golf and read nothing,
to obviate infection.

Undermasters are not above
curiosity and self-display. When the new
retail and restaurant complex
at the Wharf opens (near their boats),
they stroll and eat and buy. Perhaps
one enters the doomed but
briefly brave bookstore. You might
enjoy decoding Language poetry,
bro, but don't mess with me.

2

At the end I'll be too busy
begging for morphine
to think anything, so this passage
is a sort of self-bequest. I've always
despised Kierkegaard (almost as much
as his God), but rather admire
how at the end he balanced
outstanding debts and assets.
When the drugs kick in I'll try to solve,
one last time, in theory, my two
conundra: how to make fifty,
a hundred, at most a few thousand years
the metaphysical horizon; and my own version
of *unde malum*: Why is pain more convincing?
(They say it isn't but they lie.)
But really at best I'll think dreamily
of love and people and regrets

until breathing gets hard. If I'm lucky,
Medicare won't end or my secondary
coverage run out before I do.

3

Mannerist neck, true blond,
stacked. If you were smart,
you realized she was out of your league.
Few or no signals, but also
not the flat affect
of a lesbian in that town and era warning
you off. Something else.
If you were even smarter, you stayed and
talked.
"When I was thirteen," she said, "and
miserable,
a voice came to me in my bed;
just a few words, clichéd, forgiving,
heartening. I couldn't tell
who had spoken. It didn't matter;
it could have been myself, but not the I
who heard. And who decided to go on,
and rely on my mind. I went into physics
and flourished, despite the obstacles."
She described her work, engagingly, without
vanity.
Impressed, I muttered, "Art can serve as well."

4

The smell and lamentations –
distancing word! – of the refugees
(not "immigrants," they won't be let in)
at the end of the lawn is less obtrusive
than the sound of crickets,
exhausted by their night's exertions.
There is a layer of time
between those dirty hungry people
and me. It may be just a membrane
or thicker than my future, but it muffles the
cries

of their kids. I feel bad.
I walk to the end of the lawn and tell them,
"You must hate me."
(They all speak English, still.) "We don't hate
you,"
they say. "We're only abstractly aware of you.
Don't feel bad." Their voices are further
muted by the ministrations
of cops of some sort who shoot
and stack them, light a hecatomb on the spot.
(Intolerable in this heat, their armor
focuses their efforts.) "But really,
I want to help," I say –
to the refugees, not the cops.
At least some Diet Coke, like I give my
gardener.

Nor Melt Away

1

If I had lived a few more years
(and why shouldn't I have? Good genes,
hale satisfied centenarian),
I might have asked the following:
What is time but style?
In my youth, I wore the black uniform.
Some girls found it sexy, some scary,
which gave us a good way of judging girls.
(Men in black, it's well known, are *serious*.)
At his trial, Fat Hermann
said that in fifty years
there would be small statues of him
in every German home – very small, perhaps,
but there. He was decades off,
and might he have been visualizing
bobbleheads?
Still ... Then Grass, the novelist,
briefly a comrade, had someone
sing at the end (no doubt trying
to surrender to the Americans),
The trend is toward the bourgeois-smug.
For me it was. Without regret,
I abandoned stern nihilism
for the jaunty relativism
of commerce. Holidayed on nude beaches,
accepted my decadent children
and perverse grandchildren, even developed
some taste, as you can tell. But youth returns.

2

Griffin, archaeologist of the Anthropocene,
masked in the heat against hantavirus,
armed, exploring trailers and lean-tos
far from towns
in southeastern California and western Nevada,
found among the drifts and piles
a bundle of letters. The rubber-band
broke on touch. Neat penciled cursive,

school paper. Examinations
of feeling, immediate, honest, untainted
by literature, detailed
concern for mostly implied unspecified
problems, heartfelt considerate
advice, and hope (not, interestingly, faith)
continually urged … Nearby,
amidst receipts, bills,
tissues and droppings lay some polaroids
that had perhaps belonged. Green T-shirt,
blue dress, great hanging breasts and armflesh;
one of the faces puffy
from drink but neither visibly bruised.
Looking at them one imagined love
as high above the desert as any vulture.

3

If pain alone is real to us,
with violence as its faithful
sidekick and attorney, the old saw
"Life is a dream" has meaning.
Pain is the fuel of the dream,
whose work like that of poetry
is apotropaic: to deflect pain.
That inexplicable crowd
one day on Olympic or was it Pico
(new discount place?) was obviously dreaming.
Driving, whether on surface streets
or freeways, is a tense dream.
The position of any observer
is dreamlike. Shostakovich at the end
borrowed the xylophone from Saint-Saens's
"Skeleton Dance" for his own bones,
Rossini for an echo of his snide
youth. He believed the KGB
wouldn't get him now, something else would;
surveillance had been handed off.
"Good people on both sides"
at Nazi demonstrations
dream each other: as pain;
as opportunities for violence.
The important thing is not to use
the word "we" imprecisely,

certainly not for humanity at large.
"We" in the present case is Santa Monica.
When I was sick I went to a hospital.
I brought my notebook and three books
from the NYRB Classics series,
read, sweated, tried to read.
They found me a bed. I lay reading,
waiting for the specialist. And then I woke up.

4

An early-morning light-angle
where a ceiling meets a wall
resembles engineered effects
in shots of more expensive houses.
She has to go to the doctor.
He'll take her, and wait, though it's
unnecessary
(next week she'll return the favor).
Then they'll shop, at an overpriced chain
that has outlived its reputation,
but its fruits remain good and they want fruit.
Returning, he'll do laundry
and attack the kitchen floor
with a Swiffer. (Even to mention
the maid who comes bi-weekly could
suggest discomfort that they have a maid
and ruin the delicate effect.)
Then while she cooks he'll take his evening pills
and feed the cat, who is already
leaping onto and off
the ledge beneath the ledge that holds her
treats,
not sure that after a lifetime he'll remember.
(It may be sentimental to use the cat.)
With dinner, news, as much as bearable,
silenced when Trump appears
("That man doesn't speak in our house,"
she decreed and he approves),
unless the latest crime has been exceptional.
Later he asks what she's thinking.
She's thinking about the problems of a friend;
he, recalling an old article
decrying the tendency of mainstream poems
to end with bursts of vague philosophy.

About the Author:

Author of two book-length narrative poems, The Adventure (Story Line Press, 1986) and Happiness (Story Line Press, 1998), and two collections, A Poverty of Words (Prolific Press, 2015) and Landscape with Mutant (Smokestack Books, 2018). In print, **Pollack's** work has appeared in Hudson Review, Southern Review, Salmagundi, Poetry Salzburg Review, Manhattan Review, Skidrow Penthouse, Main Street Rag, Miramar, Chicago Quarterly Review, The Fish Anthology (Ireland), Poetry Quarterly Review, Magma (UK), Neon (UK), Orbis (UK), and elsewhere. Online, his poems have appeared in Adelaide Review, Big Bridge, Diagram, BlazeVox, Mudlark, Occupoetry, Faircloth Review, Triggerfish, and elsewhere. Adjunct professor of creative writing at George Washington University.

RED FOREST

by Dmitry Blizniuk

Red forest

You live in me.
Every morning you come to my eyes
From inside my head. They look like French windows –
Their clear cast glass extends down to your feet.
You stretch yourself on tiptoe and look out
At the green, breathing waterfall of the new day,
Staying yourself.
You stare at the well-known but unfamiliar world
At the city waking up in lilac pebbles...
I've given you a bright drop of immortality,
I've let you live in the red forest of my heart
like a bird of prey, tawny owl...
-
I used to kiss you,
Inhaling the sweet smoke
From the clay mouthpieces of your breasts.
I absorbed the brackish essence
Of your translucent clavicles and neck.
My fingers rubbed the moire glow
On your shoulder-blades.
I held your consciousness
In my hand like a fluffy dandelion.
It was enough to blow tenderly in your eyes
To puff away all your seeds
And send them slowly waltz around the bedroom
Like a thousand and one swan needles...

After that, we used to sleep, hugging each
other.
Sometimes I started in my half-sleep like a
fridge,
And you gently stroked the nape of my neck.
Our flat was ropy with wires.
It needed a renovation
Like a poor fakir needs
A new basket for his dancing snakes.
We didn't have either a magic fish capable of
granting wishes
Or even the sea,
Only a monumental view from the window,
Looking like a (removed by the moderator.)
-

I was a kid inside a ship,
And you were my mysterious sea.
I fought against the light of your candle;
No one wanted to give in,
To lose to the scalding darkness growing
between us.
I whispered "off",
But your love glowed softly.
Little by little you were becoming a part of me;
You nestled inside my brain
Like a blade nestles inside a pocket knife
handle,
Like the rib outgrowing Adam…
-

My love,
I've become a hostage of good habits
I'm plagued by the universal hunger:
Everyone I remember becomes me.
We find the extension of our soul
In a worthless stone found on the seaside,
In a woman, in an idea, in a tree or a theorem,
In a rural dullness, in the thickets of science,
In the eternal, glimmering orchards of art,
In the tiny warm palm of a baby,
In any other straws we grasp…

About the Author:

Dmitry Blizniuk is an author from Ukraine. His most recent poems have appeared   River Poets , Dream Catcher, Magma, Bombay Gin, Press53, Sheila Na Gig, Canada Quarterly, Palm Beach Poetry Festival and many others. He is a finalist for 2016 Award 'Open Eurasia', 'The Best of Kindness 2017'(USA). He is the author of "The Red Forest" /Fowlpox press, Canada 2018/. He lives in Kharkov, Ukraine

THE LAW OF SILENCE
by David Dephy

When a Poet

I am a firm believer
That as soon as a person stops lying
To himself,
He will be able to find someone
He can trust unconditionally.
And this someone is his own self.

When a poet bestows his words
To the whole world,
Every letter in every word is drenched
With his essence
That the world embraces just like it embraces
The world.

A flower "gives away" its smell
But asks for nothing in return.
It would have been unfair to have
A flower stripped of its right to "give away"
Its smell and to steal the amazing idea from it.
None of the stones lying around a fragrant
flower do this.

None of them take credit for the fragrance
And pretend that it's theirs.
It is safe for me to say that even stones protect

The law on property as they are content
With their own natural qualities,
Without trying to take over other's.

How much more important is a human?
In the epoch ruled by the internet,
Contemporary literature is as exposed
And vulnerable as never before.
I'd like to say that everything is in your hands,
But someone ask me:"How about Lord?"

I say: "For the Lord has no other hands but
yours,
my friend."

David Dephy
October 11, 2018

The Law of Silence

I asked one man: "What is silence?"
"Silence?" He said. "Is the answer
to all your questions."
I asked one tree: "What is silence?"
"You are silence," The tree told me.
"This is talking without dialogue
and without monologue with yourself.
And you are in peace."
"What is silence during a war!?"
I asked one man again, exactly that man.

He said: "Let me explain it once more,
The silence, like love, is the law of the words.
The silence is the clothes the words wear.
Anywhere, like love the human faith bears.
To define the silence with some other words,
The law of death is the life of law."

He was my shadow during the war.
He was myself my personal law.
I opposed the war with my protest meetings
in the streets and millions of us like that only
trees
are standing around - fronds in the black
smoke,
foliage of heartbeats are covering the city
with their political action committee, through
the spaces
between the words - the very home of silence -
every old man knows what the grace really is,
like the sound under stylus always timeless.

David Dephy
October 21, 2018

Smile in the Dark

Here is the door.
Here, in this dark cell
in this attraction-loving
stream of news
with its sustaining hatred
of ascetic life,
and its plans to ruin the gentle
person, the free person, and here,
in this revelation's last word,
is an uncanny capture of the political tone,
when the light of redemption is already gone.
An amazing assumption of character in which
the delicate adjustments of life are revealed
by the breath of silence.

Yes, I smiled, no doubt,
whenever I passed the dark place
and opened the door, but who passed without
much the same smile? Yes, I smiled no doubt.
I gave command and the darkness disappeared
there where silence stands without any fears
and it's so alive, yes silence stands here.

Alive like centuries of past.
Alive like presentiment of future.
Alive like smile after hopeless days' cry
Alive like sea mile across the oceans
of solitude.

David Dephy
October 23, 2018

Eastern Star

If there is no freedom within you, you won't
inspire anyone
If a star is born only in the sky and not in you,
you won't see the light
If heaven is not in you, you will never get there
If there is hell in you, you will never escape
from there

If you are not forgiving, you will never breathe
freely
If you don't give, you will never fly
If you lose hope, you will never wake up
If you don't steer your passion
You will never quench your yearning,

You told me one day - I am your song,
Your breath is the song and the song is like me,
Children are playing - soon calmness will come,
I feel your breath in front of the gate,

So far, so far, so near and so far…

You're the vineyard's gate and this gate is the
heart,
The heart is the choice, the choice is the way
You are what I think and always you are
You are what I saw and always you were

So far, so far, so near and so far…

So, let me sing in your transparent breath,
Be like the wine in your divine veins
I am wishing to let you hear the song - as I am
And let me so please you - you know I need this
too

So far, so far, so near and so far…

All the words' variations come down to one
truth

And all the ideas come down to one breath
And all the world's secrets in your heart are
revealed
Till the star of the East is the sign of the future

So near and not far… Almighty and calm…

Eastern star is trembling all over me
And also all over you – we hear and we see
The spirit of silence within our breathe
Oh yes which we take and yes, which we leave.

David Dephy
May 8, 2018

The Manifest Alpha and Omega

I will never understand the world where:

The Life is the Death.
The Death is the Love.
The Love is the Lie.
The Lie is the Truth.
The Truth is the Shame.
The Shame is the Freedom.
The Freedom is the Rudeness.
The Rudeness is the Disposition.
The Disposition is the Problem.
The Problem is the Existence.
The Existence is the Belief.
The Belief is the Demagogy.
The Demagogy is the Experience.
The Experience is the Sin.
The Sin is the Wisdom.
The Wisdom is the Devil.
The Devil is the Angel.
The Angel is the Myth.
The Myth is the History.
The History is the Past.
The Past is the Being.
The Being is the Illusion.
The Illusion is the God
And the God does not exist.

David Dephy
Sept 17, 2012

About the Author:

David Dephy - The trilingual Georgian/ American poet, novelist, essayist, performer, multimedia artist and painter, and the founder of the first Georgian poetic order Samckauly. He is the author of eight novels and fifteen collections of verse and three audio albums of poetry with orchestra and electronic bands. His short story "Before The End" was chosen for the Best European Fiction 2012, edited by Aleksandar Hemon and prefaced by Nicole Krauss, and published in the U.S. by Dalkey Archive Press. His first book-length work in English, a novel All the World's Mysteries, is forthcoming in fall 2019 from Mad Hat Press with a translation from the Georgian by Adham Smart.

In 2010 – 2011 he was an artist-in-residence at the writer's residency Ledig House in Ghent, New York.

That same year Dephy was invited to participate in the PEN World Voices festival in New York City, where he presented a live poetry event entitled "The Second Skin" with Laurie Anderson, Yusef Komunyakaa and Salman Rushdie at the Unterberg Poetry Center, 92nd Str Y.

In 2012 he made his live poetry performance with quadraphonic audio system at the Abastumani's Observatory of Georgia and in 2017 David Dephy was chosen as an Ambassador of Poetry by Austrian worldwide brand Julius Meinl in Georgia and his poetry and live performance The Poet King and The Easter Verses at the Peace Cathedral of the Evangelical Baptist Church of Georgia included in the Divine Liturgies officially.

In 2017 he emigrated from Georgia for a political reason and currently lives in New York City.

In 2017, David Dephy was invited by the Columbia University in the City of New York City – The School of the Arts, for a literary event. He made this event under the title We Will All Get Out of Here Alive and performed his poetry and prose.

In 2018 – He is the active participant of the American literary and artistic scene as a PEN American, Voices of Poetry.

His works has been anthologized in many collections of poetry and prose and has been published in the USA, Mexico, Germany, Brazil, Ukraine, Georgia.

BRAND OF BROKEN
by Madison Smith

brand of broken

They will tell you it's nature, not nurture. The disorders and the diseases. Because the list of
Bad Things That Need Fixed grows (and they know you're sensitive about it).

Generational, not situational. It's true though and you know it. It doesn't make you feel any less
guilty.

Your mother's undiagnosed bipolar left you recovering from your childhood. Your
grandmother is 67 years old and bulimic, the special kind of bulimic that everyone knows about but
refuses to talk about. Your uncle lies and drinks and cries and drinks and lies and "no one knows
why."
But you've always known that your brand of broken is inherited;
you come by your damage honestly.

This never was (but always was) your fault; your brain chemistry's awry,
but you could still try harder.

So stop talking, now. Just take the pills, now. The doctors and mothers know where you hide the
razor.

But the razors are attached to the tips of your fingers and no matter where you are,
you can get creative.

You want to be honest about all this,

but your truth has you hospitalized over and over and at some point, you start to
take it personally.

So that's when you learn how to lie. You're good at that now because the medicines aren't the only
things you hide under your tongue. Truth disintegrates and dissolves in your pooling saliva, the
gelatin coating should help it slide away easier.

But it doesn't.

It doesn't matter when you want to hold the lie close in your cheek and you're left with bitter powder burning your teeth.

The first hospital stay, you realized. You realized there wasn't enough time or money or research or therapies or drugs to fix you. Because your brand of broken *is* inherited.

And you can't fix blood.

My therapist is crunchy

like granola. Crunchy like organic tree nuts. Like crisp leaves of kale.
But she's nice so I guess there's not much I can really complain about. I like her.
She's just
              crunchy.

She asks me questions like *Have you considered meditation? Have you studied your rising moon sign?* and talks about how the air quality of my household could be affecting my mood.
And she hands me pamphlets on the benefits of aromatherapy massages.

She recommends only consuming foods that are non-GMO, gluten free, vegan, all natural, and locally sourced. *You would be amazed at the level of toxins in your body. Processed foods are poison, just poison.* Which is fine and all sure but I make ten dollars an hour with a bachelor's degree and fifty thousand dollars in student loans and medical debt so I eat what I can get, not what I want and not what I should.

I don't get the privilege of being picky.

                              I'm pretty sure eating an avocado and some fucking
                              flaxseed won't cure my bipolar disorder, anyway.

I just want drugs. I don't want to be even keeled or calm or functioning. I want numb.
A serotonin slumber.
Quit through Quetiapine.
Leave with Lexapro.
Vanish into Venlafaxine.

I want to be anesthetized.

She says,

buy a jar and we'll call it our JAR OF JOY!

She says write down the *everyday* pleasant occurrences in your life.

She says put them in our jar. *Of course* there's always good, there's always things to be thankful for. And you like to write, don't you?

She says we must hold onto them. Reflect on the positive, even the smallest joys:

> 'i passed my test
> someone held the door for me
> i showered with fancy new soap
> someone said my hair was pretty
> > i got out of bed
> today,
> > i didn't scratch my arms until they bled
> today,
> > my parents didn't find me in their backyard with a bleach bottle to my lips
> today,
> > my friends didn't call campus police to remove the kitchen knives from my dorm
> today,
> > i woke up.'

Oh, and use
colorful
patterned
paper,

She says.

splitting

Gravity means nothing to me.
Never securely attached to this earth,
A ball of lighting rattling inside a cage of flesh,
Faking stability in my every anxious breath.

I teeter on the edge of a universe of disasters
In every unsure step.

THE LOST RIVER

by Jane Varley

Hummingbirds

The varmint squirrel dropped a gnawed
      pinecone like a grenade out of a fir tree
         and a hummingbird turned

my ear inside out,
      rapidfire thrum of tiny bones.
           Time machine of thought:

Someday you will have a little girl.
No. I didn't think it then.

Not possible. Some other joy
      woke me into that moment,

some thought
        or memory (as I
      kaleidoscope the whole idea of memory).

Twenty years before, same campsite,
      we woke to see a moose
         paddling across the river

the big rack like an altar
      before a congregation.

It was the sound of the rocky river
       as much as the sight of the moose

waking us to aliveness,
        to a passion for land and water,
           a realization—
   we didn't have to stay there forever—

no, we could carry it along.
Something like that
       (I am getting caught up)

so let me just—
      let me say—
   let me—that was a blessed morning

     (blessed, not a word of religion
        but of belief)
Hats kept us warm, the blue and white tent
        looked fresh as a linen closet.
              Our coffee was called Morning Glory.

Rehoboth

Vultures

The transcendence of the sea and sand
with backdrop of blue sky, and the
silly perfection of my pink motel

looking like a set for a movie based on its
name—
Oceanus. When I walk the beach
I think of all the people who have strolled

in this same way, walking away from life
and walking toward it—no matter what
we move both ways. My brick Ohio house

and the bracings of motherhood seem far away
(I do like those tasks, that series of problems).
I reach down and pluck up the perfect shell.

Listen, the solar system weeps and then laughs.
I am a cliché of the tiny and inconsequential
yet joined with a force beyond my
comprehension.

They collect the
darkness of the pines
strange space
like an inverted cauldron
we walk inside
their false ennui
we know these birds
are single-minded
about death
enthusiastic even
hunching with their
damnable secrets
and watching our step
my dog
an animal contrast
small whine and goofy
sweet naturedness
crap-eater who sniffs
every inch of the alley
neighbor guy comes out
waves and can't see
what haunts his treetops
his face
a cartoon of good cheer
as buzzards spit
adjust their hunger
who knows
the neighbor's dreams
might be black
and sprouting wings
who knows the sound
of our soles pounding
the skeletons
over at the cemetery
underground winds
howl at the moonless sky
press your ear to soil
and you can hear
wagon trains
carrying the dead away

The Lost River

In 1983 a 7.3 earthquake shook the Lost River range in Idaho and lifted Borah
Peak, the state's highest mountain, over 7 feet.

The Lost River is a stream that descends into a depression and flows
underground until it spurts from basalt cliffs at Thousand Springs, Idaho.

Good morning. First sip of coffee so black
and bitter it clears the vision while the sun

squats on the ridge (briefly) and casts diamonds
on the water. This is how I rinse my face

in the river, how I light a fire
of perception, ash crackling against its own

internal dampness. Tie up the boots.
Steady the compass. Reading my map

I am given advice by a stranger
(strings of hair, a broken tooth, jeans could stand

on their own) for the trailhead, the do-
able climb, my perseverance at

Chickenout Ridge, but he sees someone
I am not—a serious hiker who achieves

the summit. Not me. What I crave
is the everyday impossible

as when an earthquake lifted Mt. Borah
seven feet higher and the valley floor

dropped nine. This is nature.
This is sudden cosmic change. The moon,

that watcher, saw a new face

on the mountainside. The river is gradual,

flowing southeast where it vanishes
into the plain, water ghosts leaving behind

their trail of fragrance. A friend told me I can
go to a Thousand Springs and see

a one-of-a-kind fish with the head of a prince,
the Shoshone sculpin

swimming waters that had traveled
a hundred miles underground

before bursting from the canyon wall.
If we go, we will sit with our cups

and no one will have died, and no one
(those other ghosts) will be whispering.

The crystal falls will offer white songs
cool as the interior of the sea.

Biography of a Bee

This is the biography of a bee who flew around the world
gathering nectar and pollen and single-handedly
double-wingedly made the world grow again the whole
world greening up and the flowers coming back
and the flowers were arranged in all the colors
of the spectrum a rainbow of flowers in a healthy world
and the rivers regressed to flow across the land
as the valleys inverted and sloughed off the dirty old rocks
the graffitied and drilled and abused rocks the formations
rose up and melded back to young healthy rock fired
by the hot magma fueled beauty burning so intensely
out of the center of a world that would not be destroyed
and thanks to that one single godlike bee about which
you were writing the biography.

About the Author:

Jane Varley is the author of a memoir, Flood
Stage and Rising; a chapbook of poetry,
Sketches at the Naesti Bar; and co-author on a
coaching memoir with NCAA Hall of Fame
fastpitch coach Donna Newberry. Jane has a
PhD in poetry and creative writing from the
University of North Dakota and has published
many poems and reviews of poetry and fiction
in literary magazines. A native Iowan, she lived
in the western and southern U.S. before
moving back to the Midwest, where she is a
professor at Muskingum University in Ohio.

WHISTLING PAST THE VEIL

Short stories by

A. Elizabeth Herting

Paperback: 220 pages
Publishing date: April 2, 2019
Language: English
ISBN-10: 1-949180-94-8
ISBN-13: 978-1-949180-94-7
Product Dimensions: 6 x 0.6 x 9 inches

Death. Mysterious and terrifying, exhilarating and heartbreaking. Is it the irrevocable end of our existence or a tantalyzing new beginning? Dying is the one thing we all have in common, it is the true "final frontier."

All of the stories in "Whistling Past the Veil" have previously been published and each one deals in some way with death, dying or the supernatural. From a Shakespearean deathbed to the very gates of doggie heaven and musical hell, the stories in "Whistling Past the Veil" include horror, fantasy, love, hauntings, revenge and real-life inspirational tales all connected to the ultimate eventuality and mystery of death.

A. Elizabeth Herting has had short fiction stories featured in many different publications, including podcasts, reprints and poetry. She also has experience with non-fiction and as an online copywriter.

A. Elizabeth was proud to be selected as a Finalist in the "Adelaide Literary Award, 2018 Short Story Anthology." Her story "Sourdough's Cabin" was chosen as "Readers Choice" in the November 2017 edition of "Frontier Tales" for a future anthology. She has also had stories featured in short story anthologies: "Write to Meow," "Weird Reader 2017 Edition" and "Ghostlight, the Magazine of Terror." A second collection of short stories called "Postcards From Waupaca" will be published by "Adelaide Books" in 2020. A. Elizabeth has also completed her first novel called "Wet Birds Don't Fly at Night" that she eventually hopes to find a home for.

https://aeherting.weebly.com,

twitter.com/AEHerting,

facebook.com/AElizabethHerting

VANISH TO THE MOUNTAIN SPRING

Poems by Donny Barilla

Paperback: 120 pages
Publishing date: March 1, 2019
Language: English
ISBN-10: 1-950437-05-1
ISBN-13: 978-1-950437-05-4
Product Dimensions: 6 x 0.5 x 9 inches

These poems enclosed waver and fluctuate with rhythms and hold a natural approach to musical theories, yet they do so through images and metaphors. Poems included create sounds which need arrangement such as a puzzle piece must fit with its fellow pieces. Along with following the sound of the poem, one will discover an image, or images which cover the palate of the senses. The sounds of the words, individually or together, create the themes of the book. I hold the strong belief that the art of writing and reading poems exists as theatrical one. One which calls for an audience and upholds the notion that verse, in the end, is music and image and meaning together.

Donny Barilla has four books published and has completed nine self-published books. He has been published seventy four times in journals, reviews and magazines. Twenty two of his books have found homes in libraries, public and academic. Nine book readings and signings have come his way as he hosts private reading out of his home. The Adelaide Literary Awards named him as top finalist for poetry and winner of the award for the most recent literary contest in two thousand and eighteen. Writing with an enigmatic approach to poetry and always maintaining the element of nature, his poems are filled with strong images and metaphors which blend thematically throughout the books he writes. Studying philosophy, mythology, Asian poetry, folktales and fairy tales consists of his backbone and influence. Currently, Donny works on a sizable collection of poems which covers much poetic ground. As he lives in the beautiful state of Pennsylvania, he absorbs energies of natural beauty while he lives a reclusive life.

Couchsurfing: the Musical charts both a physical and psychological journey as author explores the fast-growing travel phenomenon of Couchsurfing. Middle-aged and set in his ways, he starts as a skeptic. Who would want to spend the night in the home of a complete stranger? While knocking on the doors of thirty-five of these strangers across nine countries, starting in Tel Aviv and ending in Boston, he realizes that He would, and maybe he'll not only save money, but find himself changed for the better by the experience. Balancing the forward motion of his Couchsurfing adventures are glimpses back into the past, seen through the quirky lens of musicals that have played a part in his life.

Gary Pedler has written two adult novels, a YA novel, two story collections, and, a little to his surprise, a play. A resident of San Francisco for longer than he cares to admit, Gary qualifies as a true Bay Area denizen. Yet after a recent escape from his white-collar wage slave job, he's spent much of his time rambling around the world and, of course, writing about everything he sees. Find out more about Gary at www.garypedler.com."

COUCHSURFING: THE MUSICAL

A travel memoir by

Gary Pedler

Paperback: 232 pages
Publishing date: March 1, 2019
Language: English
ISBN-10: 1-950437-09-4
ISBN-13: 978-1-950437-09-2
Product Dimensions: 6 x 0.7 x 9 inches

SOMEDAY EVERYTHING WILL ALL MAKE SENSE

A novel by

Carol LaHines

Paperback: 220 pages
Publishing date: February 7, 2019
Language: English
ISBN-10: 1-949180-91-3
ISBN-13: 978-1-949180-91-6
Product Dimensions: 6 x 0.7 x 9 inches

"It's rare to find a character like Luther van der Loon who makes such a rich and lasting impression—so vividly wounded, exuberant in characterization. Luther embodies the anxious, angst-ridden neurotic we are afraid we will become, or maybe who we aspire to be. In his grief over his mother's accidental choking vis-à-vis death, his obsession with what is the point of life is simultaneously heartbreaking and hilarious. I could read this novel a hundred times and never tire of it." - Amy E. Wallen, Author of When We Were Ghouls: A Memoir of Ghost Stories

"An original and very funny novel about a man's obsessive longing and guilt after his mother accidentally chokes on wonton soup. We follow the endearing protagonist through a period of mourning, cleverly interwoven with musical theory and an attempt to sue the Chinese take-out restaurant, all brought to a hilarious finale with a last symposium on medieval music." - Sheila Kohler, Author of numerous award-winning novels

Carol LaHines' fiction has appeared or is forthcoming in Fence, Hayden's Ferry Review, Denver Quarterly, Cimarron Review, The Literary Review, North Dakota Quarterly, South Dakota Review, The South Carolina Review, The Chattahoochee Review, The Nebraska Review, North Atlantic Review, Sycamore Review, Permafrost, redivider, Literary Orphans, Brain Child Magazine, Literal Latte, and elsewhere. Her short story, "Papijack," was selected by judge Patrick Ryan as the recipient of the 2017 Lamar York Prize for Fiction. Her short stories and novellas have also been finalists for the Mary McCarthy Prize from Sarabande Books, the David Nathan Meyerson fiction prize, the New Letters short story award, the Pirate's Alley Faulkner Society award, and the Disquiet Literary Prize, among others. She lives in New York City and is a graduate of New York University, Gallatin Division.

40 year-old Quinn Kershaw reminisces of a chapter in his life where escaping his small hometown for a taste of the city life quickly becomes a series of events that he will never forget.

The freedom of young adulthood and new experiences lands this 21 year-old a minimum wage job in the mailroom at a downtown Los Angeles law firm. Befriended by a few scallywag attorneys, Quinn is whisked away for a weekend to the unforgiving city of Las Vegas. Unlike your typical cliché Vegas getaways, Quinn's venture takes a turn that leaves him missing his old life, and questioning why he even left it in the first place. Although "Another Day in Paradise" has a deep underlying message, its pages are filled with humor and unforgettable quirky characters.

Joseph (Joe) Sneva is a singer/songwriter from the Pacific Northwest. He tours and plays shows under his two groups: "Joe Sneva," and "The Mountain Flowers." Joe resides in Mount Vernon, WA, located 50 miles north of Seattle. This is his first novel. Instagram: @joesneva Website: www.themountainflowers.com

ANOTHER DAY IN PARADISE

A novel by

Joseph Sneva

Paperback: 106 pages
Publishing date: March 1, 2019
Language: English
ISBN-10: 1-950437-10-8
ISBN-13: 978-1-950437-10-8
Product Dimensions: 6 x 0.7 x 9 inches

MY PEARLS IN SHANGHAI

A memoir by

Marianne Song

Paperback: 220 pages
Publishing date: March 1, 2019
Language: English
ISBN-10: 1-950437-08-6
ISBN-13: 978-1-950437-08-5
Product Dimensions: 6 x 0.7 x 9 inches

My Pearls in Shanghai tells the beautiful story of author's journey from a young adult struggling to find her path to a grown, successful woman who has learned who she is. The way she explores her experiences and memories to correlate with social issues corroborate her viewpoint that arts can be far away from reality. Her education in Switzerland and China expanded her capacity of cultural tolerance arising from different ethnics. A variety of people she met, talked to, and shared her feelings with in two countries were well-melt into her memoir. The core value of Song's essays lies in how to find one's uniqueness instead of being dissolved in the voice of others. This self-discovery journey brought the conclusion that human desire is the essence of the soul, which could give the life purpose. Her memoir covers not only the cultural and artistic experience she discovered in Shanghai but also what the meaningful life is all about. Each chapter in this memoir deals with empirical philosophy.

Marianne Song is an essayist who strives to reproduce the feelings and memories with poetic images through English instead of her mother tongue, Korean to convey her raw emotions as honestly as possible, otherwise might be fabricated by self-consciousness. A memoir My Pearls in Shanghai is her first published book. Currently, she is working as a writer and English instructor in Jeju Island, Korea with an unwavering belief that someday her angst and hardships could be transformed into artistic treasure in the same way the natural wonders of Jeju were made from volcanic eruption. Whenever facing a big challenge, she quietly whispers to herself 'Don't be afraid, follow your heart.'

"In noticing the gentle detail, the human touch, Gloria Monaghan's poems do not eschew the enrichment of a sumptuous word or academic allusion; neither do they break under the weight of those ornaments in moments of modest relatability, the poet asks familiar questions in pithy ways: How is it possible? What does it mean? Who walked away? When will I forget? Poetry that ignores people may be itself ignored; these poems do not ignore. These poems please." - Zachary Bos, New England Review of Books

Gloria Monaghan is a Professor of Humanities at Wentworth Institute in Boston. She has published two books of poetry, Flawed (Finishing Line Press, 2011, nominated for the Massachusetts Book Award) and The Garden (Flutter Press 2015). Her poem "Into Grace" won the 2018 Adelaide Voices Poetry Award. Her poems have appeared in Adelaide, the Aurorean, Aries, Blue Max Review, Fox Chase, 2River, and Underground Writer's Association, among others

FALSE SPRING

A collection of poems by

Gloria Monaghan

Paperback:
Publishing date:
Language: English
ISBN-10: 1-950437-07-8
ISBN-13: 978-1-950437-07-8
Product Dimensions: 6 x 0.7 x 9 inches

www.ingramcontent.com/pod-product-compliance
Lightning Source LLC
Chambersburg PA
CBHW080719020726
47502CB00009B/2478